THE ARAB–ISRAELI CONFLICT

The Arab–Israeli conflict has been one of the most protracted and contentious disputes in the Middle East. This wide-ranging textbook examines the diplomatic and historical setting within which the conflict developed, from both the Israeli and Palestinian perspectives, and gives a comprehensive overview of the peace process.

Enabling students to easily access and study original documents through the supportive framework of a textbook, *The Arab–Israeli Conflict*:

- Presents the most important and widely cited documents in the history of the Israeli–Palestinian conflict.
- Presents these documents in an edited form to highlight key elements.
- Includes an introductory chapter which sets the context for the study of the history of the area.
- Covers a comprehensive historical period, ranging from the nineteenth century to the present day.
- Incorporates a wide range of pedagogical aids: original documents, maps, and boxed sections.

This important new textbook is an essential aid for courses on the Arab–Israeli conflict and the Middle East peace process, and will be an invaluable reference tool for all students of political science, Middle East studies, and history.

Gregory S. Mahler is Academic Dean and Professor of Politics at Earlham College. He received his B.A. from Oberlin College and his M.A. and Ph.D. from Duke University. He has published widely in the area of Israeli and Middle Eastern Politics, and his academic interests include political institutions and democratic government.

Alden R. W. Mahler is a researcher and writer at CNN International. She received her B.A. from Carleton College and her M.A. from Emory University, and served in the U.S. Peace Corps in Jordan.

THE ARAB–ISRAELI CONFLICT

An introduction and documentary reader

Gregory S. Mahler and Alden R. W. Mahler

Routledge
Taylor & Francis Group

LONDON AND NEW YORK

First published 2010
by Routledge
2 Park Square, Milton Park, Abingdon, Oxon OX14 4RN

Simultaneously published in the USA and Canada
by Routledge
270 Madison Ave, New York, NY 10016

Routledge is an imprint of the Taylor & Francis Group, an informa business

© 2010 Gregory S. Mahler and Alden R. W. Mahler

Typeset in Garamond by
Keystroke, Tettenhall, Wolverhampton
Printed and bound in Great Britain by
TJ International, Padstow, Cornwall

British Library Cataloguing in Publication Data
A catalogue record for this book is available from the British Library

Library of Congress Cataloging-in-Publication Data
Mahler, Gregory S., 1950–
   The Arab-Israeli conflict: an introduction and documentary reader/
Gregory S. Mahler and Alden Mahler.
      p. cm.
   Includes bibliographical references and index.
   1. Arab-Israeli conflict. 2. Arab-Israeli conflict—Sources. 3. Middle East—Politics
and government—1945– 4. Middle East—Politics and government—1945–
Sources. I. Mahler, Alden. II. Title.
   DS119.7.M2245 2010
   956.04—dc22   2009008512

ISBN 13: 978–0–415–77460–4 (hbk)
ISBN 13: 978–0–415–77461–1 (pbk)
ISBN 13: 978–0–203–87159–1 (ebk)

ISBN 10: 0–415–77460–8 (hbk)
ISBN 10: 0–415–77461–6 (pbk)
ISBN 10: 0–203–87159–6 (ebk)

CONTENTS

PART IV FROM A PEACE TREATY (1979) TO THE NOBEL PEACE PRIZE (1994) 165

PART V FROM INTERIM AGREEMENTS (1995) TO THE PRESENT TIME 231

LIST OF MAPS

Part I
Introduction

"And as for Ishmael, I have heard thee; behold, I have blessed him, and will make him fruitful, and will multiply him exceedingly; twelve princes shall he beget, and I will make him a great nation. But My covenant will I establish with Isaac, whom Sarah shall bear unto thee at this set time in the next year." Bereshit (Genesis) 17:20–21, JPS translation

". . .We covenanted with Abraham and Isma'il, that they should sanctify My House for those who compass it round, or use it as a retreat, or bow, or prostrate themselves (therein in prayer)." Holy Qur'an 2:125, Yusufali translation

Thus, in theory, begins the cycle of tension between Arabs and Jews.[1] It may have been Isaac or it may have been Ishmael who was the favorite child and heir of Abraham (or, of course, it may have been neither at all). The fact remains that two peoples point to this millennia-old story as their "origin myth." More importantly, two people point to the land bequeathed by the shepherd Abraham and call it their own.

Because this is not a religious text, but an academic inquiry into a modern political situation, this story cannot be the basis of our analysis or argument. Neither is it particularly useful to itemize the subsequent regimes in the region. As fascinating as the Babylonian, Assyrian, Greek, Roman, Old Kingdom, Caliphate, and Ottoman – in no particular order! – governments may have been, they will serve us as little more than a backdrop. In short: the portion of the Middle East currently known as Israel or Palestine has, for a very long time, been the object of a great deal of contention. Sometimes one group held power and sometimes another, and sometimes power was shared or contested by more than one group. Poised at the crossroads of three continents, Palestine has rarely known peace.

But the situation currently known as the Arab–Israeli conflict is a thoroughly modern and wholly political predicament. It is a story of international machinations, citizen rebellion, and (quite literally) the quest for world domination. And in its modern incarnation, the Arab–Israeli conflict has left a paper trail.

This text will allow the reader to analyze the Arab–Israeli conflict through the words of those who have lived it. From the publication of *Der Judenstaat* to the Bush Annapolis Conference, these documents speak for the times and ideas they embodied. By placing them within their historical context, we hope to allow the reader to better understand the motivations of the authors.

Map 1 Israel in
the Middle East

Based on Gregory
Mahler, Israel:
Government and
Politics/MAT
STA, 1E.
Copyright 1989
Wadsworth, a
part of Cengage
Learning Inc.
Reproduced by
permission.
www.cengage.
com/permissions.

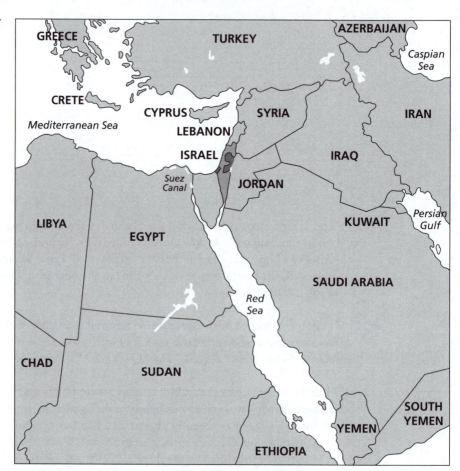

See reading #1,
"Theodor Herzl,
The Jewish State
(1896)"

In 1896, an Austrian journalist named Theodore Herzl wrote a volume that would prove to play a historically crucial role in world history, titled *The Jewish State*.

Herzl did not invent the concept of Zionism, but his book formalized a growing belief among Jews of the world about the need for a Jewish state. Anti-Semitism was an intense and apparently ever-present problem. In the decades dominated by emerging nation-states and the philosophies of self-determination and ethnic identity, the notion that the Jews too deserved a homeland – or a state[2] – appealed to many people.

The precise location of the hypothetical Jewish homeland was far from a given. Although many Jews felt a religious tie to the land that today is Israel, the movement for a homeland was itself predominantly secular. In fact, many religious Jews considered it an affront to God for man to construct a Jewish state, rather than waiting for it to occur naturally when the Messiah arrived. Without a strong religious mooring, proposals for a location ranged from rural areas of Argentina to Uganda or the island of Madagascar.

See reading #2,
"The Basle Program
(August 30, 1897)"

Eventually the focus of the early Zionist movement did turn towards Palestine, at the time a part of the centuries-old Ottoman Empire, known as the "Sick Old Man of Europe" for its persistence even as it lost territory and its government's hold became increasingly tenuous. The Ottomans had thrown their lot in with the losing side of the First World War, and found themselves pitted against the United Kingdom, France, and Russia in that conflict. The Ottoman Empire faced the insurrection of its Arab citizens. The ruler of Mecca at the time, Sharif Hussein bin Ali, saw an opportunity for self-rule at long last. Corresponding with Sir Henry McMahon, British High Commissioner in Egypt, Hussein felt assured of Great Britain's support for Arab independence, and threw his considerable influence behind the British objectives.

The Ottomans' days were numbered, and the Ottoman Empire crumbled in the First World War, leaving huge swaths of formerly Ottoman territory in a

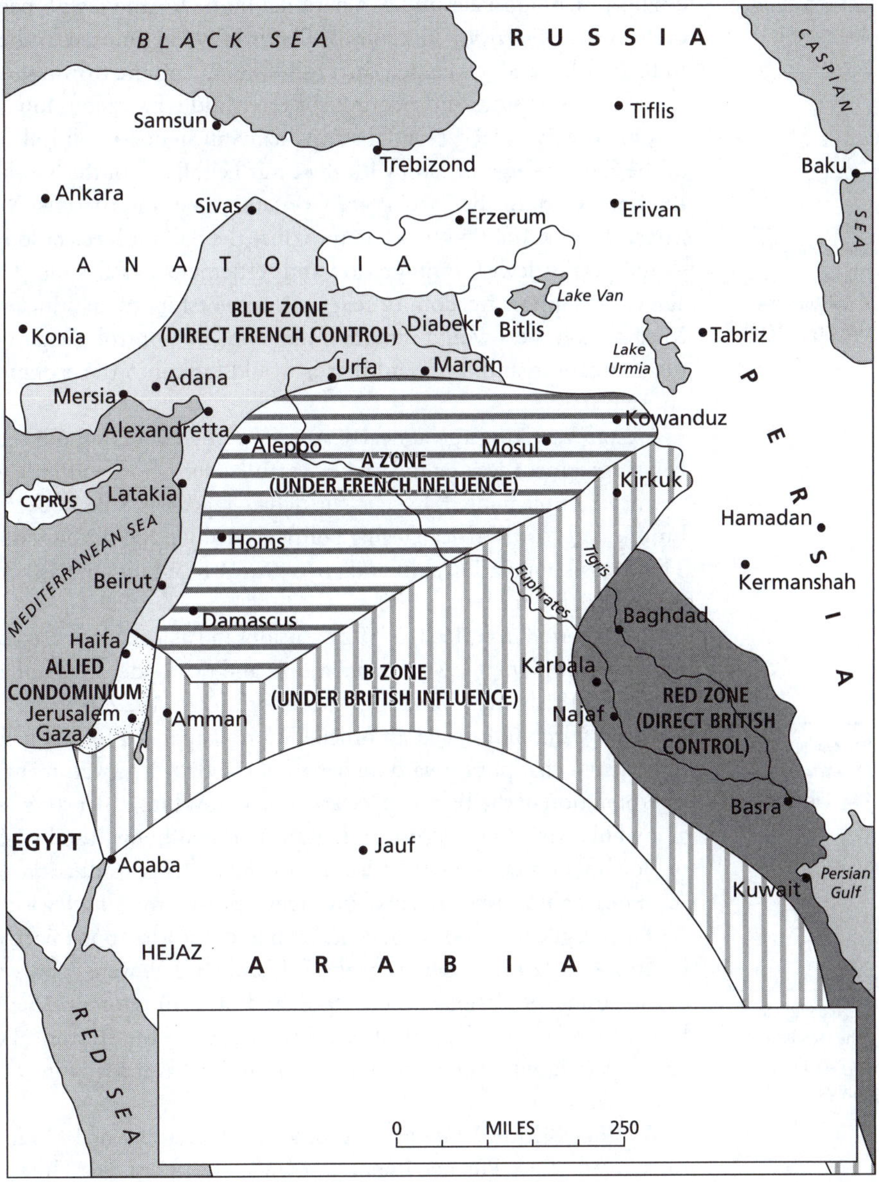

See reading #3, "The McMahon Letter (October 24, 1915)"

Map 2 The Sykes-Picot Agreement of 1916 for the Partition of the Middle East

Source: Jewish Virtual Library, A Division of the American-Israel Cooperative Enterprise, http://www.jewishvirtual library.org/jsource /History/ sykesmap.html

See reading #4, "The Sykes–Picot Agreement (1916)"

See reading #5, "The Balfour Declaration (November 2, 1917)"

See reading #6, "The Weizmann–Feisal Agreement (January 3, 1919)"

See reading #7, "The White Paper of 1922 (June, 1922)"

See reading #8, "The Mandate for Palestine (July 24, 1922)"

governmental limbo. Into that vacuum stepped the newly dominant nations of Great Britain and France. Fiercely competitive throughout their modern histories, the former allies came prepared with the Sykes–Picot agreement, which had been secretly drawn up in negotiations between the two during the war. The agreement proposed to divide all former Ottoman lands into either French or British "spheres of influence." The area known as Palestine was awarded to the British.

Over the next three decades, the question of who would permanently control Palestine was never fully settled. Both Arabs and Jews lobbied for influence and control over the land, and both felt they had been promised that control by the British government. The Balfour Declaration of 1917 implied a British goal of the establishment "in Palestine of a national home for the Jewish people" – *in* but not exclusively *comprising*. The sons of Sherif Hussein pointed to the British promises to their father and demanded their fulfillment. And the British sought to control the valuable trade routes and resources of the Middle East for as long as possible.

On January 3, 1919, Dr. Chaim Weizmann signed a political accord in the name of the Zionist Organization with the Emir Feisal, son of the Sherif of Mecca, within the framework of the Paris Peace Conference ending the First World War. In this agreement the Arabs promised to recognize the Balfour Declaration and said that they would permit Jewish immigration and settlement in Palestine. The agreement also agreed to support freedom of religion and worship in Palestine, and promised that Muslim holy sites would remain under Muslim control. As part of the agreement the Zionist Organization said that it would look into the economic possibilities of an Arab state.

Despite receiving a great deal of attention when it was announced, the Weizmann–Feisal agreement was repudiated by Arab leaders shortly after it was signed, and it was never implemented. Even as the debate raged on, Jews flocked to Palestine from Europe and North Africa, fleeing political tensions and the escalating anti-Semitism. This Jewish population shift and government instability in Palestine led to riots and general disturbance.

In the period from 1920 to 1922 tensions in Palestine increased between the native Arab and immigrant Jewish populations, and both sides were unhappy with the way that the British were handling the situation. In 1922 British Colonial Secretary Winston Churchill issued an official White Paper – a formal governmental policy statement – that put forward on behalf of the British Government a more restrictive interpretation of the Balfour Declaration. The White Paper concluded that Palestine as a whole would not become a Jewish "national home," and suggested limitations on Jewish immigration to Palestine through the introduction of the concept of "economic absorptive capacity" into regulations governing Jewish immigration.

The League of Nations issued its mandates for Mesopotamia, Syria, and Palestine in April of 1920. The details of the British mandate were approved by the Council of the League of Nations in July 1922, and came into force on September 29, 1922. In the Mandate, the League of Nations recognized the "historical connection of the Jewish people with Palestine" and the "grounds for reconstituting their national home in that country."

Another British White Paper was issued in October of 1930 in response to Arab riots in Palestine. The document, known as the "Passfield White Paper" called for a

Map 3 The British Mandate, 1920

Source: From Gregory Mahler, Israel: Government and Politics/MAT STA, 1E. Copyright 1989 Wadsworth, a part of Cengage Learning Inc. Reproduced by permission. www.cengage.com/permissions.

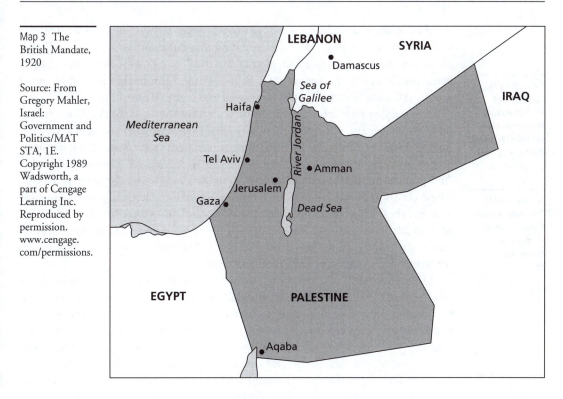

Map 4 The British Mandate, 1922

Source: From Gregory Mahler, Israel: Government and Politics/MAT STA, 1E. Copyright 1989 Wadsworth, a part of Cengage Learning Inc. Reproduced by permission. www.cengage.com/permissions.

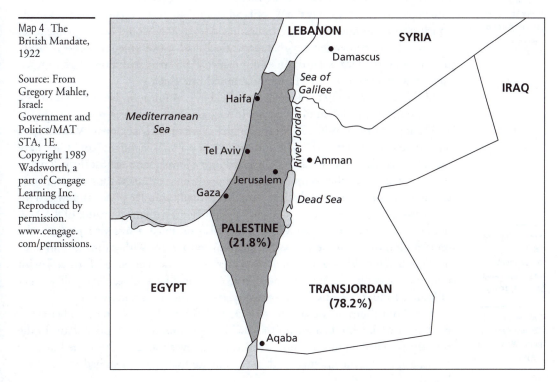

renewed attempt at establishing a Legislative Council in Palestine. The White Paper was more restrictive in its approach to the Zionist cause, and as a result the Zionist movement mounted a major campaign against the White Paper at the time. In a letter made public during February 1931, British Prime Minister Ramsay MacDonald promised Chaim Weizmann what amounted to the cancellation of that White Paper.

See reading #9, "British Prime Minister Ramsay MacDonald Letter to Chaim Weizmann (February 13, 1931)"

In November 1936 a royal commission of inquiry known as the Peel Commission (after its chairman, William Robert Wellesley Peel, Earl Peel) was sent on a fact-finding mission to Palestine by the British government in the hope that it might be able to recommend solutions to the tensions that were developing between the native Arab population and the immigrant Jewish population. It issued a report in July 1937. The Peel Report found that many of the grievances of the Palestinians were reasonable and that the "disturbances" between the two populations were based on the issues of Arab desire for national independence on one hand and conflict between Arab nationalism and Zionist goals on the other. Ultimately the Peel Commission recommended partition of the Palestinian territory.

See reading #10, "The Palestine Royal Commission (Peel Commission): Report (July 24, 1937)"

Although in 1937 the Twentieth Zionist Congress had rejected the boundaries proposed by the Peel Commission, it did agree in principle to the idea of partition of Palestine into a Jewish state and an Arab state. However, Palestinian Arab nationalists rejected any kind of partition. The British government sent a technical team in 1938, the Woodhead Commission, to make a detailed plan and to review the suggestions of the Peel Commission. The Woodhead Commission was in Palestine from April through August of 1938, and issued its report in November of that year. In its report it rejected the Peel plan, and suggested other variations on the idea of partition. Ultimately the Woodhead Commission was unable to reach a single conclusion about how to partition Palestine in a way that would be acceptable to all concerned. As a consequence of that report the British Government took the position that it found the idea of partition as impractical, and suggested more work to reach Arab–Jewish agreement on a future of a united Palestine.

See reading #11, "British Government Policy Statement Against Partition (November 11, 1938)"

In the Spring of 1939 a conference was held in London at St. James Palace to seek a solution to the problem of Palestine. It was not successful. As a result, in May of 1939 another British White Paper appeared, known as the MacDonald White Paper. This statement declared that the authors of the original mandate "could not have intended that Palestine should be converted into a Jewish state against the will of the Arab population of the country," and proposed the creation within ten years of a unitary Palestine state, to which it would eventually transfer political power. This was devastating to the Zionists, and entirely consistent with the demands of the Arab population at the time. The White Paper also outlined a five year plan for the immigration of 75,000 Jews (10,000 per year for 5 years, with a further allowance of 25,000 refugees) – and stated that after the 5-year period no further Jewish immigration could take place without Arab consent. The next year, in a policy paper of March 1940, the British went on to severely restrict land sales.

See reading #12, "British Government: The White Paper (May 17, 1939)"

The Zionist movement saw the MacDonald White Paper as "an act of betrayal," believing that it would condemn the Jewish population to a minority status in the country as well as ending any hopes of creating a Jewish state. It also argued that the White Paper was inconsistent with the Mandate that the British had received for Palestine.

See reading #13, "Zionist Reaction to the White Paper (1939)"

Map 5 The 1937
Peel Commission
Proposal

From Gregory
Mahler, Israel:
Government and
Politics/MAT
STA, 1E.
Copyright 1989
Wadsworth, a
part of Cengage
Learning Inc.
Reproduced by
permission.
www.cengage.
com/permissions.

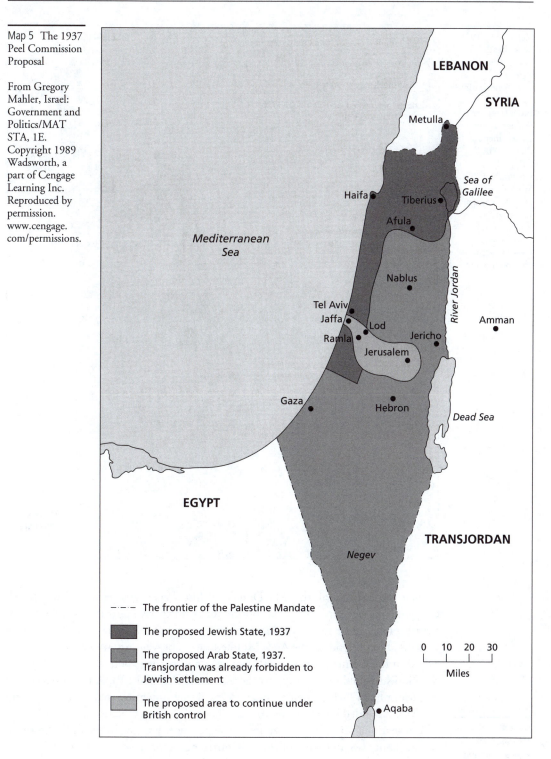

LEBANON

SYRIA

Metulla

Sea of
Galilee

Haifa
Tiberius

Afula

Mediterranean
Sea

River Jordan

Nablus

Amman

Tel Aviv

Jaffa
Lod

Ramla
Jericho

Jerusalem

Gaza
Hebron

Dead Sea

EGYPT

TRANSJORDAN

Negev

– - – - – The frontier of the Palestine Mandate

The proposed Jewish State, 1937

The proposed Arab State, 1937.
Transjordan was already forbidden to
Jewish settlement

The proposed area to continue under
British control

0   10   20   30

Miles

Aqaba

9

Map 6 The 1938
Woodhead
Commission
Partition
Recommendation

From Gregory
Mahler, Israel:
Government and
Politics/MAT
STA, 1E.
Copyright 1989
Wadsworth, a
part of Cengage
Learning Inc.
Reproduced by
permission.
www.cengage.
com/permissions.

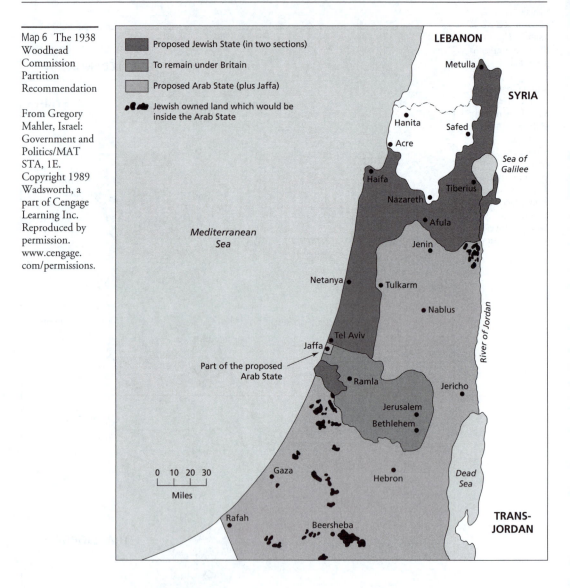

The publication of the MacDonald White Paper was seen by the British government as a reasonable policy option for the British to pursue in the context of British policy prior to the outbreak of the Second World War. The British were worried about offending the Arab Middle East – not wanting Arab governments to side with the German rulers – and they were not worried about the possibility that the Zionists would start to support the Germans. The White Paper remained British policy until 1947 when the British announced their intention to leave the area, and the British handed over the Palestine conflict to the United Nations.

See reading #14,
"The Biltmore
Program: Towards
a Jewish State
(May 11, 1942)"

International Zionist organizations were not merely sitting by passively, however. In the United States, the Biltmore Conference took place at New York City's Biltmore Hotel in early May 1942, with Zionist leaders from many different nations and over 500 delegates in attendance. The Biltmore Conference was a response to the British White Paper of 1939, and in a sense took international Zionist activism to a new level in terms of its support for the creation of a Jewish state in Palestine, something that major Zionist organizations were not prepared to do prior to the White Paper.

Arab response to the Zionist activism was not very flexible, and the Arab position continued to be that a Jewish state created in Palestine was not an acceptable outcome. In 1946 the document "Arab Office Report to Anglo-American Committee" was released, and it suggested that the Arab powers were prepared to accept a modest Zionist presence in Palestine, but that presence would have to "satisfy certain conditions," and would have to have as its goal that "over time the exclusiveness of the Jews will be neutralized by the development of loyalty to the [Palestinian] state . . ." This was not, of course, a satisfactory outcome to the Zionist activists, either the activists in Palestine or those in other areas of the world.

See Reading #15, "Arab Office Report to Anglo–American Committee (March, 1946)"

It is probably unnecessary to explain why the Second World War was a defining historical moment for the Jews of the world. In the Holocaust, Jews faced the ultimate expression of the anti-Semitism they had known for so long. After the Holocaust, anti-Semitism was indisputably real. Moreover, after the Holocaust, many world leaders sympathized with the decimated Jewish population. Suddenly, a Jewish homeland seemed less like a dramatic overreaction, and much more likely to happen.

See reading #16, "U.N. Security Council: Resolution 181 (November 29, 1947)"

In the light of the new global attitudes on the subject, and because few other options were available to them, survivors and other disaffected Jews flooded into the British holdings in Palestine. The fledgling United Nations attempted to equitably create an Israel and an Arab Palestine in United Nations General Assembly Resolution 181, but that proposal was unequivocally rejected by the Palestinian Arabs and representatives of other Arab states. Sporadic but fierce violence erupted between Jews and Arabs, and tensions ran high. As they faced the diplomatic morass, the Jews in Palestine decided to take matters into their own hands. In May of 1948, they declared to the international community the existence of the state of Israel.

See reading #17, "Declaration of the Establishment of the State of Israel (May 14, 1948)"

See reading #18, "Creation of a Conciliation Commission, General Assembly Resolution 194 (III) (December 11, 1948)"

The Arabs responded immediately – within hours. A force comprised of Syrian, Egyptian, and Jordanian troops (and backed by those countries and Iraq, Lebanon, and Saudi Arabia as well) began an invasion to "drive Israel into the sea." It was nearly a year before the two sides reached an armistice, in April of 1949. The armistice reflected the *status quo* positions of each party, and as such, Israel was awarded significantly more territory than it had been given under the United Nation's earlier partition plan. The armistice also did not allow for an independent Palestine, but put the West Bank under the control of Jordan. Israel and Jordan shared Jerusalem, and Egypt controlled the area between it and Israel known as the Gaza Strip.

Israel applied for membership in the United Nations in the Fall of 1948, but did not receive a majority vote in the Security Council at that time, which was required for membership. The next spring, in May of 1949, Israel tried again, and at that time it received a vote of 37 votes in favor of membership, 12 votes against, and 9 abstentions.

See reading #19, "Admission of Israel to the United Nations, General Assembly Resolution 273 (May 11, 1949)"

The status of Jerusalem continued to be a significant issue as part of the Middle East conflict. Resolution 303 in the General Assembly in 1949 reiterated the commitment of the United Nations to an internationalized Jerusalem, and the U.N.

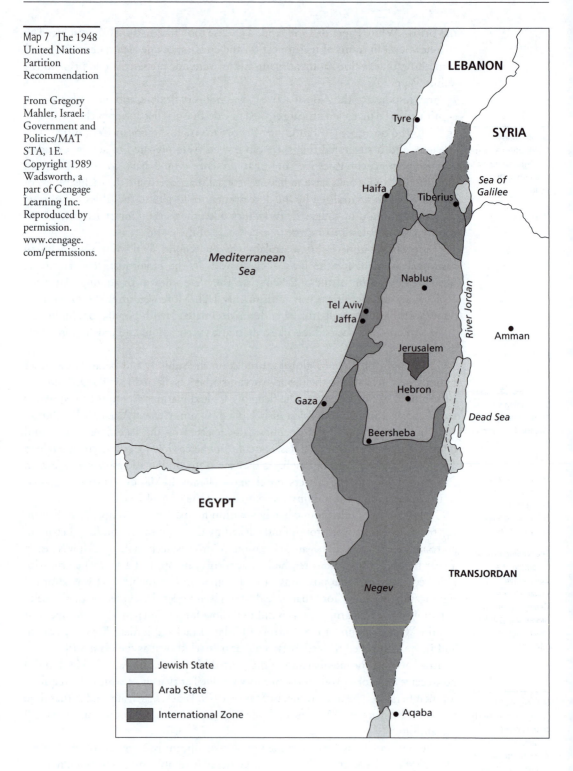

Map 7 The 1948 United Nations Partition Recommendation

From Gregory Mahler, Israel: Government and Politics/MAT STA, 1E. Copyright 1989 Wadsworth, a part of Cengage Learning Inc. Reproduced by permission. www.cengage.com/permissions.

LEBANON

SYRIA

Tyre

Haifa

Tiberius

Sea of Galilee

Mediterranean Sea

Nablus

River Jordan

Tel Aviv

Jaffa

Amman

Jerusalem

Hebron

Gaza

Dead Sea

Beersheba

EGYPT

TRANSJORDAN

Negev

Aqaba

Jewish State

Arab State

International Zone

See reading #20, "General Assembly Resolution 303: Palestine: Question of an International Regime for the Jerusalem Area and the Protection of the Holy Places (December 1949)"

designated Jerusalem a *"corpus separatum"* – separate body. In the original U.N. partition plan (Document 16, above), Jerusalem was to have been administered under the United Nations as an international city. By the end of the war of independence the city was *de facto* divided into an area controlled by Jordan in the east and an area controlled by Israel in the west.

An armistice, of course, is not a peace treaty, and the relations between Israel and its neighbors following the war did not resemble peace. The Arabs considered the existence of Israel to be absolutely unacceptable; the Arabic term "an-naqba" ("the catastrophe") is still used to refer to the creation of an Israeli state. Cross-border gunfire and conflicts, debate over land, and harassment of each other's citizens all contributed to an escalation of tensions between Israel and its neighbors.

WHAT'S THE PROBLEM?

Israelis and Palestinians each bring unique issues to the negotiating table, some of them very complex, and some derived from events of the 60 years since Israel became a state. In essence, however, the primary issues are the following.

- Palestinian refugees (including refugees currently living outside territory controlled by Israel – both in Europe and North America – as well as refugees who have relocated to areas in the West Bank and Gaza) want their land back, or fiscal remuneration for their losses, in those cases in which family property was lost in either the 1948 fighting or the 1967 fighting. Many Palestinians in exile preserve titles, deeds, and even keys to their former homes, ready for the day when they are allowed to return. The Israelis say that the Palestinians left voluntarily, and therefore they have no legitimate claim either to return to their former property or receive compensation. Despite anecdotes to the contrary, Israel maintains that it does not and has never forced Arab families to leave their homes. Moreover, Israel simply could not repatriate all the Palestinian refugees – whose numbers have increased significantly over 60 years – and continue to exist as a Jewish state.
- Israel wants to be recognized by its neighbors and the world. From the very beginning years of modern Israel, most Arab states have refused to even acknowledge the legitimacy of any Jewish state. Israel has been faced with constant, all-pervasive threats directed at its very existence, and Israeli culture and foreign policy are hugely affected by this pressure.
- Both Arabs and Israelis seek peace and security in their own homes. Because of occupation, insurgency, and terrorism, neither party can fully trust the other. Israel, essentially an occupying power, curtails Palestinians' livelihoods and opportunities. Palestinian suicide bombers kill Israeli civilians as they go about their lives. Lacking a government able to control these insurgents or to curtail these acts of violence, the Palestinians have little leverage in negotiations with the Israelis, who are often too wary of violent attacks to be willing to make concessions that might compromise security.

Map 8 1949
Armistice Lines

From Gregory
Mahler, Israel:
Government and
Politics/MAT
STA, 1E.
Copyright 1989
Wadsworth, a
part of Cengage
Learning Inc.
Reproduced by
permission.
www.cengage.
com/permissions.

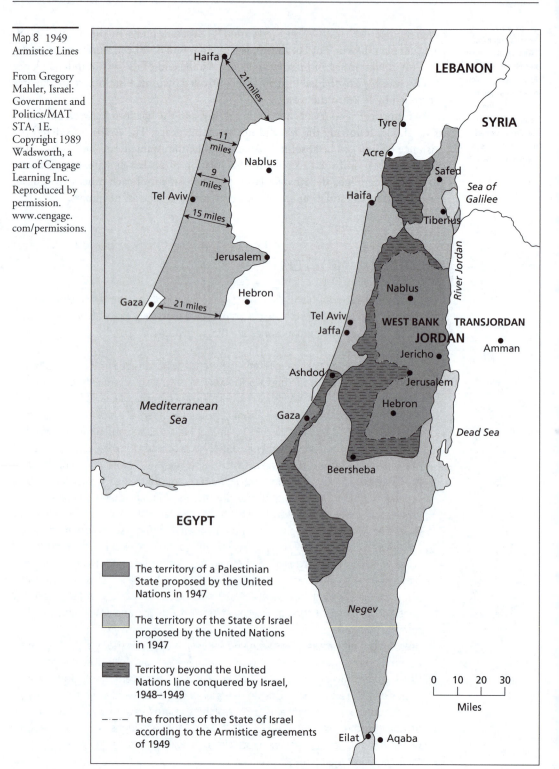

The territory of a Palestinian
State proposed by the United
Nations in 1947

The territory of the State of Israel
proposed by the United Nations
in 1947

Territory beyond the United
Nations line conquered by Israel,
1948–1949

The frontiers of the State of Israel
according to the Armistice agreements
of 1949

See reading #21, "State of Israel: Law of Return (July, 1950)"

In July of 1950, the Knesset, Israel's Parliament, enacted the Law of Return. This law, combined with the Nationality Law of 1952, gave special citizenship rights to Jews living outside Israel. The Law of Return declared that Israel is a home for all members of the Jewish people everywhere, and that those individuals who are born Jews (having a Jewish mother or grandmother), those with Jewish ancestry (having a Jewish father or grandfather), and converts to Judaism (Orthodox, Reform, or Conservative denominations) have a right to Israeli citizenship.

See reading #22, "U.N. Security Council: Resolution 95 Concerning the Passage of Ships Through the Suez Canal (September 1, 1951)"

See reading #23, "Palestine National Authority: Palestine Liberation Organization Draft Constitution (December, 1963)"

In late 1956, Egypt formed a pact of mutual defense with Syria and Jordan. Egypt also closed the Suez Canal and the Strait of Tiran to Israeli shipping traffic and developed closer relations with the Soviet Union. This was not the first time that Egypt had closed the Suez Canal to Israeli shipping. Fearing the machinations of strong neighbors, Israel allied with France and Great Britain and participated in a brief armed conflict known as the Suez Campaign. When the conflict ended, Israel found itself in possession of the Gaza Strip and portions of the Sinai peninsula in Egypt. Here the United States stepped in to facilitate negotiations, and was able to arrange for Israel to withdraw from these occupied territories in return for guaranteed, unfettered access to the Suez canal, and for free navigation and transport in the Gulf of Aqaba.[3] Once again, the immediate conflict had been resolved, but the underlying mistrust and antagonism between Israel and its neighbors continued to fester.

Meanwhile, the charter of the Palestine Liberation Organization (PLO) was prepared in 1963 by Ahmed Shukairy, a lawyer born in Palestine who represented Saudi Arabia and later Syria in the U.N. Shukairy later would become President of the PLO.

WHY DOES IT MATTER TO THE U.S.?[4]

The nation of Israel – small in size – lies thousands of miles from the United States, and yet its welfare has long been a pressing concern to the American government. Foreign policy positions on Israel have often played significant roles in U.S. presidential elections, and the U.S. sends Israel billions of dollars per year in aid. Why is Israel such a concern?

- At the outset, the United States fully endorsed the creation of the state of Israel. This enthusiasm was partially fueled by a post-Holocaust sense that traumatized Jews were entitled to a homeland, and partially by the U.S. role in the fledgling United Nations, which itself had endorsed the state.
- Israel is currently the only true democracy in the Middle East. As a nation preaching democracy as a governmental ideal, the United States is naturally inclined to support democracies like Israel. Moreover, its government makes Israel appear to be a safe, reliable ally against what have been referred to as "rogue" or "terrorist" states in the region, with whom the United States has more tenuous relations.

- As the Cold War developed, Israel rapidly became the United States' best ally in the region in the race for global influence with the Soviet Union. As Arab states moved closer to the U.S.S.R. for both fiscal and ideological reasons, the U.S. and Israel moved ever closer together.
- Although rumors persist to the contrary, there is no basis for the charge that a group of Zionist Jews is secretly running the U.S. government. Nonetheless, both Christian and Jewish lobbies in the United States do exert significant influence on the American political process in a pro-Israel direction – many Jews out of sympathy and a sense of identity with Israel, and many Christians out of a religious conviction that the existence of a state of Israel is necessary to the arrival of End Times.

Israeli settlements in northern Galilee often took fire from the Syrian front; border settlements further south were harassed by Egyptians and Jordanians. These attacks and the Israeli response strikes created an escalating, vicious cycle of grievances between Israel and its neighbors. Even worse, in early 1967, Egypt ordered the United Nations to withdraw its peacekeeping forces from the buffer zone between Israel and Egypt.

According to its procedural mandates, the United Nations could only maintain peacekeeping forces when all parties in a conflict wanted their presence. The U.N. therefore had no choice but to withdraw from the Sinai. Israel, of course, viewed this development with suspicion – a suspicion unfortunately bolstered by Egypt's closing (again) of the Straits of Tiran. This closure directly interfered with shipping to and from Israel, and directly contradicted the terms of the 1956 ceasefire.

Once again, Israel turned to the United States for its help as a facilitator. In this instance, despite having stood as the guarantor of Israel's shipping rights in 1956, the United States declined to participate. Among other reasons, this was because U.S. President Lyndon Johnson was very occupied in 1967 with America's challenges in Southeast Asia – more specifically in Vietnam – and was not interested in American forces becoming involved in the Middle East. Faced with hostile escalations from both Egypt and Syria, and with no obvious diplomatic recourse,

See reading #24, "Israeli Foreign Minister Abba Eban Speech to the Security Council of the United Nations (June 6, 1967)"

Israel attacked Egypt and Syria in early June of 1967. The Arab nations' ally, Jordan, also entered the fray, but Israel was fighting for its very existence, and fought hard. Israel gained control of the skies in the first two days, and after that time controlled a significant strategic advantage in the fighting. In a mere six days, forces from all three Arab powers had been thoroughly routed. Thousands of Palestinians found themselves displaced and unable to return to their homes. Israel, meanwhile, found itself in control of the West Bank, the Gaza Strip, the Sinai, and Syria's Golan Heights.

WHO ARE TODAY'S REFUGEES?[5]

One of the trickiest terms to define in the Arab–Israeli dialogue is "refugee." Before the rights and responsibilities of refugees can be determined, it is first necessary to figure out who they are. Definitions vary widely based on who is doing the defining.

• According to the United Nations, a Palestinian refugee is a descendant (through the male line) of any person who had been residing in Palestine from 1946 to 1948, and who lost his home and livelihood as a consequence of the Israeli declaration of independence. Currently, over a million refugees (about one-third of those defined as such by the U.N.) live in U.N. camps in Jordan, Lebanon, Syria, Gaza, and the West Bank. The U.N. does not recognize those who fled Palestine as a result of the 1967 conflict to be refugees.

• Badil, an organization dedicated to lobbying for Palestinian refugees, divides the refugees into five categories: those who left in 1948, those displaced in 1967, those who have left at some subsequent time, and those currently residing in either Gaza or the West Bank, because they are not full citizens of a stable state. In 2003, Badil estimated a total of over 7 million Palestinian refugees.

• Some pro-Israeli groups suggest that the definition of a Palestinian refugee is increasingly unfair to Israel. Even if a "refugee" is someone who was displaced from his or her home, they argue, the term is nearly never used elsewhere to apply to the descendants of those who fled, and they claim that expecting Israel to absorb nearly ten million returnees is nonsensical.

This latter territory was extremely valuable for Israel. Possession of the entire northern region of Palestine allowed Israel to much better control its water resources. More immediately, the Golan Heights served an important security function. At the very northern tip of the Great Rift Valley (which continues to the south all the way to Kenya), the Golan Heights are quite literally *above* Galilee. With very basic military technology, it was therefore extremely easy for militants in the Heights to shell and otherwise assault many Israeli settlements in the fertile Galilee area, and militants had been making good use of that geographic opportunity over the years. Now Israel could tightly control and monitor these lands with such dangerous access to Israeli citizens.

One concern following the 1967 war had to do with Israeli treatment of religious minorities in the areas newly under its control. Shortly following the end of the war, on June 27, 1967, Prime Minister Levi Eshkol addressed the spiritual leaders of all communities and assured them of Israel's determination to protect the Holy Places. That day, the Knesset passed the Protection of Holy Places Law, 1967.

See reading #25, "Protection of Holy Places Law (June 27, 1967)"

In August 1967 eight Arab heads of state attended an Arab summit conference in Khartoum, to discuss pan-Arab responses to the outcome of the 1967 War. The outcome of that meeting served as the basis of most Arab foreign policy toward Israel through the 1970s. The resolution adopted at Khartoum called for a continued

See reading #26,
"The Khartoum
Resolutions
(September 1,
1967)"

See reading #27,
"Resolution 242,
U.N. Security
Council (November
22, 1967)"

struggle against Israel, the creation of a fund to assist the economies of Egypt and Jordan, the lifting of an Arab oil boycott against the West and a new agreement to end the war in Yemen. Perhaps the most famous dimension of the Khartoum conclusion was the "three nos" clause: no peace with Israel, no recognition of Israel, and no negotiations with Israel.

Israel's impressive defeat of its enemies in 1967 was not, of course, to be the end of the story. The post-war status quo satisfied none of Israel's neighbors, who had only succeeded in increasing Israel's territorial size, and appearing weak in the public arena. Moreover, the Middle East had become involved in another global problem: the Cold War between the United States and the USSR. Israel had long been friendly to the interests of the United States, and Egypt found an eager sponsor in the Soviet Union.

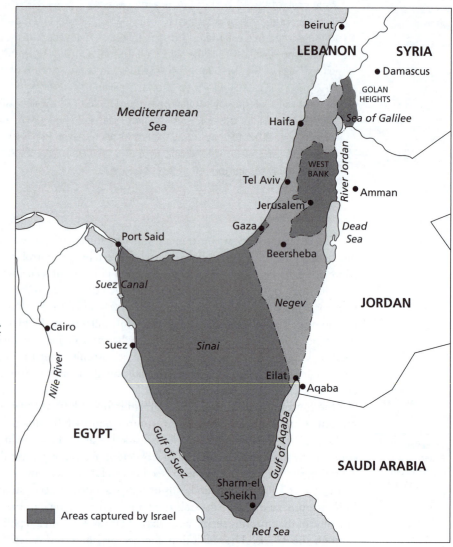

Map 9 Borders of Israel after the 1967 War

From Gregory Mahler, Israel: Government and Politics/MAT STA, 1E. Copyright 1989 Wadsworth, a part of Cengage Learning Inc. Reproduced by permission. www.cengage.com/permissions.

See reading #28,
"The Palestinian
National Charter
(July 1–17, 1968)"

See reading #29,
"The Seven Points
of Fatah (January,
1969)"

Palestinian nationalism continued to grow. In 1968 a Palestinian National Charter was published, a set of resolutions of the Palestine National Council. These resolutions were largely based upon documents dating back to January 1964, when at the Arab summit in Cairo a strategic decision was made to organize the Palestinian people. In January of 1969, at the Fifth Palestine National Congress, Fatah became the dominant faction of the PLO.

By the Fall of 1973 Israel was again seriously concerned about the developments on its borders and anticipated further Egyptian and Syrian hostilities. The United States, however, wary of military conflict between American and Soviet allies, strongly counseled Israel to avoid another preemptive strike on Egypt and Syria, and Israel complied.

Emboldened by new relationships with the Soviet Union and heavily supplied with Soviet armaments, Egypt and Syria attacked Israel on October 6, 1973. This particular day was Yom Kippur, the Jewish Day of Atonement. The holiest day of the Jewish year, Yom Kippur mandates introspection, fasting, and a general withdrawal from secular society. As such, the Israel Defense Force – heavily dependent for manpower upon military reserves that require several days to reach full strength – was especially vulnerable to an attack, and initially suffered for it with significant loss of life and territory. Egyptian forces retook much of the Sinai; allied Syrian forces retook the Golan Heights.

See reading #30,
"Resolution 338,
U.N. Security
Council (October 22,
1973)"

See reading #31,
"Palestine National
Council: Resolutions
at the 12th Session
of the Palestine
National Council
(June, 1974)"

The Israeli military found its footing, however, and eventually the military tides turned. At the end of two weeks, Israel had pushed Egypt back across the Suez. Moreover, Israel had pushed back so far on Syrian forces that its troops were within twenty miles of Damascus. The conflict known by Israelis as the Yom Kippur War, and by Arabs as the October War, came to a conclusion with Israel once again solidly the victor.

Originally the Palestine Liberation Organization called for the "total liberation of all occupied Palestine." At its Twelfth National Council in Cairo in 1974, however, it changed this goal, seeking instead to establish "a national authority in every part of Palestinian territory that is liberated."

Despite having lost territory by the conclusion of the war, many Egyptians felt that their president, Anwar al Sadat, had sent an important message to Israel and the world: that Egypt was a significant military force and not to be trifled with. Sadat was known among his fans as the "hero of the crossing,"[6] in honor of the taking of the Suez Canal.

See reading #32,
"Interim Agreement
between Israel and
Egypt (September 1,
1975)"

Seeing himself as the emergent leader of the Arab world, Sadat did something that had been unthinkable only a few years earlier. In late 1977, he reached out to his Israeli neighbors and suggested his willingness to discuss an Israeli–Egyptian peace agreement, traveling to Israel and addressing a session of the Israeli Knesset. Finally, in December of 1977, Sadat and Israeli Prime Minister Menachem Begin met in Ismailia, Egypt.

The Ismailia talks were not particularly successful. There was a fundamental disagreement about the primary issue to be resolved; Egypt sought a resolution to the question of Palestinian rights and refugee status before it would discuss a bilateral peace agreement between the two states, but Israel prioritized an open, public peace agreement between the two states that might set the tone for future developments in the region. Also, the Egyptian proposal called for a return to the 1967 east/west division of Jerusalem and offered guaranteed access to holy places for Israelis. Israel intended to maintain control of Jerusalem, with the exception of Muslim holy places, which could be controlled by some Arab authority.

Even if the two countries could have reached a peace agreement of sorts, they failed to agree about how that agreement would proceed. Israel preferred a schedule of phased withdrawal from the land it occupied, preceded by immediate and full Egyptian recognition of the state of Israel. Egypt offered exactly the opposite – a schedule of phases of diplomatic recognition, justified by the good-faith withdrawal of Israeli troops in the very short term. They differed on the status of the West Bank and Gaza: Egypt wanted Israel to remove itself entirely from their internal affairs, but Israel offered only limited self-rule with a final decision about state autonomy to be subject to later negotiations.

Finally, the Israeli and Egyptian delegations conflicted on the very touchy issue of settlements. While Israel held land formerly considered Palestinian, the land was not held in limbo. Thousands of Jews had poured into the fertile, abandoned areas and set up outposts that were rapidly flourishing. These "settlements," as they are most commonly called, served a primary Israeli purpose, precisely because they made negotiation more difficult. They created "facts on the ground" as Israeli Prime Minister Begin referred to them, that made it much more difficult for the Israeli government to even consider offering the return of those lands to Arab control. These settlements have continued to be a huge political and security issue for the state of Israel, and even in 1977 it was obvious to Sadat that their development needed to stop. Begin, however, considered the settlements perfectly legal and had no intention of curtailing them; in fact, he encouraged them.

See reading #33, "Statement to the Knesset by Prime Minister Menahem Begin (November 20, 1977)"

See reading #34, "Statement to the Knesset by President Anwar al Sadat (November 20, 1977)"

See reading #35, "Six-Point Program of the Palestine Liberation Organization (December 4, 1977)"

See reading #36, "The Camp David Accords (September 17, 1978)"

See reading #37, "Peace Treaty Between Israel and Egypt (March 26, 1979)"

Following the visit of Egyptian President Anwar Sadat to Jerusalem, the Palestine Liberation Movement met in Tripoli, Libya, and issued a reaction statement designed to bring together a group of states that would try to isolate Egypt and prevent peace with Israel. This became known as the "refusal front." On December 4, 1977, they issued a statement that included rejection of both United Nations Security Council Resolution 242 and Resolution 338, and reaffirmed the commitment of the PLO to deny the right of Israel to exist.

Eager to see a final peace agreement develop between Egypt and Israel, U.S. president Jimmy Carter stepped up American involvement in the issue. In the Fall of 1978, he invited both Begin and Sadat to the Presidential retreat at Camp David, where he set up each delegation in its own cabin. Shuttling between delegations with offers and suggestions, Carter facilitated the development of what became a final document of Egyptian–Israeli understanding. The final sticking point was the status of a luxury hotel that Israel had built in the formerly Egyptian city of Taba. After lengthy negotiations, Israel agreed to allow the status of Taba to be subjected to international arbitration,[7] and an overall agreement was reached.

Although Anwar al Sadat had been careful to combine a broad Middle East peace agreement with a specific Egyptian–Israeli peace agreement (so that he could not be accused of "selling out" the Palestinians), he was not applauded in the rest of the Arab world for his unilateral agreement with Israel. Neither were his domestic policies universally applauded. Sadat's regime became increasingly authoritarian, and in

October 1981, he was assassinated. His assassination presented an obvious problem to the Israeli government: would a new Egyptian government respect Sadat's renegade peace agreement with Israel? The new president, Hosni Mubarak, quickly reassured Israel that repudiating that agreement was not his intent, and it has in fact endured to this day.

It is important to understand one of the huge complexities of the Arab–Israeli conflict: a phenomenon that can be called "party agency." In general, Israel acts as a political unit. Although its military decisions are of course not subject to constant legislative overview, the general direction of Israeli policies about the military, settlements, and negotiation are determined by the political reality of the Israeli government. While this government has occasionally repositioned itself on a conservative– liberal spectrum, it is generally a visible movement, transparent to international understanding and analysis. The same cannot be said of the institutions representing (or claiming to represent) Arab and Palestinian interests. These institutions are many and varied, and do not always share goals or approve of one another. It is therefore difficult for Israelis to know with whom they ought best to negotiate.

WHO SPEAKS FOR THE PALESTINIANS?

Far from having a united voice, the Palestinians have been represented by a number of different groups through the years – sometimes without particular concern for the Palestinians' approval. Some of the major players:

- **The Palestinian Liberation Organization (PLO)** was founded in 1964 to liberate Palestine through military means. The PLO, under the leadership of Yasser Arafat, was recognized as the legitimate representative of the Palestinian people by the Arab League in 1974. Israel followed suit, but not until 1993, when the PLO accepted a two-state solution and declared its recognition of the state of Israel. Thereafter, the PLO has been the dominant force in the Palestinian National Authority.
- **Fatah**, also known as the **Palestine National Liberation Movement**, is one faction of the PLO. Fatah was founded by Yasser Arafat and brought to prominence under his influence. It has, in recent years, become the political, non-violent voice in Palestine, and was the undisputed primary political force until the 2006 elections. It has labored under accusations of inefficiency, corruption, and incoherency in recent years.
- **Hamas** is a Sunni Muslim group, founded by the pan-Arab Muslim Brotherhood movement. Hamas does not recognize the State of Israel and, in fact, calls for its destruction. It is considered a terrorist organization by many, including the United States, but is often hailed for its effective social services and true dedication to the quality of life of the Palestinian people and Palestinian goals. Hamas is now the controlling party in the Gaza Strip.
- **Hezbollah** is a Shi'ite Muslim group heavily subsidized by Iran and primarily concerned with affairs in Lebanon. It is also considered a terrorist organization

by the United States and many others. While it does not directly claim to speak for the Palestinians, Hezbollah has nonetheless become a key player in the Arab–Israeli conflict, calling for the destruction of Israel and encouraging or perpetrating cross-border attacks into Israel from Lebanon.

See reading #38, "Basic Law: Jerusalem, Capital of Israel (July, 1980)"

In July 1980 the Knesset passed *Basic Law: Jerusalem, Capital of Israel.* The law took the position that Jerusalem's boundaries following the 1967 War would be the permanent boundaries of the city, and was seen as an acceptance of a philo-sophical statement by Israel's right wing that territory conquered in 1967 might stay under Israeli control. The law generated much international criticism of Israel, and United Nations Security Resolution 478 in 1980 – adopted with 14 votes in favor, none against, and the United States abstaining – called for the Law to be rescinded.

While Israel saw progress to its south, the situation in the north was less tranquil. Ongoing cross-border attacks on Israeli cities near the border with Lebanon generated increasing Israeli concern. In the summer of 1981, Israel attacked Lebanon, pushing back the Palestinian Liberation Organization (PLO) and Syrian forces responsible for the cross-border attacks. The U.S. quickly stepped in to mediate a ceasefire, and the Israeli occupation lasted only about a month.

See reading #39, "Saudi Crown Prince Fadh ibn Abd al-Aziz: The Fahd Plan (August 7, 1981)"

In August 1981, Saudi Crown Prince Fahd attempted to respond to several core issues of the Arab–Israeli conflict that had not yet been addressed with an eight-point peace proposal of his own. The starting point of his plan involved Israel's withdrawal from Arab territories occupied in 1967, including East Jerusalem, and the dismantling of Israel's settlements in those territories. It also included a key place for the Palestinian people's right to self-determination and compensation for Palestinian refugees not exercising the right of return. Fahd called for an independent Palestinian state with East Jerusalem as its capital. The plan was adopted in a modified form at the Arab summit in Fez, Morocco, on September 9, 1982, and remained the Arab position until the Madrid conference in 1991.

See reading #40, "Golan Heights Law (December 14, 1981)"

In December of 1981 the Knesset passed a piece of legislation called the "Golan Heights Law," which extended Israeli law to the area of the Golan Heights, land captured by Israel from Syria in 1973. Many saw this law as an effort to pressure Syria into negotiating a peace agreement with Israel, although it did not end up producing that result. When the law was introduced in the Knesset, Prime Minister Begin stated that the time had come to implement the government's policy regarding the Golan Heights citing Syria's implacable hostility to Israel.

All was not resolved with Lebanon, however. Barely a year after its most recent withdrawal, after continued cross-border antagonism and conflict, Israel had once again had enough, and it invaded Lebanon in June of 1982. This time, its presence in Lebanon was to be much longer-lasting. The PLO fled Lebanon for a more stable haven in Tunisia, while Israel occupied a significant area of southern Lebanon. This new occupation led to one of the most controversial incidents in Israeli–Arab history: the massacres in the refugee camps of Sabra and Shatila on the morning of September 16, 1982. Although the forces behind

See reading #41, "Prime Minister Menachem Begin: The Wars of No Alternative and Operation Peace for the Galilee (August 8, 1982)"

the deaths of hundreds to thousands of Palestinians were Lebanese Christians, Israel was implicated in the disaster, because the camps were in the territory occupied by Israel after its northward push. Critics argued that the Israelis, as those nominally in charge of the territory, should have protected the victims of the slaughter.

Later, both international and Israeli inquiries determined that Israel was indirectly responsible for the deaths in the refugee camps. At the time, international and domestic dismay was sufficient to cause the resignation of then-Defense Minister Ariel Sharon in 1983. That same pressure, as well as mediation by the United States, helped lead to a 1983 agreement for Israel's withdrawal from most of southern Lebanon. In the summer of 1985, Israel withdrew from all but a small "security zone" on the Israel–Lebanon border.

See reading #42, "Agreement between Israel and Lebanon (May 17, 1983)"

Once again, even as it appeared to resolve one set of issues with its neighbors, Israel found itself facing a new set of problems. In December 1987, Palestinians in Gaza and the West Bank turned to demonstrations and protests, which quickly escalated into armed conflict with Israeli forces. Known by the term "intifadha," the Arabic word for "uprising," this period of conflict and violence helped to bring the Palestinian situation back onto the international radar. Regardless of who started what, images of Palestinian children armed with rocks facing down powerful Israeli tanks moved the international community, and Israel faced increasing pressure to find a solution for the Palestinian question.

The Middle East arena changed rapidly in the later 1980s. In 1988, King Hussein of Jordan officially relinquished control of the West Bank to a hypothetical future Palestinian state. In practice, Jordan had not controlled the West Bank in 20 years; as a theoretical concession, it nonetheless had great symbolic impact. In November 1988, the Palestine National Congress meeting in Algiers accepted a new policy outline from Yasser Arafat and called for the convening of an international peace conference for the Middle East. Arafat said that this should be done under the auspices of the United Nations Security Council, and should be based upon Security Council Resolutions 242 and 338 and the assurance of the legitimate rights of the Palestinian people. The document proclaimed the independence of Palestine without defining its borders with Jerusalem as its capital. The document also renounced terrorism but accepted the right of people to fight against foreign occupation and called for the continuation of the intifadha. In December of that year, the Palestinian National Council formally accepted UN Resolution 181, including its partition plan creating an Israeli and a Palestinian state.

See reading #43, "Palestine National Council: Declaration of Independence (November 15, 1988)"

In 1989, Israeli Prime Minister Yitzhak Shamir proposed a four-point peace plan allowing for Palestinian self-government. United States Secretary of State James Baker proposed a similar but slightly more expansive peace plan, which Israel rejected. For the first time in its history, the Israeli Knesset voted to overturn a sitting government, frustrated with its leaders' inability to move forward with the peace process. Everything seemed optimistic for the future, positive development of Arab–Israeli relations.

See reading #44, "Israel's Peace Initiative (May 14, 1989)"

See reading #45, "U.S. Secretary of State James Baker's Five-Point Plan (October 10, 1989)"

In the summer of 1990, Iraqi President Saddam Hussein invaded tiny neighboring Kuwait. He knew that the Arab world was unlikely to back his "reclamation" of Kuwait, and had an idea for generating more support. Because "the enemy of my enemy is my friend," He supposed that if Israel could be drawn into the conflict, he would be able to rely on political and financial support from the wealthy Gulf states. Accordingly, Iraq fired missiles at Jerusalem and Tel Aviv, and suggested to the Palestinian National Council that a victorious Iraq would support the creation of a real, independent Palestinian state. Yasser Arafat willingly endorsed Iraq's sovereignty over Kuwait.

The results were not what Saddam Hussein had hoped. Complying with significant pressure from the United States, Israel did not respond to Iraq's opening salvo. Instead, Israel added its political backing to the American invasion of Kuwait and southern Iraq, pushing Saddam's forces back and out of the area. The Gulf states not only failed to support Iraq, but actively joined in the American opposition. Even worse, from the context of the Arab–Israeli situation, the Gulf states kicked thousands of Palestinian refugees out of their countries, exacerbating the refugee situation elsewhere and further straining the resources of the Palestinian community.

See reading #46, "Letter of Invitation to the Madrid Peace Conference (October 30, 1991)"

After the Gulf War, U.S. President George H.W. Bush refocused his administration's energies on the political situation in the Middle East. In October 1991, the U.S. and Soviet governments sponsored the Madrid Conference to facilitate conversation between Israel and Syria, Jordan, and Lebanon. Palestinians were included as part of a Jordanian delegation and not as a delegation of their own, but the Palestinian question was a pressing issue. Also on the table were questions of bilateral peace treaties between Israel and each of its neighbors, and issues of economic cooperation and development in the region as a whole.

Several rounds of talks followed. In the fourth round, in December 1991, the Palestinians presented a demand for direct elections in a hypothetical Palestinian state. Unwilling to cede that much control so quickly, Israel rejected the demand, and talks ended. Subsequent rounds of talks allowed the parties to stumble through the process of negotiation about what a Palestinian state might look like, whether Israel would withdraw from all or some of the Golan Heights, and whether Israel would recognize Palestinian organizations like the PLO.

See reading #47, "Israel–PLO Recognition (September 9, 1993)"

Finally, in August 1993, the PLO revealed a breakthrough: Israel and Palestinian representatives had reached something approximating an agreement. The two sides formally agreed to the Oslo Accords, named after the city where the secret negotiations had occurred. The Accords allowed for partial autonomy for a Palestinian Authority, and greater autonomy in the Gaza Strip and in Jericho.

See reading #48, "Declaration of Principles on Interim Self-Government Arrangements (September 13, 1993)"

On September 13, 1993, Israeli Prime Minister Yitzhak Rabin and PLO Chairman Yasser Arafat met and watched Israeli Foreign Minister Shimon Peres and PLO Executive Council Member Abou Abbas sign the Oslo Agreement, witnessed by President Bill Clinton, former presidents George Bush and Jimmy Carter, and many other dignitaries. The next day Israel and Jordan agreed to an Israel–Jordan Common Agenda, marking the end of the state of war between the two nations and paving the way for talks leading to a formal peace treaty.

See reading #49, "Israel–Jordan Common Agenda (September 14, 1993)"

See reading #50, "Agreement on the Gaza Strip and the Jericho Area (May 4, 1994)"

Progress toward a normalization of relations continued to be made in 1994. In May 1994 the Gaza–Jericho Agreement was signed. This brought about a withdrawal of Israeli forces and administration from specific areas of the West Bank and the Gaza Strip, and also described the transfer of powers and responsibilities to the Palestine National Authority, with specific attention paid to security arrangements.

See reading #51, "The Washington Declaration (July 25, 1994)"

See reading #52, "Treaty of Peace between The Hashemite Kingdom of Jordan and the State of Israel (October 26, 1994)"

See readings #53, #54, and #55: Nobel lectures (December 10, 1994)

Jordan's King Hussein and Israeli Prime Minister Yitzhak Rabin signed the Washington Declaration at the White House on July 25, 1994. It formally ended the 46-year state of war between Jordan and Israel. The Declaration committed both Jordan and Israel to aim at the "achievement of a just, lasting and comprehensive peace between Arab states and the Palestinians, with Israel." It included agreements safeguarding Islamic control over the Muslim Holy Sites of Jerusalem. The Declaration also mandated a number of practical steps such as the establishment of direct telephone links between Jordan and Israel, the opening of two new border crossings between the two countries, linking of the Jordanian and Israeli power grids, and police cooperation in combating crime. The signing of the Washington Declaration paved the way for Jordan and Israel to reach agreement on their Treaty of Peace, which was initialed at the border crossing between Eilat, Israel, and Aqaba, Jordan, on October 17, 1994, with United States President Bill Clinton witnessing the ceremony, and formally signed on October 26, 1994.

The year 1994 also saw three Middle East leaders – Israeli Prime Minister Yitzhak Rabin, Israeli Foreign Minister Shimon Peres, and Palestinian Authority Chairman Yasser Arafat – share the Nobel Prize for Peace. The three national leaders delivered Nobel Lectures on December 10, 1994, articulating their visions of peace and the future of the Middle East.

SECRET LIAISONS[8]

Although undeniably the best-known, the negotiations leading to the Oslo Accords were not Israel's only secret negotiations with Arab leaders. For example, Israel's history with its neighbor to the east, the Hashemite Kingdom of Jordan, is peppered with tales of unofficial communications.

- In 1947, Golda Meir – who would become the first female Prime Minister of Israel – crossed the border into then-Transjordan disguised as a Muslim wife traveling with her husband. She and her "husband," a colleague, met with Jordan's King Abdullah I and pleaded with him to keep his country out of the upcoming military conflict with Israel.
- In the 1970s, Israelis met repeatedly with King Hussein of Jordan, often in his doctor's office in London.
- In March 2004, King Abdullah II flew in a helicopter to drop by Prime Minister Ariel Sharon's personal ranch. The two leaders lunched and discussed the wall/fence barrier being erected between Israeli and Palestinian lands.

See reading #56, "Israeli–Palestinian Interim Agreement (September 28, 1995)"

In September 1995, Israeli and Palestinian representatives signed an interim agreement derived from the Oslo negotiations. This "Interim Agreement on the West Bank and the Gaza Strip" called for the creation of an independent Palestinian Authority, as well as touching on issues of troop positions, Palestinian elections and self-governance, and prisoner exchanges. Those in favor of Arab–Israeli peace were

See reading #57,
"Speech by Prime
Minister Yitzhak
Rabin to the
Knesset (October 5,
1995)"

See reading #58,
"Speech by Prime
Minister Rabin at a
Peace Rally
(November 4,
1995)"

See reading #59,
"Israel–Lebanon
Ceasefire
Understanding
(April 26, 1996)"

See reading #60,
"The Wye River
Memorandum
(October 23, 1998)"

See reading #61,
"Address in the
Knesset by Prime
Minister-Elect Ehud
Barak upon the
Presentation of
His Government
(July 7, 1999)"

pleased and expectant after this rapid progress. Then, on November 4, 1995, Prime Minister Yitzhak Rabin was assassinated by a Jewish student displeased with the Oslo Accords and their subsequent developments.

In April 1996, after three weeks of fighting between Israeli and Lebanese Hezbollah forces, U.S. Secretary of State Warren Christopher was credited with brokering a peace between Israel and the Hezbollah guerrillas. Israel said it launched "Operation Grapes of Wrath" to halt Hezbollah rocket attacks on its northern settlements. Hezbollah contended that the barrage would stop when Israel left the southern Lebanon enclave it occupied in 1982. The Israel–Lebanon Ceasefire Understanding led some observers to hope that Israel's northern border would remain calm in the future.

Over the next several years, international leaders of all stripes attempted to keep the Israeli–Arab peace process moving forward. Rabin's death led to the eventual election of Likud Party Prime Minister Binyamin Netanyahu, known for his more conservative and hawkish stance on the peace process. The United States hosted a conference at the Wye River Conference Center in Maryland, where President Clinton and Secretary of State Albright met with Netanyahu and Palestinian President Yasser Arafat. The product of that meeting, known as the Wye River Memorandum, demonstrated that even a hard-line Israeli government could arrive at some form of agreement with its Palestinian neighbors.

In the spring of 1999, Labor Party member Ehud Barak was elected Prime Minister of Israel. Despite his strong military background, Barak championed peace and negotiation with Israel's Arab neighbors, and his election symbolized the ongoing hope in the Middle East that a solution to the Middle East conflict was within reach. But Barak's administration was to be short-lived.

On September 9, 2000, Ariel Sharon, leader of the opposition Likud party, and approximately 1,000 members of the Israeli police force visited the Temple Mount in Jerusalem. The top of the Temple Mount is a huge compound enclosing the al-Aqsa Mosque and the Dome of the Rock, and the area is considered the third holiest site in Islam. It is also the site of the last Temple of the Jews in Israel, and the enclosing compound includes the Wailing Wall, making the site the holiest place in the world for Jews. Long balanced under Jordanian protection, the area is a hotbed of contention and dispute.

During his visit, Sharon took the opportunity to proclaim Israel's sovereignty over the al-Aqsa and Temple Mount area. The next day, Palestinian protesters and Israeli police met and clashed in the first violent encounter of what would become known as the al-Aqsa Intifadha. Whether Sharon's visit was an intentional attempt to contribute to his political aspirations may never be known, but subsequent international investigation did condemn Sharon for his inflammatory actions. The reactions were intense and widespread, and despite desperate negotiations, the cycle of Israeli and Palestinian violence spun out of control.

The international *zeitgeist*, of course, shifted dramatically in the fall of 2001 with the attacks on financial and military targets in the United States. It is important to note that the Palestinian insurgency is *not*, traditionally, associated with the religiously fundamental forces associated with Osama bin Laden and his ilk – those moving out of Saudi Arabia and into areas like Pakistan, Afghanistan, and, in the last few years, Iraq. There has, of course, been a significant uptick in religiously oriented political action in Palestinian communities, demonstrated most clearly in the 2006 election of a religiously motivated government in the Gaza Strip. But in 2001, it was fairly safe to say that those angrily rebelling in the streets of Gaza and the West Bank were not associated with the men flying the planes into the World Trade Center in New York City.

Nonetheless, the world did change, politically and philosophically. Buoyed by the insurgency in his own country and by the international sense of insecurity and instability, Ariel Sharon was elected Prime Minister of Israel in 2001, promising security. Within a year, the Sharon administration announced the expansion of the construction of a Security Wall between Israeli and Palestinian holdings to terminate the series of suicide attacks perpetrated by Palestinians in Israeli territory. Unfortunately, this barrier also divided some Palestinian families from each other, farmers from their land, children from their schools, and employees from their jobs.

WHAT'S IN A NAME?[9]

The Arab–Israeli conflict has been plagued with persistent issues of nomenclature. Even a relatively small slip of terminology can upset one side or the other. This fact is apparent in the ongoing struggle over what to call the Israeli/West Bank barrier.

- Israelis prefer to refer to the barrier as "a fence," implying a lack of permanence and a sense of permeability. Israel's flagship daily newspaper, *Ha'aretz*, has even gone so far as to refer to the sturdier sections as "concrete section[s] of separation fence."
- At their most generous, Palestinian sources prefer the term "wall." Some pro-Palestinian groups refer to the barrier as an "apartheid wall" and compare it to the Berlin Wall.
- Amnesty International, by way of an example only, carefully maintains neutrality and chooses the term "fence/wall" wherever appropriate.
- This debate is complicated by the fact that the actual physical object of the discussion is not always the same. There are many miles of concrete wall, especially in the area near Jerusalem, typically 10 meters (30 feet) high. In these areas the word "wall" is clearly correct, and the word "fence" would not be, since the object in question is solid, made of concrete, and 30 feet high. Far more of the border between Israeli territory and Palestinian territory is delimited by what elsewhere *would* be called a "fence": something made of wire, 10 to 12 feet high.

International opinion frowned on the construction of the barrier between Israel and its Palestinian neighbors. The United Nations General Assembly condemned it, and the International Court of Justice ruled that it was illegal according to international law. But the fence/wall spoke to Israeli frustration with ongoing terrorist attacks despite negotiations. Israel had also reached the limit of its tolerance for Palestinian President Yasser Arafat, who appeared to be failing to control the attacks coming from his territory – some even accused him of blatantly endorsing such attacks. Accordingly, the Israeli military temporarily placed Arafat under house arrest and for periods of time occupied portions of the West Bank, such as the Church of the Nativity in Bethlehem.

WHAT ABOUT THE DISSENTERS?

One of the fundamental problems in the process of Israeli–Arab negotiation is that the extant Palestinian government appears to be incapable of enforcing its own declarations of peace, even if it is truly willing to offer them. In other words, the government may negotiate as much as it likes, but it cannot deliver on a promise to Israeli leaders of safety and security. It only takes one dissenter dedicated to the cause to kill himself (or herself) and kill dozens of Israelis, too. And this applies to both sides of the conflict: in 1994, a disgruntled Israeli settler opened fire on morning prayers in a mosque and killed 29 Arab worshippers there. This problem of *rejectionism* – the refusal of some factions on both sides of the conflict to participate in the state-level peace process – is one of the most frustrating aspects of Israeli–Palestinian relations.

See reading #62, "Sharm el-Sheikh Memorandum (September 4, 1999)"

The Sharm el-Sheikh Memorandum on Implementation Timeline of Outstanding Commitments of Agreements Signed and the Resumption of Permanent Status Negotiations was a memorandum signed on September 4, 1999, by the Prime Minister of Israel Ehud Barak and PLO Chairman Yasser Arafat at Sharm el Sheikh in Egypt. The United States coordinated the process and was represented by Secretary of State Madeleine Albright. The memorandum was witnessed and co-signed by President Hosni Mubarak of Egypt and King Abdullah of Jordan. The purpose of the Memorandum was to implement the Interim Agreement on the West Bank and the Gaza Strip (Oslo II) of September 1995 and to implement all other agreements between the PLO and Israel since September 1993 that were not moving forward as quickly as all parties might have liked.

See reading #63, "Protocol Concerning Safe Passage Between the West Bank and the Gaza Strip (October 5, 1999)"

Next, the Protocol Concerning Safe Passage was signed in October 1999. This document was a result of the Wye River Memorandum, and was intended to contribute to the normalization of life of the Palestinians living under occupation by making it easier to travel from the West Bank to Gaza – through Israel – and return. It was never implemented by Israel.

See reading #64, "Trilateral Statement on the Middle East Peace Summit at Camp David (July 25, 2000)"

In July 2000, U.S. President Bill Clinton invited Israeli Prime Minister Ehud Barak and Palestinian Authority Chairman Yasser Arafat to Camp David. Clinton hoped that, in his final weeks in office, he might be able to press the two leaders to reach a real and lasting agreement to move the parties forward toward a Middle East peace. The meetings were not successful. Although the final statement from the meeting made an effort to sound as though the meeting had been a success, leaders were disappointed.

See reading #65,
"Sharm El-Sheikh
Fact-Finding
Committee Final
Report (April 30,
2001)"

On April 30, 2001, the Sharm el-Sheikh Fact-Finding Committee, chaired by former U.S. Senator George Mitchell, issued its final report on what could be done to break the cycle of violence that had developed between Israel and the Palestinians, and how the Israeli–Palestinian negotiations might be re-energized, leading to a solution to the conflict. The report singled out Ariel Sharon's visit on September 28, 2000, to the Temple Mount area as significant in the start of the al-Aqsa Intifadha, and suggested that Israeli settlement building, Palestinian acts of terrorism, Israeli military responses to those acts, and injudicious public statements had all contributed to the cycle of violence in the Middle East.

The situation was not entirely bleak. In March 2002, Crown Prince Abdullah of Saudi Arabia proposed a new peace initiative at a conference in Beirut. This initiative called for a return to the 1967 borders of Israel and Palestine. In return, the Arab League promised to fully normalize relations with the State of Israel. This proposal was especially significant because it signified the willingness of the Saudi government to finally compromise. Although Israel rejected the substance of the proposal, this was the first time after nearly 40 years that Israel had had an offer of goodwill from its fiercest ideological opponent.

As Saudi Arabia and the Arab League moved toward normalization, the United States appeared to be moving away from its position as recurrent mediator. President George W. Bush did not share his predecessor's optimism that a solution to the Arab–Israeli quagmire was forthcoming; moreover, his attention was focused on the escalating situation in Iraq. In the summer of 2002, Bush gave a speech evidencing a hawkish frustration with Palestinians, calling the terrorist attacks "homicide bombings," in a somewhat redundant turn of phrase meant to emphasize their indefensibility.[10]

See reading #66,
"Roadmap to a
Solution of the
Israeli–Palestinian
Conflict (April 30,
2003)"

Bush did not walk away from the situation entirely. Along with the United Nations, the European Union, and Russia, the United States proposed what became known as the "Roadmap for Peace." The Roadmap reiterated the call for a two-state solution, but designed the normalization process to be implemented based on the achievement of certain goals. That is, rather than imposing an external timeline on the peace process, the Roadmap called on Israel and the Palestinian Authority to meet certain benchmarks of goodwill and development, at which point the next phase of the plan would begin.

See reading #67,
"The Disengagement
Plan from Gaza
Strip and Northern
Samaria
(April 18, 2004)"

See reading #68,
"Prime Minister
Ariel Sharon's
Address to the
Knesset – The
Vote on the
Disengagement
Plan (October 25,
2004)"

Chief among these benchmarks was the cessation of violence, including (and especially) suicide attacks by Palestinian insurgents. The enforcement and improvement of the Roadmap were not a priority of the Bush administration, unfortunately; President Bush did not even visit the Middle East as president until 2008, the last year of his eight-year term in office. The usefulness of the Roadmap has been questioned, as very few of its objectives have been met.

American attention soon turned almost exclusively to the new war in Iraq, which officially came to a head in 2003. Nonetheless, the peace process lurched along. In 2004, Prime Minister Ariel Sharon announced that as a result of not having a partner with whom to seriously negotiate – by which he meant that Israel could not trust negotiations with the Palestinians – Israel had decided to withdraw entirely from Gaza, leaving it to govern itself – but surrounded and thoroughly locked down by Israel on its borders. That same year, President Yasser Arafat died. Stepping into the leadership of the Palestinian Authority, new President Mahmoud Abbas was elected in 2005, promising to advance negotiations with Israel. Shortly thereafter the militant groups still embroiled in the al-Aqsa Intifadha agreed to a cease-fire with Israeli troops.

In 2006, Israel lashed out at Hezbollah on the Lebanese border after the kidnapping of several Israeli soldiers. That conflict lasted barely a month, but changed the political landscape significantly, as it was generally *not* considered a success for the Israeli forces. In fact, the Hezbollah insurgents in Lebanon gleefully claimed victory, and the missing soldiers were not returned. For the first time, it was fairly widely perceived that Israel had failed at a major military objective, rocking the government internally.

See reading #69, "U.N. Security: Council Resolution 1701 (August 11, 2006)"

In the same year, Palestinians went to the polls, and brought to life a dilemma beloved of political scientists: what happens when the winner of a democratic election is not fully a participant in the democratic process? Specifically, Palestinians elected an overwhelming majority government of Hamas members. Long listed as a terrorist organization by the U.S. Department of State, the election of Hamas represented a move away from the peace process. Even the sitting government of the Palestinian Authority, long a Fatah stronghold, was horrified. The U.S. stopped all financial assistance to the Palestinian Authority and politics there ground to a halt.

WHY HAMAS?[11]

In 2006, the Western world watched in surprise as Palestinians participated in a democratic election and a majority chose Hamas to represent them. Hamas denies the legitimacy of the State of Israel and has actively sought its destruction. Moreover, Western powers consider Hamas to be a violent terrorist organization. Why would a largely peaceful population of Palestinians choose Hamas to speak for them?

The answer, in a nutshell, is that Hamas is seen and understood differently by Palestinians than by Western observers. Palestinians looked at their previous government, run by Yasser Arafat's Fatah party, and saw corruption and inefficacy. They saw a frustrating lack of infrastructure, rampant graft, and an ongoing and apparently insolvable enmity with Israel. Like many populations chafing under an unpleasant status quo, Palestinians sought a political change.

By contrast, Hamas has been known among many Palestinians as a grassroots organization embracing reassuringly Muslim values. Hamas has successfully raised funds for hospitals, schools, and other infrastructure development in Palestine conducted completely outside government supervision. Perhaps most importantly, Hamas has served as a focus for identity politics in Palestine, returning pride and honor to Palestinians who feel humiliated by what has seemed to be decades of subjugation to everybody's will but their own.

Desperate to prevent the outbreak of civil war in the Palestinian Authority, Hamas and Fatah agreed to a Saudi proposal arranging a coalition government in Palestine. The two groups eyed each other warily until Hamas took over control of

Gaza entirely in June 2007. At that point, Fatah declared the unity government invalid and reclaimed unilateral control of the Palestinian Authority in the West Bank, and the U.S. resumed its financial assistance to that area. Gaza remains under the control of Hamas – and without the benefit of international financial assistance – to this day.

In the final year of his eight years in office as President of the United States, George W. Bush sought to leave his mark on the Middle East peace process. On November 20, 2007, plans for an Annapolis Peace Conference were announced and nations were invited to come to Annapolis to discuss the peace process. The conference marked the first time both sides came to negotiations agreeing upon a two-state solution, and was also noteworthy for the number of participants who appeared and the inclusion of a number of Arab nations that had not actively participated in the peace process before.

See reading #70, "Announcement of Annapolis Conference (November 20, 2007)"

The Annapolis Conference was held on November 27, 2007, at the United States Naval Academy in Annapolis, Maryland. The conference ended with the issuing of a joint statement from all parties. The objectives of the conference were an attempt to produce a substantive document on resolving the Israeli-Palestinian conflict along the lines of President George W. Bush's Roadmap For Peace (see Document # 66), with the eventual establishment of a Palestinian state.

See reading #71, "Joint Understanding on Negotiations (November 27, 2007)"

In May 2008, Israel celebrated the sixtieth anniversary of its independence. Mere miles away, hundreds of thousands of Palestinians and their sympathizers marked the sixtieth anniversary of the Naqba "catastrophe." Gaza continues to labor under the burden of closed borders, no income, and no infrastructure, while the Palestinian Authority deals with its own issues of poor organization, corruption, and Israeli interference. Israeli citizens continue to live with the constant threat of random shelling from Arab territories, suicide bombs in their restaurants, schools, and religious sites, and the ongoing threats of complete annihilation from bombastic leaders of neighboring countries.

This introductory chapter has barely touched upon the tensions also prevalent *among* Israel's neighbors, who often do not agree with one another on almost anything. Neither have we elaborated on the tensions within Israel itself, where secular citizens frequently butt heads with religious elements to create a contradictory, frustrating foreign policy. Most of all, it is difficult to know how to end a survey examination of the history of Israel's relations with its neighbors. In a situation that changes as rapidly and as unpredictably as this one, any predictions or assessments of the future will inevitably sound dated and inappropriate before very long.

In the end, the Israeli-Arab conflict is the story of two peoples who are not so very different. It is an indisputable fact that both share roots in the dusty lands both consider holy. Until relatively recently, neither had governed themselves as a modern state. It is probably also true that each group has realized the futility of trying to outlast the other. Whether the acknowledgement of this futility will lead to a conclusion with which both can live is a matter only time can resolve.

"Ye People of the Scripture! Why will ye argue about Abraham, when the Torah and the Gospel were not revealed till after him?" (Holy Qur'an, Pickthall translation, 003.065)

Map 10 Israel Borders Today

From Gregory Mahler, Israel: Government and Politics/MAT STA, 1E. Copyright 1989 Wadsworth, a part of Cengage Learning Inc. Reproduced by permission. www.cengage.com/permissions.

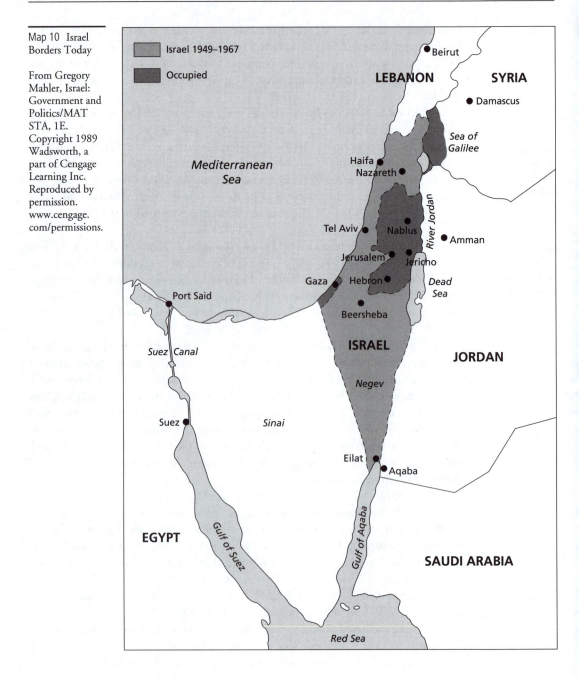

- Israel 1949–1967
- Occupied

Beirut

LEBANON

SYRIA

Damascus

Sea of Galilee

Haifa
Nazareth

Mediterranean Sea

River Jordan

Tel Aviv

Nablus

Amman

Jerusalem

Jericho

Gaza

Hebron

Dead Sea

Beersheba

ISRAEL

JORDAN

Negev

Port Said

Suez Canal

Suez

Sinai

Eilat

Aqaba

EGYPT

Gulf of Suez

Gulf of Aqaba

SAUDI ARABIA

Red Sea

Notes

1 It is important to explain the terms used to refer to the various parties in this conflict. The term "Arab," which was originally a geography-based label referring to someone from Arabia, refers to an ethnic group of the Middle East. Arabs are largely Muslim, but many are Christian. A very small number of Arabs are, in fact, Jews. That said, the term "Jew" generally refers to a *non-Arab* person of Middle Eastern descent, who may be religious (Jewish) or secular. The term "Israeli" refers to a citizen of the state of Israel after 1948. It is worth noting that Israelis may be Arabs, although they are usually Jews. Many Israelis are not orthodox Jews, though the state itself is nominally a Jewish state.

2 This is an important distinction. A state, as the term is used here, is a political entity with political sovereignty – the ability to make public policy on its own. A homeland, on the other hand, is a geographical region *within* a state that does *not* have sovereignty or the ability to make public policy on its own without the permission or acquiescence of another state.

3 The Israeli preference is to refer to this body of water as "The Gulf of Eilat." As general international consensus favors "Gulf of Aqaba," that is the term used here.

4 Israeli–United States Relations (adapted from a report by Clyde R. Mark, Congressional Research Service, updated October 17, 2002) http://www.policyalmanac.org/world/archive/crs_israeli-us_relations.shtml.

5 http://www.jcpa.org/jl/vp485.htm; http://www.badil.org/Refugees/facts&figures.htm; http://www.un.org/unrwa/refugees/index.html

6 http://books.google.com/books?id=m-Hw_PFOlLsC&pg=PA132&lpg=PA132&dq=sadat+hero+of+the+crossing&source=web&ots=760h9Ffvpg&sig=-Iy714GGbg5wf6Mb65z_ocf3L8U

7 In accordance with the outcome of that arbitration, Taba was returned to Egypt in 1989.

8 http://news.bbc.co.uk/1/hi/world/middle_east/3549203.stm; http://news.bbc.co.uk/2/hi/events/israel_at_50/profiles/81288.stm; Bronner, Ethan. "Israel has long history of secret talks with Arabs." *The Boston Globe*, 31 October 1991.

9 http://www.haaretz.com/hasen/pages/ShArt.jhtml?itemNo=326397&contrassID=2&subContrassID=1&sbSubContrassID=0&listSrc=Y; http://electronicintifada.net/v2/article1791.shtml; http://www.stopthewall.org/; http://www.tomjoad.org/wall.htm; http://www.amnesty.org/en/library/info/MDE15/016/2004.

10 http://www.nationmaster.com/encyclopedia/Suicide-bombers

11 http://www.counterpunch.org/gordon02072006.html

Part II

From Herzl (1896) to
Recognition as a State (1949)

1 Theodor Herzl, *The Jewish State* (1896)

I. Introduction

[. . .]

The world possesses slaves of extraordinary capacity for work, whose appearance has been fatal to the production of handmade goods: these slaves are the machines. . . . Only those who are ignorant of the conditions of Jews in many countries of Eastern Europe would venture to assert that Jews are either unfit or unwilling to perform manual labor.

But I do not wish to take up the cudgels for the Jews in this pamphlet. It would be useless. Everything rational and everything sentimental that can possibly be said in their defense has been said already . . .

This century has given the world a wonderful renaissance by means of its technical achievements; but at the same time its miraculous improvements have not been employed in the service of humanity. Distance has ceased to be an obstacle, yet we complain of insufficient space. Our great steamships carry us swiftly and surely over hitherto unvisited seas. Our railways carry us safely into a mountain-world hitherto tremblingly scaled on foot. Events occurring in countries undiscovered when Europe confined the Jews in Ghettos are known to us in the course of an hour. Hence the misery of the Jews is an anachronism—not because there was a period of enlightenment one hundred years ago, for that enlightenment reached in reality only the choicest spirits.

I believe that electric light was not invented for the purpose of illuminating the drawing-rooms of a few snobs, but rather for the purpose of throwing light on some of the dark problems of humanity. One of these problems, and not the least of them, is the Jewish question. In solving it we are working not only for ourselves, but also for many other over-burdened and oppressed beings.

The Jewish question still exists. It would be foolish to deny it. It is a remnant of the Middle Ages, which civilized nations do not even yet seem able to shake off, try as they will. They certainly showed a generous desire to do so when they emancipated us. The Jewish question exists wherever Jews live in perceptible numbers. Where it does not exist, it is carried by Jews in the course of their migrations. We naturally move to those places where we are not persecuted, and there our presence produces persecution. This is the case in every country, and will remain so, even in those highly civilized—for instance, France—until the Jewish question finds a solution on a political basis. The unfortunate Jews are now carrying the seeds of Anti-Semitism into England; they have already introduced it into America.

I believe that I understand Anti-Semitism, which is really a highly complex movement. I consider it from a Jewish standpoint, yet without fear or hatred. I believe that I can see what elements there are in it of vulgar sport, of common trade jealousy, of inherited prejudice, of religious intolerance, and also of pretended self-defense. I think the Jewish question is no more a social than a religious one, notwithstanding that it sometimes takes these and other forms. It is a national question, which can only be solved by making it a political world-question to be discussed and settled by the civilized nations of the world in council.

We are a people—one people.

We have honestly endeavored everywhere to merge ourselves in the social life of surrounding communities and to preserve the faith of our fathers. We are not permitted to do so. In vain are we loyal patriots, our loyalty in some places running to extremes; in vain do we make the same sacrifices of life and property as our fellow-citizens; in vain do we strive to increase the fame of our native land in science and art, or her wealth by trade and commerce. In countries where we have lived for centuries we are still cried down as strangers, and often by those whose ancestors were not yet domiciled in the land where Jews had already had experience of suffering. The majority may decide which are the strangers, for this, as indeed every point which arises in the relations between nations, is a question of might. I do not here surrender any portion of our prescriptive right, when I make this statement merely in my own name as an individual. In the world as it now is and for an indefinite period will probably remain, might precedes right. It is useless, therefore, for us to be loyal patriots, as were the Huguenots who were forced to emigrate. If we could only be left in peace. . . .

But I think we shall not be left in peace.

Oppression and persecution cannot exterminate us. No nation on earth has survived such struggles and sufferings as we have gone through. Jew-baiting has merely stripped off our weaklings; the strong among us were invariably true to their race when persecution broke out against them. This attitude was most clearly apparent in the period immediately following the emancipation of the Jews. Those Jews who were advanced intellectually and materially entirely lost the feeling of belonging to their race. Wherever our political well-being has lasted for any length of time, we have assimilated with our surroundings. I think this is not discreditable. Hence, the statesman who would wish to see a Jewish strain in his nation would have to provide for the duration of our political well-being; and even a Bismarck could not do that.

For old prejudices against us still lie deep in the hearts of the people. He who would have proofs of this need only listen to the people where they speak with frankness and simplicity: proverb and fairy-tale are both Anti-Semitic. A nation is everywhere a great child, which can certainly be educated; but its education would, even in most favorable circumstances, occupy such a vast amount of time that we could, as already mentioned, remove our own difficulties by other means long before the process was accomplished.

Assimilation, by which I understood not only external conformity in dress, habits, customs, and language, but also identity of feeling and manner—assimilation of Jews could be effected only by intermarriage. But the need for mixed marriages would have to be felt by the majority; their mere recognition by law would certainly not suffice.

[. . .]

Those who really wished to see the Jews disappear through intermixture with other nations, can only hope to see it come about in one way. The Jews must previously acquire economic power sufficiently great to overcome the old social prejudice against them . . . A previous acquisition of power could be synonymous with that economic supremacy which Jews are already erroneously declared to possess . . .

Because I have drawn this conclusion with complete indifference to everything but the quest of truth, I shall probably be contradicted and opposed by Jews who are in easy circumstances. . . . But the distinctive nationality of Jews neither can, will, nor must be destroyed. It cannot be destroyed, because external enemies consolidate it. It will not be destroyed; this is shown during two thousand years of appalling suffering. It must not be destroyed, and that, as a descendant of numberless Jews who refused to despair, I am trying once more to prove in this pamphlet. Whole branches of Judaism may wither and fall, but the trunk will remain.

[. . .]

No human being is wealthy or powerful enough to transplant a nation from one habitation to another. An idea alone can achieve that and this idea of a State may have the requisite power to do so. The Jews have dreamt this kingly dream all through the long nights of their history. "Next year in Jerusalem" is our old phrase. It is now a question of showing that the dream can be converted into a living reality.

[. . .]

II. The Jewish Question

No one can deny the gravity of the situation of the Jews. Wherever they live in perceptible numbers, they are more or less persecuted. Their equality before the law, granted by statute, has become practically a dead letter. They are debarred from filling even moderately high positions, either in the army, or in any public or private capacity. And attempts are made to thrust them out of business also: "Don't buy from Jews!"

Attacks in Parliaments, in assemblies, in the press, in the pulpit, in the street, on journeys—for example, their exclusion from certain hotels—even in places of recreation, become daily more numerous. The forms of persecution varying according to the countries and social circles in which they occur. In Russia, imposts are levied on Jewish villages; in Rumania, a few persons are put to death; in Germany, they get a good beating occasionally; in Austria, Anti-Semites exercise terrorism over all public life; in Algeria, there are traveling agitators; in Paris, the Jews are shut out of the so-called best social circles and excluded from clubs. Shades of anti-Jewish feeling are innumerable. But this is not to be an attempt to make out a doleful category of Jewish hardships.

I do not intend to arouse sympathetic emotions on our behalf. That would be foolish, futile, and undignified proceeding. I shall content myself with putting the following questions to the Jews: Is it not true that, in countries where we live in perceptible numbers, the position of Jewish lawyers, doctors, technicians, teachers, and employees of all descriptions becomes daily more intolerable? Is it not true, that the Jewish middle classes are seriously threatened? Is it not true, that the passions of the mob are incited against our wealthy people? Is it not true, that our poor endure greater sufferings than any other proletariat? I think that this external pressure makes itself felt everywhere. In our economically upper classes it causes discomfort, in our middle classes continual and grave anxieties, in our lower classes absolute despair.

Everything tends, in fact, to one and the same conclusion, which is clearly enunciated in that classic Berlin phrase: "Juden Raus" (Out with the Jews !)

I shall now put the Question in the briefest possible form: Are we to "get out" now, and where to?

Or, may we yet remain? And, how long?

Let us first settle the point of staying where we are. Can we hope for better days, can we possess our souls in patience, can we wait in pious resignation till the princes and peoples of this earth are more mercifully disposed towards us? I say that we cannot hope for a change in the current of feeling. And why not? Even if we were as near to the hearts of princes as are their other subjects, they could not protect us. They would only feel popular hatred by showing us too much favor. By "too much," I really mean less than is claimed as a right by every ordinary citizen, or by every race. The nations in whose midst Jews live are all either covertly or openly Anti-Semitic.

[. . .]

We are one people—our enemies have made us one without our consent, as repeatedly happens in history. Distress binds us together, and, thus united, we suddenly discover our strength. Yes, we are strong enough to form a State, and, indeed, a model State. We possess all human and material resources necessary for the purpose . . .

THE PLAN

The whole plan is in its essence perfectly simple, as it must necessarily be if it is to come within the comprehension of all.

Let the sovereignty be granted us over a portion of the globe large enough to satisfy the rightful requirements of a nation; the rest we shall manage for ourselves.

The creation of a new State is neither ridiculous nor impossible. We have in our day witnessed the process in connection with nations which were not largely members of the middle class, but poorer, less educated, and consequently weaker than ourselves. The Governments of all countries scourged by Anti-Semitism will be keenly interested in assisting us to obtain the sovereignty we want.

The plan, simple in design, but complicated in execution, will be carried out by two agencies: The Society of Jews and the Jewish Company.

The Society of Jews will do the preparatory work in the domains of science and politics, which the Jewish Company will afterwards apply practically.

The Jewish Company will be the liquidating agent of the business interests of departing Jews, and will organize commerce and trade in the new country.

We must not imagine the departure of the Jews to be a sudden one. It will be gradual, continuous, and will cover many decades. The poorest will go first to cultivate the soil. In accordance with a preconceived plan, they will construct roads, bridges, railways and telegraph installations; regulate rivers; and build their own dwellings; their labor will create trade, trade will create markets and markets will attract new settlers, for every man will go voluntarily, at his own expense and his own risk. The labor expended on the land will enhance its value, and the Jews will soon perceive that a new and permanent sphere of operation is opening here for that spirit of enterprise which has heretofore met only with hatred and obloquy.

If we wish to found a State today, we shall not do it in the way which would have been the only possible one a thousand years ago. It is foolish to revert to old stages of civilization, as many Zionists would like to do. Supposing, for example, we were obliged to clear a country of wild beasts, we should not set about the task in the fashion of Europeans of the fifth century. We should not take spear and lance and go out singly in pursuit of bears; we would organize a large and active hunting party, drive the animals together, and throw a melinite bomb into their midst.

If we wish to conduct building operations, we shall not plant a mass of stakes and piles on the shore of a lake, but we shall build as men build now. Indeed, we shall build in a bolder and more stately style than was ever adopted before, for we now possess means which men never yet possessed.

The emigrants standing lowest in the economic scale will be slowly followed by those of a higher grade. Those who at this moment are living in despair will go first. They will be led by the mediocre intellects which we produce so superabundantly and which are persecuted everywhere.

This pamphlet will open a general discussion on the Jewish Question, but that does not mean that there will be any voting on it. Such a result would ruin the cause from the outset, and dissidents must remember that allegiance or opposition is entirely voluntary. He who will not come with us should remain behind.

Let all who are willing to join us, fall in behind our banner and fight for our cause with voice and pen and deed.

Those Jews who agree with our idea of a State will attach themselves to the Society, which will thereby be authorized to confer and treat with Governments in the name of our people. The Society will thus be acknowledged in its relations with Governments as a State-creating power. This acknowledgment will practically create the State.

Should the Powers declare themselves willing to admit our sovereignty over a neutral piece of land, then the Society will enter into negotiations for the possession of this land. Here two territories come under consideration, Palestine and Argentine. In both countries important experiments in colonization have been made, though on the mistaken principle of a gradual infiltration of Jews. An infiltration is bound to end badly. It continues till the inevitable moment when the native population feels itself threatened, and forces the Government to stop a further influx of Jews. Immigration is consequently futile unless we have the sovereign right to continue such immigration.

[. . .]

PALESTINE OR ARGENTINE?

Shall we choose Palestine or Argentine? We shall take what is given us, and what is selected by Jewish public opinion. The Society will determine both these points.

Argentine is one of the most fertile countries in the world, extends over a vast area, has a sparse population and a mild climate. The Argentine Republic would derive considerable profit from the cession of a portion of its territory to us. The present infiltration of Jews has certainly produced some discontent, and it would be necessary to enlighten the Republic on the intrinsic difference of our new movement.

Palestine is our ever-memorable historic home. The very name of Palestine would attract our people with a force of marvelous potency. If His Majesty the Sultan were to give us Palestine, we could in return undertake to regulate the whole finances of Turkey. We should there form a portion of a rampart of Europe against Asia, an outpost of civilization as opposed to barbarism. We should as a neutral State remain in contact with all Europe, which would have to guarantee our existence. The sanctuaries of Christendom would be safeguarded by assigning to them an extra-territorial status such as is well-known to the law of nations. We should form a guard of honor about these sanctuaries, answering for the fulfillment of this duty with our existence. This guard of honor would be the great symbol of the solution of the Jewish question after eighteen centuries of Jewish suffering.

[. . .]

III. The Jewish Company

IV. Local Groups

V. Society of Jews and Jewish State

[. . .]

We know and see for ourselves that States still continue to be created. Colonies secede from the mother country. Vassals fall away from their suzerain; newly opened territories are immediately formed into free States. It is true that the Jewish State is conceived as a peculiarly modern structure on unspecified territory. But a State is formed, not by pieces of land, but rather by a number of men united under sovereign rule. The people is the subjective, land the objective foundation of a State, and the subjective basis is the more important of the two. One sovereignty, for example, which has no objective basis at all, is perhaps the most respected one in the world. I refer to the sovereignty of the Pope.

[. . .]

The Society will have scientific and political tasks, for the founding of a Jewish State, as I conceive it, presupposes the application of scientific methods. We cannot journey out of Egypt today in the primitive fashion of ancient times. We shall previously obtain an accurate account of our number and strength.

[. . .]

Thus the Society will find out for the first time whether the Jews really wish to go to the Promised Land, and whether they must go there. Every Jewish community in the world will send contributions to the Society towards a comprehensive collection of Jewish statistics . . .

Externally, the Society will attempt, as I explained before in the general part, to be acknowledged as a State-forming power. The free assent of many Jews will confer on it the requisite authority in its relations with Governments.

Internally, that is to say, in its relation with the Jewish people, the Society will create all the first indispensable institutions; it will be the nucleus out of which the public institutions of the Jewish State will later on be developed.

Our first object is, as I said before, supremacy, assured to us by international law, over a portion of the globe sufficiently large to satisfy our just requirements.

What is the next step?

THE OCCUPATION OF THE LAND

When nations wandered in historic times, they let chance carry them, draw them, fling them hither and thither, and like swarms of locusts they settled down indifferently anywhere. For in historic times the earth was not known to man. But this modern Jewish migration must proceed in accordance with scientific principles.

[. . .]

CONSTITUTION

One of the great commissions which the Society will have to appoint will be the council of State jurists. These must formulate the best, that is, the best modern constitution possible. I believe that a good constitution should be of moderately elastic nature. In another work I have explained in detail what forms of government I hold to be the best. I think a democratic monarchy and an aristocratic republic are the finest forms of a State, because in them the form of State and the principle of government are opposed to each other, and thus preserve a true balance of power.

[. . .]

Politics must take shape in the upper strata and work downwards. But no member of the Jewish State will be oppressed, every man will be able and will wish to rise in it. Thus a great upward tendency will pass through our people; every individual by trying to raise himself, raising also the whole body of citizens. The ascent will take a normal form, useful to the State and serviceable to the National Idea.

Hence I incline to an aristocratic republic. This would satisfy the ambitious spirit in our people, which has now degenerated into petty vanity. Many of the institutions of Venice pass through my mind; but all that which caused the ruin of Venice must be carefully avoided. We shall learn from the historic mistakes of others, in the same way as we learn from our own; for we are a modern nation, and wish to be the most modern in the world. Our people, who are receiving the new country from the Society, will also thankfully accept the new constitution it offers them. Should any opposition manifest itself, the Society will suppress it. The Society cannot permit the exercise of its functions to be interpreted by short-sighted or ill-disposed individuals.

LANGUAGE

It might be suggested that our want of a common current language would present difficulties. We cannot converse with one another in Hebrew. Who amongst us has a sufficient acquaintance with Hebrew to ask for a railway ticket in that language! Such a thing cannot be done. Yet the difficulty is very easily circumvented. Every man can preserve the language in which his thoughts are at home. Switzerland affords a conclusive proof of the possibility of a federation of tongues. We shall remain in the new country what we now are here, and we shall never cease to cherish with sadness the memory of the native land out of which we have been driven.

We shall give up using those miserable stunted jargons, those Ghetto languages which we still employ, for these were the stealthy tongues of prisoners. Our national teachers will give due attention to this matter; and the language which proves itself to be of greatest utility for general intercourse will be adopted without compulsion as our national tongue. Our community of race is peculiar and unique, for we are bound together only by the faith of our fathers.

THEOCRACY

Shall we end by having a theocracy? No, indeed. Faith unites us, knowledge gives us freedom. We shall therefore prevent any theocratic tendencies from coming to the fore on the part of our priesthood. We shall keep our priests within the confines of their temples in the same way as we shall keep our professional army within the confines of their barracks. . . .

Every man will be as free and undisturbed in his faith or his disbelief as he is in his nationality. And if it should occur that men of other creeds and different nationalities come to live amongst us, we should accord them honorable protection and equality before the law. We have learnt toleration in Europe. This is not sarcastically said; for the Anti-Semitism of today could only in a very few places be taken for old religious intolerance. It is for the most part a movement among civilized nations by which they try to chase away the spectres of their own past.

[. . .]

THE FLAG

We have no flag, and we need one. If we desire to lead many men, we must raise a symbol above their heads.

I would suggest a white flag, with seven golden stars. The white field symbolizes our pure new life; the stars are the seven golden hours of our working-day. For we shall march into the Promised Land carrying the badge of honor.

VI. Conclusion

OUTLINES

[. . .]

I have tried to meet certain objections; but I know that many more will be made, based on high grounds and low. To the first class of objections belongs the remark that the Jews are not the only people in the world who are in a condition of distress. Here I would reply that we may as well begin by removing a little of this misery, even if it should at first be no more than our own.

It might further be said that we ought not to create new distinctions between people; we ought not to raise fresh barriers, we should rather make the old disappear. But men who think in this way are amiable visionaries; and the idea of a native land will still flourish when the dust of their bones will have vanished tracelessly in the winds. Universal brotherhood is not even a beautiful dream. Antagonism is essential to man's greatest efforts. But the Jews, once settled in their own State, would probably have no more enemies. As for those who remain behind, since prosperity enfeebles and causes them to diminish, they would soon disappear altogether. I think the Jews will always have sufficient enemies, such as every nation has. But once fixed in their own land, it will no longer be possible for them to scatter all over the world. The diaspora cannot be reborn, unless the civilization of the whole earth should collapse; and such a consummation could be feared by none but foolish men. . . .

Here it is, fellow Jews! Neither fable nor deception! Every man may test its reality for himself, for every man will carry over with him a portion of the Promised Land— one in his head, another in his arms, another in his acquired possessions.

Now, all this may appear to be an interminably long affair. Even in the most favorable circumstances, many years might elapse before the commencement of the foundation of the State. In the meantime, Jews in a thousand different places would suffer insults, mortifications, abuse, blows, depredation, and death. No; if we only begin to carry out the plans, Anti-Semitism would stop at once and for ever. For it is the conclusion of peace.

The news of the formation of our Jewish Company will be carried in a single day to the remotest ends of the earth by the lightning speed of our telegraph wires. . . .

Prayers will be offered up for the success of our work in temples and in churches also; for it will bring relief from an old burden, which all have suffered.

But we must first bring enlightenment to men's minds. The idea must make its way into the most distant, miserable holes where our people dwell. They will awaken from gloomy brooding, for into their lives will come a new significance. Every man need think only of himself, and the movement will assume vast proportions.

And what glory awaits those who fight unselfishly for the cause!

Therefore I believe that a wondrous generation of Jews will spring into existence. The Maccabeans will rise again.

Let me repeat once more my opening words: The Jews who wish for a State will have it. We shall live at last as free men on our own soil, and die peacefully in our own homes.

The world will be freed by our liberty, enriched by our wealth, magnified by our greatness.

And whatever we attempt there to accomplish for our own welfare, will react powerfully and beneficially for the good of humanity.

2 The Basle Program, Resolutions of the First Zionist Congress (August 30, 1897)

Zionism seeks to establish a home for the Jewish people in Palestine secured under public law. The Congress contemplates the following means to the attainment of this end:

1. The promotion by appropriate means of the settlement in Palestine of Jewish farmers, artisans, and manufacturers.

2. The organization and uniting of the whole of Jewry by means of appropriate institutions, both local and international, in accordance with the laws of each country.

3. The strengthening and fostering of Jewish national sentiment and national consciousness. Preparatory steps toward obtaining the consent of governments, where necessary, in order to reach the goals of Zionism.

The handwritten copy of the program also states:

4. Preparatory steps toward obtaining the consent of governments, where necessary, in order to reach the goals of Zionism.

3 Sir Henry McMahon: The McMahon Letter (October 24, 1915)

24 October 1915

I have received your letter of the 29th Shawal, 1333, with much pleasure and your expression of friendliness and sincerity have given me the greatest satisfaction.

I regret that you should have received from my last letter the impression that I regarded the question of limits and boundaries with coldness and hesitation; such was not the case, but it appeared to me that the time had not yet come when that question could be discussed in a conclusive manner.

I have realised, however, from your last letter that you regard this question as one of vital and urgent importance. I have, therefore, lost no time in informing the Government of Great Britain of the contents of your letter, and it is with great pleasure that I communicate to you on their behalf the following statement, which I am confident you will receive with satisfaction.

The two districts of Mersina and Alexandretta and portions of Syria lying to the west of the districts of Damascus, Homs, Hama and Aleppo cannot be said to be purely Arab, and should be excluded from the limits demanded.

With the above modification, and without prejudice to our existing treaties with Arab chiefs, we accept those limits.

As for those regions lying within those frontiers wherein Great Britain is free to act without detriment to the interests of her ally, France, I am empowered in the name of the Government of Great Britain to give the following assurances and make the following assurances and make the following reply to your letter:

1. Subject to the above modifications, Great Britain is prepared to recognise and support the independence of the Arabs in all the regions within the limits demanded by the Sherif of Mecca.
2. Great Britain will guarantee the Holy Places against all external aggression and will recognise their inviolability.
3. When the situation admits, Great Britain will give to the Arabs her advice and will assist them to establish what may appear to be the most suitable forms of government for those various territories.
4. On the other hand, it is understood that the Arabs have decided to seek the advice and guidance of Great Britain only, and that such European advisers and officials as may be required for the formation of a sound form of administration will be British.

5. With regard to the *vilayets* of Bagdad and Basra, the Arabs will recognise that the established position and interests of Great Britain necessitate special administrative arrangements in order to secure these territories from foreign aggression to promote the welfare of the local populations and to safeguard our mutual economic interests.

I am convinced that this declaration will assure you beyond all possible doubt of the sympathy of Great Britain towards the aspirations of her friends the Arabs and will result in a firm and lasting alliance, the immediate results of which will be the expulsion of the Turks from the Arab countries and the freeing of the Arab peoples from the Turkish yoke, which for so many years has pressed heavily upon them.

I have confined myself in this letter to the more vital and important questions, and if there are any other matters dealt with in your letters which I have omitted to mention, we may discuss them at some convenient date in the future.

It was with very great relief and satisfaction that I heard of the safe arrival of the Holy Carpet and the accompanying offerings which, thanks to the clearness of your directions and the excellence of your arrangements, were landed without trouble or mishap in spite of the dangers and difficulties occasioned by the present sad war. May God soon bring a lasting peace and freedom of all peoples.

I am sending this letter by the hand of your trusted and excellent messenger, Sheikh Mohammed ibn Arif ibn Uraifan, and he will inform you of the various matters of interest, but of less vital importance, which I have not mentioned in this letter.

(Compliments).
(Signed): A. HENRY MCMAHON

4 The Sykes-Picot Agreement (1916)

The Sykes-Picot Agreement

It is accordingly understood between the French and British governments:

That France and Great Britain are prepared to recognize and protect an independent Arab state or a confederation of Arab states (a) and (b) marked on the annexed map, under the suzerainty of an Arab chief. That in area (a) France, and in area (b) Great Britain, shall have priority of right of enterprise and local loans. That in area (a) France, and in area (b) Great Britain, shall alone supply advisers or foreign functionaries at the request of the Arab state or confederation of Arab states.

That in the blue area France, and in the red area Great Britain, shall be allowed to establish such direct or indirect administration or control as they desire and as they may think fit to arrange with the Arab state or confederation of Arab states.

That in the brown area there shall be established an international administration, the form of which is to be decided upon after consultation with Russia, and subsequently in consultation with the other allies, and the representatives of the sheriff of Mecca.

That Great Britain be accorded (1) the ports of Haifa and Acre, (2) guarantee of a given supply of water from the Tigris and Euphrates in area (a) for area (b). His majesty's government, on their part, undertake that they will at no time enter into negotiations for the cession of Cyprus to any third power without the previous consent of the French government.

That Alexandretta shall be a free port as regards the trade of the British empire, and that there shall be no discrimination in port charges or facilities as regards British shipping and British goods; that there shall be freedom of transit for British goods through Alexandretta and by railway through the blue area, or (b) area, or area (a); and there shall be no discrimination, direct or indirect, against British goods on any railway or against British goods or ships at any port serving the areas mentioned.

That Haifa shall be a free port as regards the trade of France, her dominions and protectorates, and there shall be no discrimination in port charges or facilities as regards French shipping and French goods. There shall be freedom of transit for French goods through Haifa and by the British railway through the brown area, whether those goods are intended for or originate in the blue area, area (a), or area (b), and there shall be no discrimination, direct or indirect, against French goods on any railway, or against French goods or ships at any port serving the areas mentioned.

That in area (a) the Baghdad railway shall not be extended southwards beyond Mosul, and in area (b) northwards beyond Samarra, until a railway connecting Baghdad and Aleppo via the Euphrates valley has been completed, and then only with the concurrence of the two governments.

That Great Britain has the right to build, administer, and be sole owner of a railway connecting Haifa with area (b), and shall have a perpetual right to transport troops along such a line at all times. It is to be understood by both governments that this railway is to facilitate the connection of Baghdad with Haifa by rail, and it is further understood that, if the engineering difficulties and expense entailed by keeping this connecting line in the brown area only make the project unfeasible, that the French government shall be prepared to consider that the line in question may also traverse the Polgon Banias Keis Marib Salkhad tell Otsda Mesmie before reaching area (b).

For a period of twenty years the existing Turkish customs tariff shall remain in force throughout the whole of the blue and red areas, as well as in areas (a) and (b), and no increase in the rates of duty or conversions from ad valorem to specific rates shall be made except by agreement between the two powers.

There shall be no interior customs barriers between any of the above mentioned areas. The customs duties leviable on goods destined for the interior shall be collected at the port of entry and handed over to the administration of the area of destination.

It shall be agreed that the French government will at no time enter into any negotiations for the cession of their rights and will not cede such rights in the blue area to any third power, except the Arab state or confederation of Arab states, without the previous agreement of His Majesty's government, who, on their part, will give a similar undertaking to the French government regarding the red area.

The British and French government, as the protectors of the Arab state, shall agree that they will not themselves acquire and will not consent to a third power acquiring territorial possessions in the Arabian peninsula, nor consent to a third power installing a naval base either on the east coast, or on the islands, of the Red Sea. This, however, shall not prevent such adjustment of the Aden frontier as may be necessary in consequence of recent Turkish aggression.

The negotiations with the Arabs as to the boundaries of the Arab states shall be continued through the same channel as heretofore on behalf of the two powers.

It is agreed that measures to control the importation of arms into the Arab territories will be considered by the two governments.

I have further the honor to state that, in order to make the agreement complete, His Majesty's government are proposing to the Russian government to exchange notes analogous to those exchanged by the latter and your excellency's government on the 26th April last. Copies of these notes will be communicated to your excellency as soon as exchanged. I would also venture to remind your excellency that the conclusion of the present agreement raises, for practical consideration, the question of claims of Italy to a share in any partition or rearrangement of Turkey in Asia, as formulated in Article 9 of the agreement of the 26th April, 1915, between Italy and the allies.

His Majesty's government further consider that the Japanese government should be informed of the arrangements now concluded.

[See map of Sykes-Picot agreement showing Palestine under International Control on page 5.]

5 The Balfour Declaration (November 2, 1917)

Foreign Office
November 2nd, 1917

Dear Lord Rothschild,

I have much pleasure in conveying to you, on behalf of His Majesty's Government, the following declaration of sympathy with Jewish Zionist aspirations which has been submitted to, and approved by, the Cabinet.

"His Majesty's Government view with favour the establishment in Palestine of a national home for the Jewish people, and will use their best endeavours to facilitate the achievement of this object, it being clearly understood that nothing shall be done which may prejudice the civil and religious rights of existing non-Jewish communities in Palestine, or the rights and political status enjoyed by Jews in any other country."

I should be grateful if you would bring this declaration to the knowledge of the Zionist Federation.

Yours sincerely,
Arthur James Balfour

6 The Weizmann–Feisal Agreement (January 3, 1919)

Agreement between Emir Feisal Ibn al-Hussein al-Hashemi, and the President of the World Zionist Organization, Dr. Chaim Weizmann

His Royal Highness the Emir Feisal, representing and acting on behalf of the Arab Kingdom of Hedjaz, and Dr. Chaim Weizmann, representing and acting on behalf of the Zionist Organization, mindful of the racial kinship and ancient bonds existing between the Arabs and the Jewish people, and realizing that the surest means of working out the consummation of their natural aspirations is through the closest possible collaboration in the development of the Arab State and Palestine, and being desirous further of confirming the good understanding which exists between them, have agreed upon the following:

Article I

The Arab State and Palestine in all their relations and undertakings shall be controlled by the most cordial goodwill and understanding, and to this end Arab and Jewish duly accredited agents shall be established and maintained in the respective territories.

Article II

Immediately following the completion of the deliberations of the Peace Conference, the definite boundaries between the Arab State and Palestine shall be determined by a Commission to be agreed upon by the parties hereto.

Article III

In the establishment of the Constitution and Administration of Palestine, all such measures shall be adopted as will afford the fullest guarantees for carrying into effect the British Government's Declaration of the 2nd of November, 1917.

Article IV

All necessary measures shall be taken to encourage and stimulate immigration of Jews into Palestine on a large scale, and as quickly as possible to settle Jewish immigrants upon the land through closer settlement and intensive cultivation of the soil. In taking such measures the Arab peasant and tenant farmers shall be protected in their rights and shall be assisted in forwarding their economic development.

Article V

No regulation or law shall be made prohibiting or interfering in any way with the free exercise of religion; and further, the free exercise and enjoyment of religious profession and worship, without discrimination or preference, shall forever be allowed. No religious test shall ever be required for the exercise of civil or political rights.

Article VI

The Mohammedan Holy Places shall be under Mohammedan control.

Article VII

The Zionist Organization proposes to send to Palestine a Commission of experts to make a survey of the economic possibilities of the country, and to report upon the best means for its development. The Zionist Organization will place the aforementioned Commission at the disposal of the Arab State for the purpose of a survey of the economic possibilities of the Arab State and to report upon the best means for its development. The Zionist Organization will use its best efforts to assist the Arab State in providing the means for developing the natural resources and economic possibilities thereof.

Article VIII

The parties hereto agree to act in complete accord and harmony on all matters embraced herein before the Peace Congress.

Article IX

Any matters of dispute which may arise between the contracting parties shall be referred to the British Government for arbitration.

Given under our hand at London, England, the third day of January, one thousand nine hundred and nineteen

Chaim Weizmann   *Feisal Ibn-Hussein*

Reservation by the Emir Feisal

If the Arabs are established as I have asked in my manifesto of 4 January, addressed to the British Secretary of State for Foreign Affairs, I will carry out what is written in this agreement. If changes are made, I cannot be answerable for failing to carry out this agreement.

7 The White Paper of 1922 (June, 1922) (The "Churchill White Paper")

The Secretary of State for the Colonies has given renewed consideration to the existing political situation in Palestine, with a very earnest desire to arrive at a settlement of the outstanding questions which have given rise to uncertainty and unrest among certain sections of the population. After consultation with the High Commissioner for Palestine [Sir Herbert Samuel] the following statement has been drawn up. It summarizes the essential parts of the correspondence that has already taken place between the Secretary of State and a delegation from the Moslem Christian Society of Palestine, which has been for some time in England, and it states the further conclusions which have since been reached.

The tension which has prevailed from time to time in Palestine is mainly due to apprehensions, which are entertained both by sections of the Arab and by sections of the Jewish population. These apprehensions, so far as the Arabs are concerned are partly based upon exaggerated interpretations of the meaning of the Balfour Declaration favouring the establishment of a Jewish National Home in Palestine, made on behalf of His Majesty's Government on 2nd November, 1917.

Unauthorized statements have been made to the effect that the purpose in view is to create a wholly Jewish Palestine. Phrases have been used such as that Palestine is to become "as Jewish as England is English." His Majesty's Government regard any such expectation as impracticable and have no such aim in view. Nor have they at any time contemplated, as appears to be feared by the Arab delegation, the disappearance or the subordination of the Arabic population, language, or culture in Palestine. They would draw attention to the fact that the terms of the Declaration referred to do not contemplate that Palestine as a whole should be converted into a Jewish National Home, but that such a Home should be founded 'in Palestine.' In this connection it has been observed with satisfaction that at a meeting of the Zionist Congress, the supreme governing body of the Zionist Organization, held at Carlsbad in September, 1921, a resolution was passed expressing as the official statement of Zionist aims "the determination of the Jewish people to live with the Arab people on terms of unity and mutual respect, and together with them to make the common home into a flourishing community, the upbuilding of which may assure to each of its peoples an undisturbed national development."

It is also necessary to point out that the Zionist Commission in Palestine, now termed the Palestine Zionist Executive, has not desired to possess, and does not possess, any share in the general administration of the country. Nor does the special position assigned to the Zionist Organization in Article IV of the Draft Mandate for Palestine imply any such functions. That special position relates to the measures to be taken in Palestine affecting the Jewish population, and contemplates that the organization may assist in the general development of the country, but does not entitle it to share in any degree in its government.

Further, it is contemplated that the status of all citizens of Palestine in the eyes of the law shall be Palestinian, and it has never been intended that they, or any section of them, should possess any other juridical status. So far as the Jewish population of Palestine are concerned it appears that some among them are apprehensive that His Majesty's Government may depart from the policy embodied in the Declaration of 1917. It is necessary, therefore, once more to affirm that these fears are unfounded, and that that Declaration, re affirmed by the Conference of the Principal Allied Powers at San Remo and again in the Treaty of Sevres, is not susceptible of change.

During the last two or three generations the Jews have recreated in Palestine a community, now numbering 80,000, of whom about one fourth are farmers or workers upon the land. This community has its own political organs; an elected assembly for the direction of its domestic concerns; elected councils in the towns; and an organization for the control of its schools. It has its elected Chief Rabbinate and Rabbinical Council for the direction of its religious affairs. Its business is conducted in Hebrew as a vernacular language, and a Hebrew Press serves its needs. It has its distinctive intellectual life and displays considerable economic activity. This community, then, with its town and country population, its political, religious, and social organizations, its own language, its own customs, its own life, has in fact "national" characteristics. When it is asked what is meant by the development of the Jewish National Home in Palestine, it may be answered that it is not the imposition of a Jewish nationality upon the inhabitants of Palestine as a whole, but the further development of the existing Jewish community, with the assistance of Jews in other parts of the world, in order that it may become a centre in which the Jewish people as a whole may take, on grounds of religion and race, an interest and a pride. But in order that this community should have the best prospect of free development and provide a full opportunity for the Jewish people to display its capacities, it is essential that it should know that it is in Palestine as of right and not on the sufferance. That is the reason why it is necessary that the existence of a Jewish National Home in Palestine should be internationally guaranteed, and that it should be formally recognized to rest upon ancient historic connection.

This, then, is the interpretation which His Majesty's Government place upon the Declaration of 1917, and, so understood, the Secretary of State is of opinion that it does not contain or imply anything which need cause either alarm to the Arab population of Palestine or disappointment to the Jews.

For the fulfillment of this policy it is necessary that the Jewish community in Palestine should be able to increase its numbers by immigration. This immigration cannot be so great in volume as to exceed whatever may be the economic capacity of the country at the time to absorb new arrivals. It is essential to ensure that the immigrants should not be a burden upon the people of Palestine as a whole, and that they should not deprive any section of the present population of their employment.

Hitherto the immigration has fulfilled these conditions. The number of immigrants since the British occupation has been about 25,000.

It is necessary also to ensure that persons who are politically undesirable be excluded from Palestine, and every precaution has been and will be taken by the Administration to that end.

It is intended that a special committee should be established in Palestine, consisting entirely of members of the new Legislative Council elected by the people, to confer with the administration upon matters relating to the regulation of immigration. Should any difference of opinion arise between this committee and the Administration, the matter will be referred to His Majesty's Government, who will give it special consideration. In addition, under Article 81 of the draft Palestine Order in Council, any religious community or considerable section of the population of Palestine will have a general right to appeal, through the High Commissioner and the Secretary of State, to the League of Nations on any matter on which they may consider that the terms of the Mandate are not being fulfilled by the Government of Palestine.

With reference to the Constitution which it is now intended to establish in Palestine, the draft of which has already been published, it is desirable to make certain points clear. In the first place, it is not the case, as has been represented by the Arab Delegation, that during the war His Majesty's Government gave an undertaking that an independent national government should be at once established in Palestine. This representation mainly rests upon a letter dated the 24th October, 1915, from Sir Henry McMahon, then His Majesty's High Commissioner in Egypt, to the Sherif of Mecca, now King Hussein of the Kingdom of the Hejaz. That letter is quoted as conveying the promise to the Sherif of Mecca to recognise and support the independence of the Arabs within the territories proposed by him. But this promise was given subject to a reservation made in the same letter, which excluded from its scope, among other territories, the portions of Syria lying to the west of the District of Damascus. This reservation has always been regarded by His Majesty's Government as covering the vilayet of Beirut and the independent Sanjak of Jerusalem. The whole of Palestine west of the Jordan was thus excluded from Sir Henry McMahon's pledge.

Nevertheless, it is the intention of His Majesty's government to foster the establishment of a full measure of self government in Palestine. But they are of the opinion that, in the special circumstances of that country, this should be accomplished by gradual stages and not suddenly. The first step was taken when, on the institution of a Civil Administration, the nominated Advisory Council, which now exists, was established. It was stated at the time by the High Commissioner that this was the first step in the development of self governing institutions, and it is now proposed to take a second step by the establishment of a Legislative Council containing a large proportion of members elected on a wide franchise. It was proposed in the published draft that three of the members of this Council should be non official persons nominated by the High Commissioner, but representations having been made in opposition to this provision, based on cogent considerations, the Secretary of State is prepared to omit it. The legislative Council would then consist of the High Commissioner as President and twelve elected and ten official members. The Secretary of State is of the opinion that before a further measure of self government is extended to Palestine and the Assembly placed in control over the Executive, it would be wise to allow some time to elapse. During this period the institutions of the country will have become well established; its financial credit will be based on firm foundations, and the Palestinian officials will have been enabled to gain experience of sound methods of government. After a few years the situation will be again reviewed, and if the experience of the working of the constitution now to be established so warranted, a larger share of authority would then be extended to the elected representatives of the people.

The Secretary of State would point out that already the present administration has transferred to a Supreme Council elected by the Moslem community of Palestine the entire control of Moslem Religious endowments (Waqfs), and of the Moslem religious Courts. To this Council the Administration has also voluntarily restored considerable revenues derived from ancient endowments which have been sequestrated by the Turkish Government. The Education Department is also advised by a committee representative of all sections of the population, and the Department of Commerce and Industry has the benefit of the cooperation of the Chambers of Commerce which have been established in the principal centres. It is the intention of the Administration to associate in an increased degree similar representative committees with the various Departments of the Government.

The Secretary of State believes that a policy upon these lines, coupled with the maintenance of the fullest religious liberty in Palestine and with scrupulous regard for the rights of each community with reference to its Holy Places, cannot but commend itself to the various sections of the population, and that upon this basis may be built up that a spirit of cooperation upon which the future progress and prosperity of the Holy Land must largely depend.

8 The Mandate for Palestine (July 24, 1922)

The Council of the League of Nations

Whereas the Principal Allied Powers have agreed, for the purpose of giving effect to the provisions of Article 22 of the Covenant of the League of Nations, to entrust to a Mandatory selected by the said Powers the administration of the territory of Palestine, which formerly belonged to the Turkish Empire, within such boundaries as may be fixed by them; and

Whereas the Principal Allied Powers have also agreed that the Mandatory should be responsible for putting into effect the declaration originally made on November 2nd, 1917, by the Government of His Britannic Majesty, and adopted by the said Powers, in favour of the establishment in Palestine of a national home for the Jewish people, it being clearly understood that nothing should be done which might prejudice the civil and religious rights of existing non-Jewish communities in Palestine, or the rights and political status enjoyed by Jews in any other country; and

Whereas recognition has thereby been given to the historical connection of the Jewish people with Palestine and to the grounds for reconstituting their national home in that country; and

Whereas the Principal Allied Powers have selected His Britannic Majesty as the Mandatory for Palestine; and

Whereas the mandate in respect of Palestine has been formulated in the following terms and submitted to the Council of the League for approval; and

Whereas His Britannic Majesty has accepted the mandate in respect of Palestine and undertaken to exercise it on behalf of the League of Nations in conformity with the following provisions; and

Whereas by the afore-mentioned Article 22 (paragraph 8), it is provided that the degree of authority, control or administration to be exercised by the Mandatory, not having been previously agreed upon by the Members of the League, shall be explicitly defined by the Council of the League of Nations;

Confirming the said mandate, defines its terms as follows:

Article 1.

The Mandatory shall have full powers of legislation and of administration, save as they may be limited by the terms of this mandate.

Article 2.

The Mandatory shall be responsible for placing the country under such political, administrative and economic conditions as will secure the establishment of the Jewish national home, as laid down in the preamble, and the development of self-governing institutions, and also for safeguarding the civil and religious rights of all the inhabitants of Palestine, irrespective of race and religion.

Article 3.

The Mandatory shall, so far as circumstances permit, encourage local autonomy.

Article 4.

An appropriate Jewish agency shall be recognised as a public body for the purpose of advising and co-operating with the Administration of Palestine in such economic, social and other matters as may affect the establishment of the Jewish national home and the interests of the Jewish population in Palestine, and, subject always to the control of the Administration, to assist and take part in the development of the country.

The Zionist organisation, so long as its organisation and constitution are in the opinion of the Mandatory appropriate, shall be recognised as such agency. It shall take steps in consultation with His Britannic Majesty's Government to secure the cooperation of all Jews who are willing to assist in the establishment of the Jewish national home.

Article 5.

The Mandatory shall be responsible for seeing that no Palestine territory shall be ceded or leased to, or in any way placed under the control of, the Government of any foreign Power.

Article 6.

The Administration of Palestine, while ensuring that the rights and position of other sections of the population are not prejudiced, shall facilitate Jewish immigration under suitable conditions and shall encourage, in co-operation with the Jewish agency referred to in Article 4, close settlement by Jews on the land, including State lands and waste lands not required for public purposes.

Article 7.

The Administration of Palestine shall be responsible for enacting a nationality law. There shall be included in this law provisions framed so as to facilitate the acquisition of Palestinian citizenship by Jews who take up their permanent residence in Palestine.

Article 8.

The privileges and immunities of foreigners, including the benefits of consular jurisdiction and protection as formerly enjoyed by Capitulation or usage in the Ottoman Empire, shall not be applicable in Palestine.
[. . .]

Article 9.

The Mandatory shall be responsible for seeing that the judicial system established in Palestine shall assure to foreigners, as well as to natives, a complete guarantee of their rights.

Respect for the personal status of the various peoples and communities and for their religious interests shall be fully guaranteed. In particular, the control and administration of Wakfs shall be exercised in accordance with religious law and the dispositions of the founders.

Article 10.

Pending the making of special extradition agreements relating to Palestine, the extradition treaties in force between the Mandatory and other foreign Powers shall apply to Palestine.

Article 11.

The Administration of Palestine shall take all necessary measures to safeguard the interests of the community in connection with the development of the country, and, subject to any international obligations accepted by the Mandatory, shall have full power to provide for public ownership or control of any of the natural resources of the country or of the public works, services and utilities established or to be established therein. . . .

The Administration may arrange with the Jewish agency mentioned in Article 4 to construct or operate, upon fair and equitable terms, any public works, services and utilities, and to develop any of the natural resources of the country, in so far as these matters are not directly undertaken by the Administration. . . .

Article 12.

The Mandatory shall be entrusted with the control of the foreign relations of Palestine and the right to issue exequaturs to consuls appointed by foreign Powers. He shall also be entitled to afford diplomatic and consular protection to citizens of Palestine when outside its territorial limits.

Article 13.

All responsibility in connection with the Holy Places and religious buildings or sites in Palestine, including that of preserving existing rights and of securing free access to the Holy Places, religious buildings and sites and the free exercise of worship, while ensuring the requirements of public order and decorum, is assumed by the Mandatory, who shall be responsible solely to the League of Nations, in all matters connected herewith, provided that nothing in this article shall prevent the Mandatory from entering into such arrangements as he may deem reasonable with the Administration for the purpose of carrying the provisions of this article into effect; and provided also that nothing in this mandate shall be construed as conferring upon the Mandatory authority to interfere with the fabric or the management of purely Moslem sacred shrines, the immunities of which are guaranteed.

Article 14.

A special Commission shall be appointed by the Mandatory to study, define and determine the rights and claims in connection with the Holy Places and the rights and claims relating to the different religious communities in Palestine. . . .

Article 15.

The Mandatory shall see that complete freedom of conscience and the free exercise of all forms of worship, subject only to the maintenance of public order and morals, are ensured to all. No discrimination of any kind shall be made between the inhabitants of Palestine on the ground of race, religion or language. No person shall be excluded from Palestine on the sole ground of his religious belief.

The right of each community to maintain its own schools for the education of its own members in its own language, while conforming to such educational requirements of a general nature as the Administration may impose, shall not be denied or impaired.

Article 16.

The Mandatory shall be responsible for exercising such supervision over religious or eleemosynary bodies of all faiths in Palestine as may be required for the maintenance of public order and good government. Subject to such supervision, no measures shall be taken in Palestine to obstruct or interfere with the enterprise of such bodies or to discriminate against any representative or member of them on the ground of his religion or nationality.

Article 17.

The Administration of Palestine may organise on a voluntary basis the forces necessary for the preservation of peace and order, and also for the defence of the country, subject, however, to the supervision of the Mandatory, but shall not use them for purposes other than those above specified save with the consent of the Mandatory, Except for such purposes, no military, naval or air forces shall be raised or maintained by the Administration of Palestine.

[. . .] The Mandatory shall be entitled at all times to use the roads, railways and ports of Palestine for the movement of armed forces and the carriage of fuel and supplies.

Article 18.

The Mandatory shall see that there is no discrimination in Palestine against the nationals of any State Member of the League of Nations (including companies incorporated under its laws) as compared with those of the Mandatory or of any foreign State in matters concerning taxation, commerce or navigation, the exercise of industries or professions, or in the treatment of merchant vessels or civil aircraft. . . .

Subject as aforesaid and to the other provisions of this mandate, the Administration of Palestine may, on the advice of the Mandatory, impose such taxes and customs duties as it may consider necessary, and take such steps as it may think best to promote the development of the natural resources of the country and to safeguard the interests of the population. . . .

Article 19.

The Mandatory shall adhere on behalf of the Administration of Palestine to any general international conventions already existing, or which may be concluded hereafter with the approval of the League of Nations, respecting the slave traffic, the traffic in arms and ammunition, or the traffic in drugs, or relating to commercial equality, freedom of transit and navigation, aerial navigation and postal, telegraphic and wireless communication or literary, artistic or industrial property.

Article 20.

The Mandatory shall co-operate on behalf of the Administration of Palestine, so far as religious, social and other conditions may permit, in the execution of any common policy adopted by the League of Nations for preventing and combating disease, including diseases of plants and animals.

Article 21 . . . [On a Law of Antiquities]

Article 22.

English, Arabic and Hebrew shall be the official languages of Palestine. Any statement or inscription in Arabic on stamps or money in Palestine shall be repeated in Hebrew, and any statement or inscription in Hebrew shall be repeated in Arabic.

Article 23.

The Administration of Palestine shall recognise the holy days of the respective communities in Palestine as legal days of rest for the members of such communities.

Article 24.

The Mandatory shall make to the Council of the League of Nations an annual report to the satisfaction of the Council as to the measures taken during the year to carry out the provisions of the mandate. Copies of all laws and regulations promulgated or issued during the year shall be communicated with the report.

Article 25.

In the territories lying between the Jordan and the eastern boundary of Palestine as ultimately determined, the Mandatory shall be entitled, with the consent of the Council of the League of Nations, to postpone or withhold application of such provisions of this mandate as he may consider inapplicable to the existing local conditions, and to make such provision for the administration of the territories as he may consider suitable to those conditions, provided that no action shall be taken which is inconsistent with the provisions of Articles 15, 16 and 18.

Article 26.

The Mandatory agrees that, if any dispute whatever should arise between the Mandatory and another Member of the League of Nations relating to the interpretation or the application of the provisions of the mandate, such dispute, if it cannot be settled by negotiation, shall be submitted to the Permanent Court of International Justice provided for by Article 14 of the Covenant of the League of Nations.

Article 27.

The consent of the Council of the League of Nations is required for any modification of the terms of this mandate.

Article 28.

In the event of the termination of the mandate hereby conferred upon the Mandatory, the Council of the League of Nations shall make such arrangements as may be deemed necessary for safeguarding in perpetuity, under guarantee of the League, the rights secured by Articles 13 and 14, and shall use its influence for securing, under the guarantee of the League, that the Government of Palestine will fully honour the financial obligations legitimately incurred by the Administration of Palestine during the period of the mandate, including the rights of public servants, to pensions or gratuities.

The present instrument shall be deposited in original in the archives of the League of Nations and certified copies shall be forwarded by the Secretary-General of the League of Nations to all Members of the League.

Done at London the twenty-fourth day of July, one thousand nine hundred and twenty-two.

9 British Prime Minister Ramsay MacDonald Letter to Chaim Weizmann (February 13, 1931)

13 February 1931

Dear Dr. Weizmann:

In order to remove certain misconceptions and misunderstandings which have arisen as to the policy of his Majesty's Government with regard to Palestine, as set forth in the White Paper of October, 1930, and which were the subject of a debate in the House of Commons on Nov. 17, and also to meet certain criticisms put forward by the Jewish Agency, I have pleasure in forwarding you the following statement of our position, which will fall to be read as the authoritative interpretation of the White Paper on the matters with which this letter deals.

It has been said that the policy of his Majesty's Government involves a serious departure from the obligations of the mandate as hitherto understood; that it misconceives the mandatory obligations, and that it foreshadows a policy which is inconsistent with the obligations of the mandatory to the Jewish people.

His Majesty's Government did not regard it as necessary to quote *in extenso* the declarations of policy which have been previously made, but attention is drawn to the fact that, not only does the White Paper of 1930 refer to and endorse the White Paper of 1922, which has been accepted by the Jewish Agency, but it recognizes that the undertaking of the mandate is an undertaking to the Jewish people and not only to the Jewish population of Palestine. The White Paper places in the foreground of its statement my speech in the House of Commons on the 3rd of April, 1930, in which I announced, in words that could not have been made more plain, that it was the intention of his Majesty's Government to continue to administer Palestine in accordance with the terms of the mandate as approved by the Council of the League of Nations. That position has been reaffirmed and again made plain by my speech in the House of Commons on the 17th of November. In my speech on the 3rd of April, I used the following language:

His Majesty's Government will continue to administer Palestine in accordance with the terms of the mandate as approved by the Council of the League of Nations. This is an international obligation from which there can be no question of receding.

Under the terms of the mandate his Majesty's Government are responsible for promoting the establishment of a national home for the Jewish people, it being clearly understood that nothing shall be done which might prejudice the civil and religious rights of existing non-Jewish communities in Palestine or the rights and political status enjoyed by Jews in any other country.

A double undertaking is involved, to the Jewish people on the one hand and to the non-Jewish population of Palestine on the other; and it is the firm resolve of his Majesty's Government to give effect, in equal measure, to both parts of the declaration and to do equal justice to all sections of the population of Palestine. That is the duty from which they will not shrink and to discharge of which they will apply all the resources at their command.

That declaration is in conformity not only with the articles but also with the preamble of the mandate, which is hereby explicitly reaffirmed.

In carrying out the policy of the mandate the mandatory cannot ignore the existence of the differing interests and viewpoints. These, indeed, are not in themselves irreconcilable, but they can only be reconciled if there is a proper realization that the full solution of the problem depends upon an understanding between the Jews and the Arabs. Until that is reached, considerations of balance must inevitably enter into the definition of policy.

A good deal of criticism has been directed to the White Paper upon the assertion that it contains injurious allegations against the Jewish people and Jewish labor organizations. Any such intention on the part of his Majesty's Government is expressly disavowed. It is recognized that the Jewish Agency have all along given willing cooperation in carrying out the policy of the mandate and that the constructive work done by the Jewish people in Palestine has had beneficial effects on the development and well-being of the country as a whole. His Majesty's Government also recognizes the value of the services of labor and trades union organizations in Palestine, to which they desire to give every encouragement.

A question has arisen as to the meaning to be attached to the words "safeguarding the civil and religious rights of all inhabitants of Palestine irrespective of race and religion" occurring in Article II, and the words "insuring that the rights and position of other sections of the population are not prejudiced" occurring in Article VI of the mandate. The words "safeguarding the civil and religious rights" occurring in Article II cannot be read as meaning that the civil and religious rights of individual citizens are unalterable. In the case of Suleiman Murra, to which reference has been made, the Privy Council, in construing these words of Article II said "It does not mean . . . that all the civil rights of every inhabitant of Palestine which existed at the date of the mandate are to remain unaltered throughout its duration; for if that were to be a condition of the mandatory jurisdiction, no effective legislation would be possible." The words, accordingly, must be read in another sense, and the key to the true purpose and meaning of the sentence is to be found in the concluding words of the article, "irrespective of race and religion." These words indicate that in respect of civil and religious rights the mandatory is not to discriminate between persons on the ground of religion or race, and this protective provision applies equally to Jews, Arabs and all sections of the population.

The words "rights and position of other sections of the population," occurring in Article VI, plainly refer to the non-Jewish community. These rights and position are not to be prejudiced; that is, are not to be impaired or made worse. The effect of the policy of immigration and settlement on the economic position of the non-Jewish community cannot be excluded from consideration. But the words are not to be read as implying that existing economic conditions in Palestine should be crystallized. On the contrary, the obligation to facilitate Jewish immigration and to encourage close settlement by Jews on the land remains a positive obligation of the mandate and it can be fulfilled without prejudice to the rights and position of other sections of the population of Palestine.

We may proceed to the contention that the mandate has been interpreted in a manner highly prejudicial to Jewish interests in the vital matters of land settlement and immigration. It has been said that the policy of the White Paper would place an embargo on immigration and would suspend, if not indeed terminate, the close settlement of the Jews on the land, which is a primary purpose of the mandate. In support of this contention particular stress has been laid upon the passage referring to State lands in the White Paper, which says that "it would not be possible to make available for Jewish settlement in view of their actual occupation by Arab cultivation and of the importance of making available suitable land on which to place the Arab cultivators who are now landless."

The language of this passage needs to be read in the light of the policy as a whole. It is desirable to make it clear that the landless Arabs, to whom it was intended to refer in the passage quoted, were such Arabs as can be shown to have been displaced from the lands which they occupied in consequence of the land passing into Jewish hands, and who have not obtained other holdings on which they establish themselves, or other equally satisfactory occupation . . . The recognition of this obligation in no way detracts from the larger purposes of development which his Majesty's Government regards as the most effectual means of furthering the establishment of a national home for the Jews . . .

Further, the statement of policy of his Majesty's Government did not imply a prohibition of acquisition of additional lands by Jews. It contains no such prohibition, nor is any such intended. What it does contemplate is such temporary control of land disposition and transfers as may be necessary not to impair the harmony and effectiveness of the scheme of land settlement to be undertaken. His Majesty's Government feels bound to point out that it alone of the governments which have been responsible for the administration of Palestine since the acceptance of the mandate has declared its definite intention to initiate an active policy of development, which it is believed will result in a substantial and lasting benefit to both Jews and Arabs.

Cognate to this question is the control of immigration. It must first of all be pointed out that such control is not in any sense a departure from previous policy. From 1920 onward, when the original immigration ordinance came into force, regulations for the control of immigration have been issued from time to time, directed to prevent illicit entry and to define and facilitate authorized entry. The right of regulation has at no time been challenged.

But the intention of his Majesty's Government appears to have been represented as being that "no further immigration of Jews is to be permitted as long as it might prevent any Arab from obtaining employment." His Majesty's Government never proposed to pursue such a policy. They were concerned to state that, in the regulation of Jewish immigration, the following principles should apply: viz., that "it is essential to insure that the immigrants should not be burden on the people of Palestine as a whole, and that they should not deprive any section of the present population of their employment." *(White Paper 1922.)*

In one aspect, his Majesty's Government have to be mindful of their obligations to facilitate Jewish immigration under suitable conditions, and to encourage close settlement by Jews on the land; in the other aspect, they have to be equally mindful of their duty to insure that no prejudice results to the rights and position of the non-Jewish community. It is because of this apparent conflict of obligation that his Majesty's Government have felt bound to emphasize the necessity of the proper application of the absorptive principle.

That principle is vital to any scheme of development, the primary purpose of which must be the settlement both of Jews and of displaced Arabs on the land. It is for that reason that his Majesty's Government have insisted, and are compelled to insist, that government immigration regulations must be properly applied. The considerations relevant to the limits of absorptive capacity are purely economic considerations.

His Majesty's Government did not prescribe and do not contemplate any stoppage or prohibition of Jewish immigration in any of its categories. . . . With regard to public and municipal works failing to be financed out of public funds, the claim of Jewish labor to a due share of the employment available, taking into account Jewish contributions to public revenue, shall be taken into consideration. As regards other kinds of employment, it will be necessary in each case to take into account the factors bearing upon the demand for labor, including the factor of unemployment among both the Jews and the Arabs.

Immigrants with prospects of employment other than employment of a purely ephemeral character will not be excluded on the sole ground that the employment cannot be guaranteed to be of unlimited duration.

In determining the extent to which immigration at any time may be permitted it is necessary also to have regard to the declared policy of the Jewish Agency to the effect that "in all the works or undertakings carried out or furthered by the Agency it shall be deemed to be a matter of principle that Jewish labor shall be employed." His Majesty's Government do not in any way challenge the right of the Agency to formulate or approve and endorse this policy. The principle of preferential, and indeed exclusive, employment of Jewish labor by Jewish organizations is a principle which the Jewish Agency are entitled to affirm. But it must be pointed out that if in consequence of this policy Arab labor is displaced or existing unemployment becomes aggravated, that is a factor in the situation to which the mandatory is bound to have regard.

His Majesty's Government desire to say, finally, as they have repeatedly and unequivocally affirmed, that the obligations imposed upon the mandatory by its acceptance of the mandate are solemn international obligations from which there is not now, nor has there been at any time, an intention to depart. To the tasks imposed by the mandate, his Majesty's Government have set their hand, and they will not withdraw it. But if their efforts are to be successful, there is need for cooperation, confidence, readiness on all sides to appreciate the difficulties and complexities of the problem, and, above all, there must be a full and unqualified recognition that no solution can be satisfactory or permanent which is not based upon justice, both to the Jewish people and to the non-Jewish communities of Palestine.

Ramsay MacDonald

10 The Palestine Royal Commission (Peel Commission): Report (July 24, 1937)

C.495.M.336.1937.VI.
Geneva, November 30th, 1937.

LEAGUE OF NATIONS

****

REPORT
of the
PALESTINE ROYAL COMMISSION

presented by the Secretary of State for the Colonies
to the United Kingdom Parliament
by Command of His Britannic Majesty
(July 1937)
Distributed at the request of the United Kingdom Government.

PALESTINE

Royal Commission

****

SUMMARY OF REPORT

SUMMARY OF THE REPORT OF THE PALESTINE ROYAL
COMMISSION.

The Members of the Palestine Royal Commission were :-

Rt. Hon. EARL PEEL, G.C.S.I., G.B.E. (Chairman).
Rt. Hon. Sir HORACE RUMBOLD, Bart., G.C.B., G.C.M.G., M.V.O. (Vice-Chairman).
Sir LAURIE HAMMOND, K.C.S.I., C.B.E.

Sir MORRIS CARTER, C.B.E.
Sir HAROLD MORRIS, M.B.E., K.C.
Professor REGINALD COUPLAND, C.I.E.

Mr. J. M. MARTIN was Secretary.

****

The Commission was appointed in August, 1936, with the following terms of reference:-

> To ascertain the underlying causes of the disturbances which broke out in Palestine in the middle of April; to enquire into the manner in which the Mandate for Palestine is being implemented in relation to the obligations of the Mandatory towards the Arabs and the Jews respectively; and to ascertain whether, upon a proper construction of the terms of the Mandate, either the Arabs or the Jews have any legitimate grievances on account of the way in which the Mandate has been or is being implemented; and if the Commission is satisfied that any such grievances are well-founded, to make recommendation for their removal and for the prevention of their recurrence.

The following is a summary of the Commission's Report: -

SUMMARY

****

PART I: THE PROBLEM

Chapter I.—The Historical Background

Chapter II.—The War and the Mandate

In order to obtain Arab support in the War, the British Government promised the Sherif of Mecca in 1915 that, in the event of an Allied victory, the greater part of the Arab provinces of the Turkish Empire would become independent. The Arabs understood that Palestine would be included in the sphere of independence.

In order to obtain the support of World Jewry, the British Government in 1917 issued the Balfour Declaration. The Jews understood that, if the experiment of establishing a Jewish National Home succeeded and a sufficient number of Jews went to Palestine, the National Home might develop in course of time into a Jewish State.

At the end of the War, the Mandate System was accepted by the Allied and Associated Powers as the vehicle for the execution of the policy of the Balfour Declaration, and, after a period of delay, the Mandate for Palestine was approved by the League of Nations and the United States . . .

Chapter III.—Palestine from 1920 to 1936

During the first years of the Civil Administration, which was set up in 1920, a beginning was made on the one hand with the provision of public services, which mainly affected the Arab majority of the population, and on the other hand with the establishment of the Jewish National Home. There were outbreaks of disorder in 1920 and 1921, but in 1925 it was thought that the prospects of ultimate harmony between the Arabs and the Jews seemed so favourable that the forces for maintaining order were substantially reduced.

These hopes proved unfounded because, although Palestine as a whole became more prosperous, the causes of the outbreaks of 1920 and 1921, namely, the demand of the Arabs for national independence and their antagonism to the National Home, remained unmodified and were indeed accentuated by the "external factors," namely, the pressure of the Jews of Europe on Palestine and the development of Arab nationalism in neighbouring countries.

These same causes brought about the outbreaks of 1929 and 1933. By 1936 the external factors had been intensified by—

(1) the sufferings of the Jews in Germany and Poland, resulting in a great increase of Jewish immigration into Palestine; and

(2) the prospect of Syria and the Lebanon soon obtaining the same independence as Iraq and Saudi Arabia. Egypt was also on the eve of independence.

Chapter IV.—The Disturbances of 1936

These disturbances (which are briefly summarized) were similar in character to the four previous outbreaks, although more serious and prolonged. As in 1933, it was not only the Jews who were attacked, but the Palestine Government. A new feature was the part played by the Rulers of the neighbouring Arab States in bringing about the end of the strike.

The underlying causes of the disturbances of 1936 were—

(1) The desire of the Arabs for national independence;
(2) their hatred and fear of the establishment of the Jewish National Home.

These two causes were the same as those of all the previous outbreaks and have always been inextricably linked together. Of several subsidiary factors, the more important were—

(1) the advance of Arab nationalism outside Palestine;
(2) the increased immigration of Jews since 1933;
(3) the opportunity enjoyed by the Jews for influencing public opinion in Britain;
(4) Arab distrust in the sincerity of the British Government;
(5) Arab alarm at the continued Jewish purchase of land;
(6) the general uncertainty as to the ultimate intentions of the Mandatory Power.

Chapter V.—The Present Situation

The Jewish National Home is no longer an experiment. The growth of its population has been accompanied by political, social and economic developments along the lines laid down at the outset. The chief novelty is the urban and industrial development. The contrast between the modern democratic and primarily European character of the National Home and that of the Arab world around it is striking. The temper of the Home is strongly nationalist. There can be no question of fusion or assimilation between Jewish and Arab cultures. The National Home cannot be half-national.

Crown Colony government is not suitable for such a highly educated, democratic community as the National Home and fosters an unhealthy irresponsibility.

The National Home is bent on forcing the pace of its development, not only because of the desire of the Jews to escape from Europe, but because of anxiety as to the future in Palestine.

The Arab population shows a remarkable increase since 1920, and it has had some share in the increased prosperity of Palestine. Many Arab landowners have benefited from the sale of land and the profitable investment of the purchase money. The *fellaheen* are better off on the whole than they were in 1920. This Arab progress has been partly due to the import of Jewish capital into Palestine and other factors associated with the growth of the National Home. In particular, the Arabs have benefited from social services which could not have been provided on the existing scale without the revenue obtained from the Jews.

Such economic advantage, however, as the Arabs have gained from Jewish immigration will decrease if the political breach between the races continues to widen.

Arab nationalism is as intense a force as Jewish. The Arab leaders' demand for national self-government and the shutting down of the Jewish National Home has remained unchanged since 1929 . . .

The only solution of the problem put forward by the Arab Higher Committee was the immediate establishment of all independent Arab Government, which would deal with the 400,000 Jews now in Palestine as it thought fit. To that it is replied that belief in British good faith would not be strengthened anywhere in the world if the National Home were now surrendered to Arab rule.

The Jewish Agency and the Va'ad Leumi asserted that the problem would be solved if the Mandate were firmly applied in full accordance with Jewish claims: thus there should be no new restriction on immigration nor anything to prevent the Jewish population becoming in course of time a majority in Palestine . . .

PART II: THE OPERATION OF THE MANDATE

Chapter VI.—Administration

Chapter VII.—Public Security

Chapter VIII.—Financial and Fiscal Questions

Chapter IX.—The Land

Chapter X.—Immigration

Chapter XI.—Trans-Jordan

Chapter XII.—Health

Chapter XIII.—Public Works and Services

Chapter XIV.—The Christians

The religious stake of the Christians in the Holy Places is just as great as that of the Jews or Moslems. The Christians of the world cannot be indifferent to the justice and well-being of their co-religionists in the Holy Land . . .

In political matters the Christian Arabs have thrown in their lot with their Moslem brethren.

Chapter XV.—Nationality Law and Acquisition of Palestinian Citizenship

Chapter XVI.—Education

Chapter XVII.—Local Government

Chapter XVIII.—Self-governing Institutions

Chapter XIX.—Conclusion and Recommendations

The Commission recapitulate the conclusions set out in this part of the Report, and summarize the Arab and Jewish grievances and their own recommendations for the removal of such as are legitimate. They add, however, that these are not the recommendations which their terms of reference require. They will not, that is to say, remove the grievances nor prevent their recurrence. They are the best palliatives the Commission can devise for the disease from which Palestine is suffering, but they are only palliatives. They cannot cure the trouble. The disease is so deep-rooted that in the Commissioners' firm conviction the only hope of a cure lies in a surgical operation.

PART III: THE POSSIBILITY OF A LASTING SETTLEMENT

Chapter XX.—The Force of Circumstances

The problem of Palestine is briefly restated.

Under the stress of the World War the British Government made promises to Arabs and Jews in order to obtain their support. On the strength of those promises both parties formed certain expectations.

The application to Palestine of the Mandate System in general and of the specific Mandate in particular implies the belief that the obligations thus undertaken towards the Arabs and the Jews respectively would prove in course of time to be mutually compatible owing to the conciliatory effect on the Palestinian Arabs of the material prosperity which Jewish immigration would bring in Palestine as a whole. That belief has not been justified, and there seems to be no hope of its being justified in the future.

But the British people cannot on that account repudiate their obligations, and, apart from obligations, the existing circumstances in Palestine would still require the most strenuous efforts on the part of the Government which is responsible for the welfare of the country.

The existing circumstances are summarized as follows.

An irrepressible conflict has arisen between two national communities within the narrow bounds of one small country. There is no common ground between them. Their national aspirations are incompatible. The Arabs desire to revive the traditions of the Arab golden age. The Jews desire to show what they can achieve when restored to the land in which the Jewish nation was born. Neither of the two national ideals permits of combination in the service of a single State.

The conflict has grown steadily more bitter since 1920 and the process will continue. Conditions inside Palestine especially the systems of education, are strengthening the national sentiment of the two peoples. The bigger and more prosperous they grow the greater will be their political ambitions, and the conflict is aggravated by the uncertainty of the future. Who in the end will govern Palestine?" it is asked. Meanwhile, the external factors will continue to operate with increasing force. On the one hand in less than three years' time Syria and the Lebanon will attain their national sovereignty, and the claim of the Palestinian Arabs to share in the freedom of all Asiatic Arabia will thus be fortified. On the other hand the hardships and anxieties of the Jews in Europe are not likely to grow less and the appeal to the good faith and humanity of the British people will lose none of its force.

Meanwhile, the Government of Palestine, which is at present an unsuitable form for governing educated Arabs and democratic Jews, cannot develop into a system of self-government as it has elsewhere, because there is no such system which could ensure justice both to the Arabs and to the Jews. Government therefore remains unrepresentative and unable to dispel the conflicting grievances of the two dissatisfied and irresponsible communities it governs.

In these circumstances peace can only be maintained in Palestine under the Mandate by repression. This means the maintenance of security services at so high a cost that the services directed to "the well-being and development" of the population cannot be expanded and may even have to be curtailed. The moral objections to repression are self-evident. Nor need the undesirable reactions of it on opinion outside Palestine be emphasized. Moreover, repression will not solve the problem. It will exacerbate the quarrel. It will not help towards the establishment of a single self-governing Palestine. It is not easy to pursue the dark path of repression without seeing daylight at the end of it.

The British people will not flinch from the task of continuing to govern Palestine under the Mandate if they are in honour bound to do so, but they would be justified in asking if there is no other way in which their duty can be done.

Nor would Britain wish to repudiate her obligations. The trouble is that they have proved irreconcilable, and this conflict is the more unfortunate because each of the obligations taken separately accords with British sentiment and British interest. The development of self-government in the Arab world on the one hand is in accordance with British principles, and British public opinion is wholly sympathetic with Arab aspirations towards a new age of unity and prosperity in the Arab world. British interest similarly has always been bound up with the peace of the Middle East and British statesmanship can show an almost unbroken record of friendship with the Arabs. There is a strong British tradition, on the other hand, of friendship with the Jewish people, and it is in the British interest to retain as far as may be the confidence of the Jewish people.

The continuance of the present system means the gradual alienation of two peoples who are traditionally the friends of Britain.

The problem cannot be solved by giving either the Arabs or the Jews all they want. The answer to the question which of them in the end will govern Palestine must be Neither. No fair-minded statesman can think it right either that 400,000 Jews, whose entry into Palestine has been facilitated by he British Government and approved by the League of Nations, should be handed over to Arab rule, or that, if the Jews should become a majority, a million Arabs should be handed over to their rule. But while neither race can fairly rule all Palestine, each race might justly rule part of it.

The idea of Partition has doubtless been thought of before as a solution of the problem, but it has probably been discarded as being impracticable. The difficulties are certainly very great, but when they are closely examined they do not seem so insuperable as the difficulties inherent in the continuance of the Mandate or in any other alternative arrangement. Partition offers a chance of ultimate peace. No other plan does.

Chapter XXI.—Cantonisation

The political division of Palestine could be effected in a less thorough manner than by Partition. It could be divided like Federal States into provinces and cantons, which would be self-governing in such matters as immigration and land sales as well as social services. The Mandatory Government would remain as a central or federal government controlling such matters as foreign relations, defence, customs and the like.

Cantonisation is attractive at first sight because it seems to solve the three major problems of land, immigration and self-government, but there are obvious weaknesses in it. First, the working of federal systems depends on sufficient community of interest or tradition to maintain harmony between the Central Government and the cantons. In Palestine both Arabs and Jews would regard the Central Government as an alien and interfering body. Secondly, the financial relations between the Central Government and the cantons would revive the existing quarrel between Arabs and Jews as to the distribution of a surplus of federal revenue or as to the contributions of the cantons towards a federal deficit. Unrestricted Jewish immigration into the Jewish canton might lead to a demand for the expansion of federal services at the expense of the Arab canton. Thirdly, the costly task of maintaining law and order would still rest mainly on the Central Government. Fourthly, Cantonisation like

Partition cannot avoid leaving a minority of each race in the area controlled by the other. The solution of this problem requires such bold measures as can only be contemplated if there is a prospect of final peace. Partition opens up such a prospect. Cantonisation does not. Lastly, Cantonisation does not settle the question of national self-government. Neither the Arabs nor the Jews would feel their political aspirations were satisfied with purely cantonal self-government.

Cantonisation, in sum, presents most, if not all, of the difficulties presented by Partition without Partition's one supreme advantage—the possibilities it offers of eventual peace.

Chapter XXII.—A Plan of Partition

While the Commission would not be expected to embark on the further protracted inquiry which would be needed for working out a scheme of Partition in full detail, it would be idle to put forward the principle of Partition and not to give it any concrete shape. Clearly it must be shown that an actual plan can be devised which meets the main requirements of the case.

1. A Treaty System

The Mandate for Palestine should terminate and be replaced by a Treaty System in accordance with the precedent set in Iraq and Syria.

A new Mandate for the Holy Places should be instituted to fulfil the purposes defined in Section 2 below.

Treaties of alliance should be negotiated by the Mandatory with the Government of Trans-Jordan and representatives of the Arabs of Palestine on the one hand and with the Zionist Organisation on the other. These Treaties would declare that, within as short a period as may be convenient, two sovereign independent States would be established—the one an Arab State consisting of Trans-Jordan united with that part of Palestine which lies to the east and south of a frontier such as we suggest in Section 3 below; the other a Jewish State consisting of that part of Palestine which lies to the north and west of that frontier . . .

2. The Holy Places

The Partition of Palestine is subject to the overriding necessity of keeping the sanctity of Jerusalem and Bethlehem inviolate and of ensuring free and safe access to them for all the world. That, in the fullest sense of the mandatory phrase, is "a sacred trust of civilization"—a trust on behalf not merely of the peoples of Palestine but of multitudes in other lands to whom those places, one or both, are Holy Places. . . .

3. The Frontier

The natural principle for the Partition of Palestine is to separate land from the areas in which the Jews have acquired land and settled from those which are who are wholly or mainly occupied by Arabs. This offers a fair and practicable basis for Partition, provided that in accordance with the spirit of British obligations, (1) a reasonable allowance is made within the boundaries of the Jewish State for the growth of population and colonization, and (2) reasonable compensation is given to the Arab State for the loss of land and revenue . . .

4. Inter-State Subvention

The Jews contribute more *per capita* to the revenues of Palestine than the Arabs, and the Government has thereby been enabled to maintain public services for the Arabs at a higher level than would otherwise have been possible. Partition would mean, on the one hand, that the Arab Area would no longer profit from the taxable capacity of the Jewish Area. On the other hand, (1) the Jews would acquire a new right of sovereignty in the Jewish Area; (2) that Area, as we have defined it, would be larger than the existing area of Jewish land and settlement; (3) the Jews would be freed from their present liability for helping to promote the welfare of Arabs outside that Area. It is suggested, therefore, that the Jewish State should pay a subvention to the Arab State when Partition comes into effect. There have been recent precedents for equitable financial arrangements of this kind in those connected with the separation of Sind from Bombay and of Burma from the Indian Empire, and in accordance with those precedents a Finance Commission should be appointed to consider and report as to what the amount of the subvention should be . . .

5. British Subvention [. . .]

6. Tariffs and Ports [. . .]

7. Nationality [. . .]

8. Civil Services [. . .]

9. Industrial Concessions [. . .]

10. Exchange of Land and Population [. . .]

The Treaties should provide that, if Arab owners of land in the Jewish State or Jewish owners of land in the Arab State should wish to sell their land and any plantations or crops thereon, the Government of the State concerned should be responsible for the purchase of such land, plantations and crops at a price to be fixed, if required, by the Mandatory Administration . . .

Chapter X.—Conclusion

Considering the attitude which both the Arab and the Jewish representatives adopted in giving evidence, the Commission think it improbable that either party will be satisfied at first sight with the proposals submitted for the adjustment of their rival claims. For Partition means that neither will get all it wants. It means that the Arabs must acquiesce in the exclusion from their sovereignty of a piece of territory, long occupied and once ruled by them. It means that the

Jews must be content with less than the Land of Israel they once ruled and have hoped to rule again. But it seems possible that on reflection both parties will come to realize that the drawbacks of Partition are outweighed by its advantages. For, if it offers neither party all it wants, it offers each what it wants most, namely freedom and security.

The advantages to the Arabs of Partition on the lines we have proposed may be summarized as follows:-

(i) They obtain their national independence and can co-operate on an equal footing with the Arabs of the neighbouring countries in the cause of Arab unity and progress.

(ii) They are finally delivered from the fear of being swamped by the Jews, and from the possibility of ultimate subjection to Jewish rule.

(iii) In particular, the final limitation of the Jewish National Home within a fixed frontier and the enactment of a new Mandate for the protection of the Holy Places, solemnly guaranteed by the League of Nations, removes all anxiety lest the Holy Places should ever come under Jewish control.

(iv) As a set-off to the loss of territory the Arabs regard as theirs, the Arab State will receive a subvention from the Jewish State. It will also, in view of the backwardness of Trans-Jordan, obtain a grant of £2,000,000 from the British Treasury; and, if an agreement can be reached as to the exchange of land and population, a further grant will be made for the conversion, as far as may prove possible, of uncultivable land in the Arab State into productive land from which the cultivators and the State alike will profit.

The advantages of Partition to the Jews may be summarized as follows:-

(i) Partition secures the establishment of the Jewish National Home and relieves it from the possibility of its being subjected in the future to Arab rule.

(ii) Partition enables the Jews in the fullest sense to call their National Home their own; for it converts it into a Jewish State. Its citizens will be able to admit as many Jews into it as they themselves believe can be absorbed. They will attain the primary objective of Zionism—a Jewish nation, planted in Palestine, giving its nationals the same status in the world as other nations give theirs. They will cease at last to live a minority life.

To both Arabs and Jews Partition offers a prospect—and there is none in any other policy—of obtaining the inestimable boon of peace. It is surely worth some sacrifice on both sides if the quarrel which the Mandate started could he ended with its termination. It is not a natural or old-standing feud. The Arabs throughout their history have not only been free from anti-Jewish sentiment but have also shown that the spirit of compromise is deeply rooted in their life. Considering what the possibility of finding a refuge in Palestine means to many thousands of suffering Jews, is the loss occasioned by Partition, great as it would be, more than Arab generosity can bear? In this, as in so much else connected with Palestine, it is not only the peoples of that country who have to be considered. The Jewish Problem is not the least of the many problems which are disturbing international relations at this critical time and obstructing the path to peace and prosperity. If the Arabs at some sacrifice could help to solve that problem, they would earn the gratitude not of the Jews alone but of all the Western World . . .

11 British Government: Policy Statement Against Partition (November 11, 1938)

PALESTINE

Statement by His Majesty's Government in the United Kingdom

Presented by the Secretary of State for the Colonies
to Parliament by Command of His Majesty

PALESTINE

STATEMENT BY HIS MAJESTY'S GOVERNMENT
IN THE UNITED KINGDOM

1. The Royal Commission, presided over by the late Earl Peel, published its report in July, 1937, and proposed a solution of the Palestine problem by means of a scheme of partition under which independent Arab and Jewish States would be established while other areas would be retained under mandatory administration. In their statement of policy following upon the publication of the report, His Majesty's Government in the United Kingdom announced their general agreement with the arguments and conclusions of the Royal Commission, and expressed the view that a scheme of partition on the general lines recommended by the Commission represented the best and most hopeful solution of the deadlock.

2. The proposal of the Commission was framed in the light of the information available at the time, and it was generally recognized that further detailed examination would be necessary before it could be decided whether such a solution would prove practicable. This proposal was subsequently discussed in Parliament and at meetings of the Permanent Mandates Commission and the Council and Assembly of the League of Nations, when His Majesty's Government received authority to explore the practical application of the principle of partition. A despatch of 23rd December, 1937, from the Secretary of State for the Colonies to the High Commissioner for Palestine, announced the intention of His Majesty's Government to undertake the further investigations required for the drawing up of a more precise and detailed scheme. It was pointed out that the final decision could not be taken in merely general terms and that the further enquiry would provide the necessary material on which to judge,

when the best possible partition scheme had been formulated, its equity and practicability. The despatch also defined the functions and terms of reference of the technical Commission who were appointed to visit Palestine for the purpose of submitting in due course to His Majesty's Government proposals for such a detailed scheme.

3. His Majesty's Government have now received the report of the Palestine Partition Commission who have carried out their investigations with great thoroughness and efficiency, and have collected material which will be very valuable in the further consideration of policy. Their report is now published, together with a summary of their conclusions. It will be noted that the four members of the Commission advise unanimously against the adoption of the scheme of partition outlined by the Royal Commission. . . . The report points out that under either plan, while the budget of the Jewish State is likely to show a substantial surplus, the budgets of the Arab State (including Trans-Jordan) and of the Mandated Territories are likely to show substantial deficits. The Commission reject as impracticable the Royal Commission's recommendation for a direct subvention from the Jewish State to the Arab State. They think that, on economic grounds, a customs union between the States and the Mandated Territories is essential and they examine the possibility of finding the solution for the financial and economic problems of partition by means of a scheme based upon such a union. They consider that any such scheme would be inconsistent with the grant of fiscal independence to the Arab and Jewish States. Their conclusion is that, on a strict interpretation of their terms of reference, they have no alternative but to report that they are unable to recommend boundaries for the proposed areas which will afford a reasonable prospect of the eventual establishment of self-supporting Arab and Jewish States.

4. His Majesty's Government, after careful study of the Partition Commission's report, have reached the conclusion that this further examination has shown that the political, administrative and financial difficulties involved in the proposal to create independent Arab and Jewish States inside Palestine are so great that this solution of the problem is impracticable.

5. His Majesty's Government will therefore continue their responsibility for the government of the whole of Palestine. They are now faced with the problem of finding alternative means of meeting the needs of the difficult situation described by the Royal Commission which will be consistent with their obligations to the Arabs and the Jews . . . It is clear that the surest foundation for peace and progress in Palestine would be an understanding between the Arabs and the Jews, and His Majesty's Government are prepared in the first instance to make a determined effort to promote such an understanding. With this end in view, they propose immediately to invite representatives of the Palestinian Arabs and of neighbouring States on the one hand and of the Jewish Agency on the other, to confer with them as soon as possible in London regarding future policy, including the question of immigration into Palestine. As regards the representation of the Palestinian Arabs, His Majesty's Government must reserve the right to refuse to receive those leaders whom they regard as responsible for the campaign of assassination and violence.

6. His Majesty's Government hope that these discussions in London may help to promote agreement as to future policy regarding Palestine . . .

7. In considering and settling their policy His Majesty's Government will keep constantly in mind the international character of the Mandate with which they have been entrusted and their obligations in that respect.

12 British Government: The White Paper (May 17, 1939)

PALESTINE

Statement of Policy

*Presented by the Secretary of State for the Colonies to Parliament
by Command of His Majesty
May, 1939*

STATEMENT OF POLICY

In the Statement on Palestine, issued on 9th November, 1938, His Majesty's Government announced their intention to invite representatives of the Arabs of Palestine, of certain neighbouring countries and of the Jewish Agency to confer with them in London regarding future policy. It was their sincere hope that, as a result of full, free and frank discussion, some understanding might be reached. . . . Neither the Arab nor the Jewish delegations felt able to accept these proposals, and the conferences therefore did not result in an agreement. Accordingly His Majesty's Government are free to formulate their own policy, and after careful consideration they have decided to adhere generally to the proposals which were finally submitted to, and discussed with, the Arab and Jewish delegations.

2. The Mandate for Palestine, the terms of which were confirmed by the Council of the League of Nations in 1922, has governed the policy of successive British Governments for nearly 20 years. It embodies the Balfour Declaration and imposes on the Mandatory four main obligations. These obligations are set out in Articles 2, 6 and 13 of the Mandate. There is no dispute regarding the interpretation of one of these obligations, that touching the protection of and access to the Holy Places and religious buildings or sites. The other three main obligations are generally as follows:

(i) To place the country under such political, administrative and economic conditions as will secure the establishment in Palestine of a national home for the Jewish people, to facilitate Jewish immigration under suitable conditions, and to encourage, in co-operation with the Jewish Agency, close settlement by Jews on the land.

(ii) To safeguard the civil and religious rights of all the inhabitants of Palestine irrespective of race and religion, and, whilst facilitating Jewish immigration and settlement, to ensure that the rights and position of other sections of the population are not prejudiced.

(iii) To place the country under such political, administrative and economic conditions as will secure the development of self-governing institutions.

3. The Royal Commission and previous Commissions of Enquiry have drawn attention to the ambiguity of certain expressions in the Mandate, such as the expression "a national home for the Jewish people", and they have found in this ambiguity and the resulting uncertainty as to the objectives of policy a fundamental cause of unrest and hostility between Arabs and Jews . . . the establishment of self-supporting independent Arab and Jewish States within Palestine has been found to be impracticable. It has therefore been necessary for His Majesty's Government to devise an alternative policy which will, consistently with their obligations to Arabs and Jews, meet the needs of the situation in Palestine. Their views and proposals are set forth below under the three heads, (I) The Constitution, (II) Immigration, and (III) Land.

I.—The Constitution.

4. It has been urged that the expression "a national home for the Jewish people" offered a prospect that Palestine might in due course become a Jewish State or Commonwealth. His Majesty's Government do not wish to contest the view, which was expressed by the Royal Commission, that the Zionist leaders at the time of the issue of the Balfour Declaration recognised that an ultimate Jewish State was not precluded by the terms of the Declaration. But, with the Royal Commission, His Majesty's Government believe that the framers of the Mandate in which the Balfour Declaration was embodied could not have intended that Palestine should be converted into a Jewish State against the will of the Arab population of the country. That Palestine was not to be converted into a Jewish State might be held to be implied in the passage from the Command Paper of 1922 which reads as follows:—

"Unauthorised statements have been made to the effect that the purpose in view is to create a wholly Jewish Palestine. Phrases have been used such as that 'Palestine is to become as Jewish as England is English'. His Majesty's Government regard any such expectation as impracticable and have no such aim in view. Nor have they at any time contemplated . . . the disappearance or the subordination of the Arabic population, language or culture in Palestine. They would draw attention to the fact that the terms of the (Balfour) Declaration referred to do not contemplate that Palestine as a whole should be converted into a Jewish National Home, but that such a Home should be founded *in Palestine*".

But this statement has not removed doubts, and His Majesty's Government therefore now declare unequivocally that it is not part of their policy that Palestine should become a Jewish State. They would indeed regard it as contrary to their obligations to the Arabs under the Mandate, as well as to the assurances which have been given to the Arab people in the past, that the Arab population of Palestine should be made the subjects of a Jewish State against their will.

5. The nature of the Jewish National Home in Palestine was further described in the Command Paper of 1922 . . .

6. His Majesty's Government adhere to this interpretation of the Declaration of 1917 and regard it as an authoritative and comprehensive description of the character of the Jewish National Home in Palestine. It envisaged the further development of the existing Jewish community with the assistance of Jews in other parts of the world. Evidence that His Majesty's Government have been carrying out their obligation in this respect is to be found in the facts that, since the statement of 1922 was published, more than 300,000 Jews have immigrated to Palestine, and that the population of the National Home has risen to some 450,000, or approaching a third of the entire population of the country. Nor has the Jewish community failed to take full advantage of the opportunities given to it. The growth of the Jewish National Home and its achievements in many fields are a remarkable constructive effort which must command the admiration of the world and must be, in particular, a source of pride to the Jewish people.

7. In the recent discussions the Arab delegations have repeated the contention that Palestine was included within the area in which Sir Henry McMahon, on behalf of the British Government, in October, 1915, undertook to recognise and support Arab independence. The validity of this claim, based on the terms of the correspondence which passed between Sir Henry McMahon and the Sharif of Mecca, was thoroughly and carefully investigated by British and Arab representatives during the recent conferences in London. Their Report, which has been published, states that both the Arab and the British representatives endeavoured to understand the point of view of the other party but that they were unable to reach agreement upon an interpretation of the correspondence. There is no need to summarise here the arguments presented by each side. His Majesty's Government regret the misunderstandings which have arisen as regards some of the phrases used. For their part they can only adhere, for the reasons given by their representatives in the Report, to the view that the whole of Palestine west of Jordan was excluded from Sir Henry McMahon's pledge, and they therefore cannot agree that the McMahon correspondence forms a just basis for the claim that Palestine should be converted into an Arab State.

8. His Majesty's Government are charged as the Mandatory authority "to secure the development of self-governing institutions" in Palestine. Apart from this specific obligation, they would regard it as contrary to the whole spirit of the Mandate system that the population of Palestine should remain forever under Mandatory tutelage. It is proper that the people of the country should as early as possible enjoy the rights of self-government which are exercised by the people of neighbouring countries. His Majesty's Government are unable at present to foresee the exact constitutional forms

which government in Palestine will eventually take, but their objective is self-government, and they desire to see established ultimately an independent Palestine State. It should be a State in which the two in Palestine, Arabs and Jews, share authority in government in such a way that the essential interests of each are secured.

9. The establishment of an independent State and the complete relinquishment of Mandatory control in Palestine would require such relations between the Arabs and the Jews as would make good government possible. Moreover, the growth of self-governing institutions in Palestine, as in other countries, must be an evolutionary process. A transitional period will be required before independence is achieved, throughout which ultimate responsibility for the Government of the country will be retained by His Majesty's Government as the Mandatory authority, while the people of the country are taking an increasing share in the Government, and understanding and co-operation amongst them are growing. It will be the constant endeavour of His Majesty's Government to promote good relations between the Arabs and the Jews.

10. In the light of these considerations His Majesty's Government make the following declaration of their intentions regarding the future government of Palestine:—

(1) The objective of His Majesty's Government is the establishment within ten years of an independent Palestine State in such treaty relations with the United Kingdom as will provide satisfactorily for the commercial and strategic requirements of both countries in the future. This proposal for the establishment of the independent State would involve consultation with the Council of the League of Nations with a view to the termination of the Mandate.

(2) The independent State should be one in which Arabs and Jews share in government in such a way as to ensure that the essential interests of each community are safeguarded.

(3) The establishment of the independent State will be preceded by a transitional period throughout which His Majesty's Government will retain responsibility for the government of the country. During the transitional period the people of Palestine will be given an increasing part in the government of their country. Both sections of the population will have an opportunity to participate in the machinery of government, and the process will be carried on whether or not they both avail themselves of it.

(4) As soon as peace and order have been sufficiently restored in Palestine steps will be taken to carry out this policy of giving the people of Palestine an increasing part in the government of their country, the objective being to place Palestinians in charge of all the Departments of Government, with the assistance of British advisers and subject to the control of the High Commissioner. With this object in view His Majesty's Government will be prepared immediately to arrange that Palestinians shall be placed in charge of certain Departments, with British advisers. The Palestinian heads of Departments will sit on the Executive Council, which

advises the High Commissioner. Arab and Jewish representatives will be invited to serve as heads of Departments approximately in proportion to their respective populations. The number of Palestinians in charge of Departments will be increased as circumstances permit until all heads of Departments are Palestinians, exercising the administrative and advisory functions which are at present performed by British officials. When that stage is reached consideration will be given to the question of converting the Executive Council into a Council of Ministers with a consequential change in the status and functions of the Palestinian heads of Departments.

(5) His Majesty's Government make no proposals at this stage regarding the establishment of an elective legislature. Nevertheless they would regard this as an appropriate constitutional development, and, should public opinion in Palestine hereafter show itself in favour of such a development, they will be prepared, provided that local conditions permit, to establish the necessary machinery.

(6) At the end of five years from the restoration of peace and order, an appropriate body representative of the people of Palestine and of His Majesty's Government will be set up to review the working of the constitutional arrangements during the transitional period and to consider and make recommendations regarding the constitution of the independent Palestine State.

(7) His Majesty's Government will require to be satisfied that in the treaty contemplated by sub-paragraph (I) or in the constitution contemplated by sub-paragraph (6) adequate provision has been made for:—

(a) the security of, and freedom of access to, the Holy Places, and the protection of the interests and property of the various religious bodies.

(b) the protection of the different communities in Palestine in accordance with the obligations of His Majesty's Government to both Arabs and Jews and for the special position in Palestine of the Jewish National Home.

(c) such requirements to meet the strategic situation as may be regarded as necessary by His Majesty's Government in the light of the circumstances then existing . . .

(8) His Majesty's Government will do everything in their power to create conditions which will enable the independent Palestine State to come into being within ten years. If, at the end of ten years, it appears to His Majesty's Government that, contrary to their hope, circumstances require the postponement of the establishment of the independent State, they will consult with representatives of the people of Palestine, the Council of the League of Nations and the neighbouring Arab States before deciding on such a postponement. If His Majesty's Government come to the conclusion that postponement is unavoidable, they will invite the co-operation of these parties in framing plans for the future with a view to achieving the desired objective at the earliest possible date . . .

II.—Immigration.

12. Under Article 6 of the Mandate, the Administration of Palestine, "while ensuring that the rights and position of other sections of the population are not prejudiced", is required to "facilitate Jewish immigration under suitable conditions". Beyond this, the extent to which Jewish immigration into Palestine is to be permitted is nowhere defined in the Mandate. But in the Command Paper of 1922 it was laid down that for the fulfilment of the policy of establishing a Jewish National Home

> "it is necessary that the Jewish community in Palestine should be able to increase its numbers by immigration. This immigration cannot be so great in volume as to exceed whatever may be the economic capacity of the country at the time to absorb new arrivals. It is essential to ensure that the immigrants should not be a burden upon the people of Palestine as a whole, and that they should not deprive any section of the present population of their employment."

In practice, from that date onwards until recent times, the economic absorptive capacity of the country has been treated as the sole limiting factor, and in the letter which Mr. Ramsay MacDonald, as Prime Minister, sent to Dr. Weizmann in February 1931 it was laid down as a matter of policy that economic absorptive capacity was the sole criterion. This interpretation has been supported by resolutions of the Permanent Mandates Commission. But His Majesty's Government do not read either the Statement of Policy of 1922 or the letter of 1931 as implying that the Mandate requires them, for all time and in all circumstances, to facilitate the immigration of Jews into Palestine subject only to consideration of the country's economic absorptive capacity. Nor do they find anything in the Mandate or in subsequent Statements of Policy to support the view that the establishment of a Jewish National Home in Palestine cannot be effected unless immigration is allowed to continue indefinitely.

If immigration has an adverse effect on the economic position in the country, it should clearly be restricted; and equally, if it has a seriously damaging effect on the political position in the country, that is a factor that should not be ignored. Although it is not difficult to contend that the large number of Jewish immigrants who have been admitted so far have been absorbed economically, the fear of the Arabs that this influx will continue indefinitely until the Jewish population is in a position to dominate them has produced consequences which are extremely grave for Jews and Arabs alike and for the peace and prosperity of Palestine. The lamentable disturbances of the past three years are only the latest and most sustained manifestation of this intense Arab apprehension. The methods employed by Arab terrorists against fellow-Arabs and Jews alike must receive unqualified condemnation. But it cannot be denied that fear of indefinite Jewish immigration is widespread amongst the Arab population and that this fear has made possible disturbances which have given a serious setback to economic progress, depleted the Palestine exchequer, rendered life and property insecure, and produced a bitterness between the Arab and Jewish populations which is deplorable between citizens of the same country.

If in these circumstances immigration is continued up to the economic absorptive capacity of the country, regardless of all other considerations, a fatal enmity between the two peoples will be perpetuated, and the situation in Palestine may become a permanent source of friction amongst all peoples in the Near and Middle East. His Majesty's Government cannot take the view that either their obligations under the Mandate, or considerations of common sense and justice, require that they should ignore these circumstances in framing immigration policy.

13. In the view of the Royal Commission, the association of the policy of the Balfour Declaration with the Mandate system implied the belief that Arab hostility to the former would sooner or later be overcome. It has been the hope of British Governments ever since the Balfour Declaration was issued that in time the Arab population, recognizing the advantages to be derived from Jewish settlement and development in Palestine, would become reconciled to the further growth of the Jewish National Home. This hope has not been fulfilled. The alternatives before His Majesty's Government are either (i) to seek to expand the Jewish National Home indefinitely by immigration, against the strongly expressed will of the Arab people of the country; or (ii) to permit further expansion of the Jewish National Home by immigration only if the Arabs are prepared to acquiesce in it. The former policy means rule by force. Apart from other considerations, such a policy seems to His Majesty's Government to be contrary to the whole spirit of Article 22 of the Covenant of the League of Nations, as well as to their specific obligations to the Arabs in the Palestine Mandate. Moreover, the relations between the Arabs and the Jews in Palestine must be based sooner or later on mutual tolerance and goodwill; the peace, security and progress of the Jewish National Home itself require this. Therefore His Majesty's Government, after earnest consideration, and taking into account the extent to which the growth of the Jewish National Home has been facilitated over the last twenty years, have decided that the time has come to adopt in principle the second of the alternatives referred to above.

14. It has been urged that all further Jewish immigration into Palestine should be stopped forthwith. His Majesty's Government cannot accept such a proposal. It would damage the whole of the financial and economic system of Palestine and thus affect adversely the interests of Arabs and Jews alike. Moreover, in the view of His Majesty's Government, abruptly to stop further immigration would be unjust to the Jewish National Home. But, above all, His Majesty's Government are conscious of the present unhappy plight of large numbers of Jews who seek a refuge from certain European countries, and they believe that Palestine can and should make a further contribution to the solution of this pressing world problem. In all these circumstances, they believe that they will be acting consistently with their Mandatory obligations to both Arabs and Jews, and in the manner best calculated to serve the interests of the whole people of Palestine, by adopting the following proposals regarding immigration:—

(1) Jewish immigration during the next five years will be at a rate which, if economic absorptive capacity permits, will bring the Jewish population up to

approximately one-third of the total population of the country. Taking into account the expected natural increase of the Arab and Jewish populations, and the number of illegal Jewish immigrants now in the country, this would allow for the admission, as from the beginning of April this year, of some 75,000 immigrants over the next five years. These immigrants would, subject to the criterion of economic absorptive capacity, be admitted as follows:—

(a) For each of the next five years a quota of 10,000 Jewish immigrants will be allowed, on the understanding that a shortage in any one year may be added to the quotas for subsequent years, within the five-year period, if economic absorptive capacity permits.

(b) In addition, as a contribution towards the solution of the Jewish refugee problem, 25,000 refugees will be admitted as soon as the High Commissioner is satisfied that adequate provision for their maintenance is ensured, special consideration being given to refugee children and dependants.

(2) The existing machinery for ascertaining economic absorptive capacity will be retained, and the High Commissioner will have the ultimate responsibility for deciding the limits of economic capacity. Before each periodic decision is taken, Jewish and Arab representatives will be consulted.

(3} After the period of five years no further Jewish immigration will be permitted unless the Arabs of Palestine are prepared to acquiesce in it.

(4) His Majesty's Government are determined to check illegal immigration, and further preventive measure are being adopted. The numbers of any Jewish illegal immigrants who, despite these measures, may succeed in coming into the country and cannot be deported will be deducted from the yearly quotas.

15. His Majesty's Government are satisfied that, when the immigration over five years which is now contemplated has taken place, they will not be justified in facilitating, nor will they be under any obligation to facilitate, the further development of the Jewish National Home by immigration regardless of the wishes of the Arab population.

III.—Land [. . .]

13 Zionist Reaction to the White Paper (1939)

1. The new policy for Palestine laid down by the Mandatory in the White Paper now issued denies to the Jewish people the right to rebuild their national home in their ancestral country. It transfers the authority over Palestine to the present Arab majority and puts the Jewish population at the mercy of that majority. It decrees the stoppage of Jewish immigration as soon as the Jews form a third of the total population. It puts up a territorial ghetto for Jews in their own homeland.

2. The Jewish people regard this policy as a breach of faith and a surrender to Arab terrorism. It delivers Britain's friends into the hands of those who are biting her and must lead to a complete breach between Jews and Arabs which will banish every prospect of peace in Palestine. It is a policy in which the Jewish people will not acquiesce. The new regime now announced will be devoid of any moral basis and contrary to international law. Such a regime can only be established and maintained by force.

3. The Royal Commission invoked by the White Paper indicated the perils of such a policy, saying it was convinced that an Arab Government would mean the frustration of all their (Jews') efforts and ideals and would convert the national home into one more cramped and dangerous ghetto. It seems only too probable that the Jews would fight rather than submit to Arab rule. And repressing a Jewish rebellion against British policy would be as unpleasant a task as the repression of the Arab rebellion has been. The Government has disregarded this warning.

4. The Jewish people have no quarrel with the Arab people. Jewish work in Palestine has not had an adverse effect upon the life and progress of the Arab people. The Arabs are not landless or homeless as are the Jews. They are not in need of emigration. Jewish colonization has benefited Palestine and all its inhabitants. Insofar as the Balfour Declaration contributed to British victory in the Great War, it contributed also, as was pointed out by the Royal Commission, to the liberation of the Arab peoples. The Jewish people has shown its will to peace even during the years of disturbances. It has not given way to temptation and has not retaliated to Arab violence. But neither have the Jews submitted to terror nor will they submit to it even after the Mandatory has decided to reward the terrorists by surrendering the Jewish National Home.

5. It is in the darkest hour of Jewish history that the British Government proposes to deprive the Jews of their last hope and to close the road back to their Homeland. It is a cruel blow, doubly cruel because it comes from the government of a great nation which has extended a helping hand to the Jews, and whose position must rest on foundations of moral authority and international good faith. This blow will not subdue the Jewish people. The historic bond between the people and the land of Israel cannot be broken. The Jews will never accept the closing to them of the gates of Palestine nor let their national home be converted into a ghetto. The Jewish pioneers who, during the past three generations, have shown their strength in the unbuilding of a derelict country, will from now on display the same strength in defending Jewish immigration, the Jewish home and Jewish freedom.

14 The Biltmore Program: Towards a Jewish State (May 11, 1942)

Declaration adopted by the Extraordinary Zionist Conference at the Biltmore Hotel of New York City, May 11, 1942.

1. American Zionists assembled in this Extraordinary Conference reaffirm their unequivocal devotion to the cause of democratic freedom and international justice to which the people of the United States, allied with the other United Nations, have dedicated themselves, and give expression to their faith in the ultimate victory of humanity and justice over lawlessness and brute force.

2. This Conference offers a message of hope and encouragement to their fellow Jews in the Ghettos and concentration camps of Hitler-dominated Europe and prays that their hour of liberation may not be far distant.

3. The Conference sends its warmest greetings to the Jewish Agency Executive in Jerusalem, to the Va'ad Leumi, and to the whole Yishuv in Palestine, and expresses its profound admiration for their steadfastness and achievements in the face of peril and great difficulties . . .

4. In our generation, and in particular in the course of the past twenty years, the Jewish people have awakened and transformed their ancient homeland; from 50,000 at the end of the last war their numbers have increased to more than 500,000. They have made the waste places to bear fruit and the desert to blossom. Their pioneering achievements in agriculture and in industry, embodying new patterns of cooperative endeavour, have written a notable page in the history of colonization.

5. In the new values thus created, their Arab neighbours in Palestine have shared. The Jewish people in its own work of national redemption welcomes the economic, agricultural and national development of the Arab peoples and states. The Conference reaffirms the stand previously adopted at Congresses of the World Zionist Organization, expressing the readiness and the desire of the Jewish people for full cooperation with their Arab neighbours.

6. The Conference calls for the fulfillment of the original purpose of the Balfour Declaration and the Mandate which recognizing 'the historical connection of the

Jewish people with Palestine' was to afford them the opportunity, as stated by President Wilson, to found there a Jewish Commonwealth.

The Conference affirms its unalterable rejection of the White Paper of May 1939 and denies its moral or legal validity. The White Paper seeks to limit, and in fact to nullify Jewish rights to immigration and settlement in Palestine, and, as stated by Mr. Winston Churchill in the House of Commons in May 1939, constitutes 'a breach and repudiation of the Balfour Declaration'. The policy of the White Paper is cruel and indefensible in its denial of sanctuary to Jews fleeing from Nazi persecution; and at a time when Palestine has become a focal point in the war front of the United Nations, and Palestine Jewry must provide all available manpower for farm and factory and camp, it is in direct conflict with the interests of the allied war effort.

7. In the struggle against the forces of aggression and tyranny, of which Jews were the earliest victims, and which now menace the Jewish National Home, recognition must be given to the right of the Jews of Palestine to play their full part in the war effort and in the defence of their country, through a Jewish military force fighting under its own flag and under the high command of the United Nations.

8. The Conference declares that the new world order that will follow victory cannot be established on foundations of peace, justice and equality, unless the problem of Jewish homelessness is finally solved.

The Conference urges that the gates of Palestine be opened; that the Jewish Agency be vested with control of immigration into Palestine and with the necessary authority for upbuilding the country, including the development of its unoccupied and uncultivated lands; and that Palestine be established as a Jewish Commonwealth integrated in the structure of the new democratic world.

Then and only then will the age old wrong to the Jewish people be righted.

15 Arab Office Report to Anglo–American Committee (March, 1946)

[. . .]

(8) In the Arab view, any solution or the problem created by Zionist aspirations must satisfy certain conditions:

(i) It must recognize the right of the indigenous inhabitants of Palestine to continue in occupation of the country and to preserve its traditional character.

(ii) It must recognize that questions like immigration which affect the whole nature and destiny of the country should be decided in accordance with democratic principles by the will of the population.

(iii) It must accept the principle that the only way by which the will of the population can be expressed is through the establishment of responsible representative government. . . .

(iv) This representative Government should be based upon the principle of absolute equality of all citizens irrespective of race and religion. . . .

(vi) The settlement should recognize the fact that by geography and history Palestine is inescapably part of the Arab world; that the only alternative to its being part of the Arab world and accepting the implication of its position is complete isolation, which would he disastrous from every point of view; and that whether they like it or not the Jews in Palestine are dependent upon the goodwill of the Arabs.

(vii) The settlement should be such as to make possible a satisfactory definition within the framework of U.N.O. the relations between Palestine and the Western powers who posses interests in the country.

(viii) The settlement should take into account that Zionism is essentially a political movement aiming at the creation of a Jewish state and should therefore avoid making any concessions which might encourage Zionists in the hope that their aim can be achieved in any circumstances.

(ix) In accordance with these principles, the Arabs urge the establishment in Palestine of a democratic government representative of all sections of the population on a level of absolute equality; the termination of the Mandate once the Government has been established; and the entry of Palestine into the United Nations Organization as a full member of the working community.

(9) Pending the establishment of a representative Government, all further Jewish immigration should be stopped, in pursuance of the principle that a decision on so important a matter should only be taken with the consent of the inhabitants of the

country and that until representative institutions are established there is no way of determining consent. Strict measures should also continue to be taken to check illegal immigration. Once a Palestinian state has come into existence, if any section of the population favours a policy of further immigration it will be able to press its case in accordance with normal democratic procedure; but in this as in other matters the minority must abide by the decision of the majority.

Similarly, all further transfer of land from Arabs to Jews should be prohibited prior to the creation of self-governing institutions. The Land Transfer Regulations should be made more stringent and extended to the whole area of the country, and severer measures be taken to prevent infringement of them. Here again once self-government exists matters concerning land will be decided in the normal democratic manner.

(10) The Arabs are irrevocably opposed to political Zionism, but in no way hostile to the Jews as such nor to their Jewish fellow citizens of Palestine. Those Jews who have already entered Palestine, and who have obtained or shall obtain Palestinian citizenship by due legal process will be full citizens of the Palestinian state, enjoying full civil and political rights and a fair share in government and administration. There is no question of their being thrust into the position of a "minority" in the bad sense of a closed community, which dwells apart from the main stream of the State's life and which exists by sufferance of the majority. They will be given the opportunity of belonging to and helping to mould the full community of the Palestinian state, joined to the Arabs by links of interest and goodwill, not the goodwill of the strong to the powerless, but of one citizen to another.

It is to be hoped that in course of time the exclusiveness of the Jews will be neutralized by the development of loyalty to the state and the emergence of new groupings which cut across communal divisions. This however will take time and during the transitional period the Arabs recognize the need for giving special consideration to the particular position and the needs of the Jews. No attempt would be made to interfere with their communal organization, their personal status or their religious observances. Their schools and cultural institutions would be left to operate unchecked except for that general control which all governments exercise over education. In the districts in which they are most closely settled they would possess municipal autonomy and Hebrew would be an official language of administration, justice, and education.

(11) The Palestinian State would be an Arab state not (as should be clear from the preceding paragraph) in any narrow racial sense, nor in the sense that non-Arabs should be placed in a position of inferiority, but because the form and policy of its government would be based on a recognition of two facts: first that the majority of the citizens are Arabs, and secondly that Palestine is part of the Arab world and has no future except through close cooperation with the other Arab states. Thus among the main objects of the Government would be to preserve and enrich the country's Arab heritage, and to draw closer the relations between Palestine and the other Arab countries. The Cairo Pact of March 1945, provided for the representation of Palestine on the Council of the Arab League even before its independence should be a reality; once it was really self-governing it would participate fully in all the work of the

League, in the cultural and economic no less than the political sphere. This would be of benefit to the Jewish not less than the Arab citizens of Palestine since it would ensure those good relations with the Arab world without which their economic development would be impossible.

(12) The state would apply as soon as possible for admission into U.N.O. and would of course be prepared to bear its full share of the burdens of establishing a world security system. It would willingly place at the disposal of the Security Council whatever bases or other facilities were required, provided those bases were really used for the purpose which they were intended and not in order to interfere in the internal affairs of the country, and provided also Palestine and the other Arab states were adequately represented on the controlling body.

The state would recognize also the world's interest in the maintenance of a satisfactory regime for the Moslem, Christian and Jewish Holy Places. In the Arab view however the need for such a regime does not involve foreign interference in or control of Palestine; no opportunity should be given to Great Powers to use the Holy Places as instruments of policy. The Holy Places can be most satisfactorily and appropriately guarded by a Government representative of the inhabitants, who include adherents of all three faiths and have every interest in preserving the holy character of their country.

Nor in the Arab view would any sort of foreign interference or control be justified by the need to protect the Christian minorities The Christians are Arabs, who belong fully to the national community and share fully in its struggle. They would have all the rights and duties of citizens of a Palestinian state, and would continue to have their own communal organizations and institutions. They themselves would ask for no more, having learnt from the example of other Middle Eastern countries the dangers of an illusory foreign "protection" of minorities.

(13) In economic and social matters the Government of Palestine would follow a progressive policy with the aim of raising the standard of living and increasing the welfare of all sections of the population, and using the country's natural resources in the way most beneficial to all. Its first task naturally would be to improve the condition of the Arab peasants and thus to bridge the economic and social gulf which at present divides the two communities. Industry would be encouraged, but only in so far as its economic basis was sound and as part of a general policy of economic development for the whole Arab world; commercial and financial contact with the other Arab countries would so far as be possible strengthened, and tariffs decreased or abolished.

(14) The Arabs believe that no other proposals would satisfy the conditions of a just and lasting settlement. In their view there are insuperable objections of principle or of practice to all other suggested solutions of the problem.

(15) The idea of partition and the establishment of a Jewish state in a part of Palestine is inadmissible for the same reasons of principle as the idea of establishing a Jewish state in the whole country. If it is unjust to the Arabs to impose a Jewish state on the

whole of Palestine, it is equally unjust to impose it in any part of the country. Moreover, as the Woodhead Commission showed, there are grave practical difficulties in the way of partition; commerce would be strangled, communications dislocated and the public finances upset. It would also be impossible to devise frontiers which did not leave a large Arab minority in the Jewish state. This minority would not wittingly accept its subjection to the Zionists and it would not allow itself to be transferred to the Arab state. Moreover, partition would not satisfy the Zionists. It cannot be too often repeated that Zionism is a political movement aimed at the domination at least of the whole of Palestine; to give it a foothold in part of Palestine would be to encourage it to press for more and to provide it with a base for its activities. Because of this, because of the pressure of population and in order to escape from its isolation it would inevitably be thrown into enmity with the surrounding Arab states and this enmity would disturb the stability of the whole Middle East.

(16) Another proposal is for the establishment of a bi-national state; based upon political parity, in Palestine and its incorporation into a Syrian or Arab Federation. The Arabs would reject this as denying the majority its normal position and rights. There are also serious practical objections to the idea of a bi-national state which cannot exist unless there is a strong sense of unity and common interest overriding the differences between the two parties. Moreover, the point made in regard to the previous suggestion may be repeated here: this scheme would in no way satisfy the Zionists. It would simply encourage them to hope for more and improve their chances of obtaining it . . .

16 U.N. Security Council: Resolution 181, The Partition of Palestine (November 29, 1947)

The General Assembly,

Having met in special session at the request of the mandatory Power to constitute and instruct a Special Committee to prepare for the consideration of the question of the future Government of Palestine at the second regular session;

Having constituted a Special Committee and instructed it to investigate all questions and issues relevant to the problem of Palestine, and to prepare proposals for the solution of the problem, and

Having received and examined the report of the Special Committee (document A/364)(1) including a number of unanimous recommendations and a plan of partition with economic union approved by the majority of the Special Committee,

Considers that the present situation in Palestine is one which is likely to impair the general welfare and friendly relations among nations;

Takes note of the declaration by the mandatory Power that it plans to complete its evacuation of Palestine by 1 August 1948;

Recommends to the United Kingdom, as the mandatory Power for Palestine, and to all other Members of the United Nations the adoption and implementation, with regard to the future Government of Palestine, of the Plan of Partition with Economic Union set out below;

Requests that

a. The Security Council take the necessary measures as provided for in the plan for its implementation;
b. The Security Council consider, if circumstances during the transitional period require such consideration, whether the situation in Palestine constitutes a threat to the peace. If it decides that such a threat exists, and in order to maintain international peace and security, the Security Council should supplement the authorization of the General Assembly by taking measures, under Articles 39 and

41 of the Charter, to empower the United Nations Commission, as provided in this resolution, to exercise in Palestine the functions which are assigned to it by this resolution;

c. The Security Council determine as a threat to the peace, breach of the peace or act of aggression, in accordance with Article 39 of the Charter, any attempt to alter by force the settlement envisaged by this resolution;

d. The Trusteeship Council be informed of the responsibilities envisaged for it in this plan;

Calls upon the inhabitants of Palestine to take such steps as may be necessary on their part to put this plan into effect;

Appeals to all Governments and all peoples to refrain from taking any action which might hamper or delay the carrying out of these recommendations, and

Authorizes the Secretary-General to reimburse travel and subsistence expenses of the members of the Commission referred to in Part 1, Section B, Paragraph I below, on such basis and in such form as he may determine most appropriate in the circumstances, and to provide the Commission with the necessary staff to assist in carrying out the functions assigned to the Commission by the General Assembly.

[. . .]

PLAN OF PARTITION WITH ECONOMIC UNION

Part I.—Future Constitution and Government of Palestine

A. TERMINATION OF MANDATE, PARTITION AND INDEPENDENCE

1. The Mandate for Palestine shall terminate as soon as possible but in any case not later than 1 August 1948.
2. The armed forces of the mandatory Power shall be progressively withdrawn from Palestine, the withdrawal to be completed as soon as possible but in any case not later than 1 August 1948 . . .
3. Independent Arab and Jewish States and the Special International Regime for the City of Jerusalem, set forth in Part III of this Plan, shall come into existence in Palestine two months after the evacuation of the armed forces of the mandatory Power has been completed but in any case not later than 1 October 1948 . . .
4. The period between the adoption by the General Assembly of its recommendation on the question of Palestine and the establishment of the independence of the Arab and Jewish States shall be a transitional period.

B. STEPS PREPARATORY TO INDEPENDENCE

1. A Commission shall be set up consisting of one representative of each of five Member States. The Members represented on the Commission shall be elected

by the General Assembly on as broad a basis, geographically and otherwise, as possible.

2. The administration of Palestine shall, as the mandatory Power withdraws its armed forces, be progressively turned over to the Commission . . .

3. On its arrival in Palestine the Commission shall proceed to carry out measures for the establishment of the frontiers of the Arab and Jewish States and the City of Jerusalem in accordance with the general lines of the recommendations of the General Assembly on the partition of Palestine. . . .

4. The Commission, after consultation with the democratic parties and other public organizations of the Arab and Jewish States, shall select and establish in each State as rapidly as possible a Provisional Council of Government . . .

5. Subject to the provisions of these recommendations, during the transitional period the Provisional Councils of Government, acting under the Commission, shall have full authority in the areas under their control including authority over matters of immigration and land regulation.

6. [. . .]

7. The Commission shall instruct the Provisional Councils of Government of both the Arab and Jewish States, after their formation, to proceed to the establishment of administrative organs of government, central and local.

8. The Provisional Council of Government of each State shall, within the shortest time possible, recruit an armed militia from the residents of that State, sufficient in number to maintain internal order and to prevent frontier clashes. . . .

9. The Provisional Council of Government of each State shall, not later than two months after the withdrawal of the armed forces of the mandatory Power, hold elections to the Constituent Assembly which shall be conducted on democratic lines. . . . Arabs and Jews residing in the City of Jerusalem who have signed a notice of intention to become citizens, the Arabs of the Arab State and the Jews of the Jewish State, shall be entitled to vote in the Arab and Jewish States respectively. Women may vote and be elected to the Constituent Assemblies. During the transitional period no Jew shall be permitted to establish residence in the area of the proposed Arab State, and no Arab shall be permitted to establish residence in the area of the proposed Jewish State, except by special leave of the Commission.

10. The Constituent Assembly of each State shall draft a democratic constitution for its State and choose a provisional government to succeed the Provisional Council of Government appointed by the Commission. . . .

C. DECLARATION

A declaration shall be made to the United Nations by the Provisional Government of each proposed State before independence. It shall contain, inter alia, the following clauses:

General Provision

The stipulations contained in the Declaration are recognized as fundamental laws of the State and no law, regulation or official action shall conflict or interfere with these stipulations, nor shall any law, regulation or official action prevail over them.

Chapter I: Holy Places, Religious Buildings and Sites

1. Existing rights in respect of Holy Places and religious buildings or sites shall not be denied or impaired.
2. In so far as Holy Places are concerned, the liberty of access, visit, and transit shall be guaranteed, in conformity with existing rights, to all residents and citizens of the other State and of the City of Jerusalem, as well as to aliens, without distinction as to nationality, subject to requirements of national security, public order and decorum.

   Similarly, freedom of worship shall be guaranteed in conformity with existing rights, subject to the maintenance of public order and decorum.
3. Holy Places and religious buildings or sites shall be preserved. No act shall be permitted which may in any way impair their sacred character. If at any time it appears to the Government that any particular Holy Place, religious, building or site is in need of urgent repair, the Government may call upon the community or communities concerned to carry out such repair. The Government may carry it out itself at the expense of the community or community concerned if no action is taken within a reasonable time.
4. No taxation shall be levied in respect of any Holy Place, religious building or site which was exempt from taxation on the date of the creation of the State.

   No change in the incidence of such taxation shall be made which would either discriminate between the owners or occupiers of Holy Places, religious buildings or sites, or would place such owners or occupiers in a position less favourable in relation to the general incidence of taxation than existed at the time of the adoption of the Assembly's recommendations. . . .

Chapter 2: Religious and Minority Rights

1. Freedom of conscience and the free exercise of all forms of worship, subject only to the maintenance of public order and morals, shall be ensured to all.
2. No discrimination of any kind shall be made between the inhabitants on the ground of race, religion, language or sex.
3. All persons within the jurisdiction of the State shall be entitled to equal protection of the laws.
4. The family law and personal status of the various minorities and their religious interests, including endowments, shall be respected.
5. Except as may be required for the maintenance of public order and good government, no measure shall be taken to obstruct or interfere with the enterprise of religious or charitable bodies of all faiths or to discriminate against any representative or member of these bodies on the ground of his religion or nationality.
6. The State shall ensure adequate primary and secondary education for the Arab and Jewish minority, respectively, in its own language and its cultural traditions.

The right of each community to maintain its own schools for the education of its own members in its own language, while conforming to such educational requirements of a general nature as the State may impose, shall not be denied or impaired. Foreign educational establishments shall continue their activity on the basis of their existing rights.

7. No restriction shall be imposed on the free use by any citizen of the State of any language in private intercourse, in commerce, in religion, in the Press or in publications of any kind, or at public meetings.

8. No expropriation of land owned by an Arab in the Jewish State (or by a Jew in the Arab State) shall be allowed except for public purposes. In all cases of expropriation full compensation as fixed by the Supreme Court shall be said previous to dispossession.

Chapter 3: Citizenship, International Conventions and Financial Obligations

1. **Citizenship** [. . .]
2. **International conventions** [. . .]
3. **Financial obligations** [. . .]

Chapter 4: Miscellaneous Provisions [. . .]

D. ECONOMIC UNION AND TRANSIT

1. The Provisional Council of Government of each State shall enter into an undertaking with respect to Economic Union and Transit. . . .

The Economic Union of Palestine

2. The objectives of the Economic Union of Palestine shall be:
    a. A customs union;
    b. A joint currency system providing for a single foreign exchange rate;
    c. Operation in the common interest on a non-discriminatory basis of railways inter-State highways; postal, telephone and telegraphic services and ports and airports involved in international trade and commerce;
    d. Joint economic development, especially in respect of irrigation, land reclamation and soil conservation;
    e. Access for both States and for the City of Jerusalem on a non-discriminatory basis to water and power facilities.

Freedom of Transit and Visit

The undertaking shall contain provisions preserving freedom of transit and visit for all residents or citizens of both States and of the City of Jerusalem, subject to security considerations; provided that each State and the City shall control residence within its borders. . . .

E. ASSETS [. . .]

F. ADMISSION TO MEMBERSHIP IN THE UNITED NATIONS

When the independence of either the Arab or the Jewish State as envisaged in this plan has become effective and the declaration and undertaking, as envisaged in this plan, have been signed by either of them, sympathetic consideration should be given to its application for admission to membership in the United Nations in accordance with article 4 of the Charter of the United Nations.

Part II.—Boundaries

A. THE ARAB STATE [. . .]

B. THE JEWISH STATE [. . .]

C. THE CITY OF JERUSALEM

The boundaries of the City of Jerusalem are as defined in the recommendations on the City of Jerusalem. . . .

Part III.—City of Jerusalem

A. SPECIAL REGIME

The City of Jerusalem shall be established as a *corpus separatum* under a special international regime and shall be administered by the United Nations. The Trusteeship Council shall be designated to discharge the responsibilities of the Administering Authority on behalf of the United Nations.

B. BOUNDARIES OF THE CITY [. . .]

C. STATUTE OF THE CITY [. . .]

Adopted at the 128th plenary meeting:

In favour: 33
Australia, Belgium, Bolivia, Brazil, Byelorussian S.S.R., Canada, Costa Rica, Czechoslovakia, Denmark, Dominican Republic, Ecuador, France, Guatemala, Haiti, Iceland, Liberia, Luxemburg, Netherlands, New Zealand, Nicaragua, Norway, Panama, Paraguay, Peru, Philippines, Poland, Sweden, Ukrainian S.S.R., Union of South Africa, U.S.A., U.S.S.R., Uruguay, Venezuela.

Against: 13
Afghanistan, Cuba, Egypt, Greece, India, Iran, Iraq, Lebanon, Pakistan, Saudi Arabia, Syria, Turkey, Yemen.

Abstained: 10
Argentina, Chile, China, Colombia, El Salvador, Ethiopia, Honduras, Mexico, United Kingdom, Yugoslavia.

17 Declaration of the Establishment of the State of Israel (May 14, 1948)

Text:

ERETZ-ISRAEL [(Hebrew)—the Land of Israel, Palestine] was the birthplace of the Jewish people. Here their spiritual, religious and political identity was shaped. Here they first attained to statehood, created cultural values of national and universal significance and gave to the world the eternal Book of Books.

After being forcibly exiled from their land, the people kept faith with it throughout their Dispersion and never ceased to pray and hope for their return to it and for the restoration in it of their political freedom.

Impelled by this historic and traditional attachment, Jews strove in every successive generation to re-establish themselves in their ancient homeland. In recent decades they returned in their masses. Pioneers, *ma'pilim* [(Hebrew)—immigrants coming to Eretz-Israel in defiance of restrictive legislation] and defenders, they made deserts bloom, revived the Hebrew language, built villages and towns, and created a thriving community controlling its own economy and culture, loving peace but knowing how to defend itself, bringing the blessings of progress to all the country's inhabitants, and aspiring towards independent nationhood.

In the year 5657 (1897), at the summons of the spiritual father of the Jewish State, Theodore Herzl, the First Zionist Congress convened and proclaimed the right of the Jewish people to national rebirth in its own country.

This right was recognized in the Balfour Declaration of the 2nd November, 1917, and re-affirmed in the Mandate of the League of Nations which, in particular, gave international sanction to the historic connection between the Jewish people and Eretz-Israel and to the right of the Jewish people to rebuild its National Home.

The catastrophe which recently befell the Jewish people—the massacre of millions of Jews in Europe—was another clear demonstration of the urgency of solving the problem of its homelessness by re-establishing in Eretz-Israel the Jewish State, which would open the gates of the homeland wide to every Jew and confer upon the Jewish people the status of a fully privileged member of the comity of nations.

Survivors of the Nazi holocaust in Europe, as well as Jews from other parts of the world, continued to migrate to Eretz-Israel, undaunted by difficulties, restrictions and dangers, and never ceased to assert their right to a life of dignity, freedom and honest toil in their national homeland.

In the Second World War, the Jewish community of this country contributed its full share to the struggle of the freedom- and peace-loving nations against the forces of Nazi wickedness and, by the blood of its soldiers and its war effort, gained the right to be reckoned among the peoples who founded the United Nations.

On the 29th November, 1947, the United Nations General Assembly passed a resolution calling for the establishment of a Jewish State in Eretz-Israel; the General Assembly required the inhabitants of Eretz-Israel to take such steps as were necessary on their part for the implementation of that resolution. This recognition by the United Nations of the right of the Jewish people to establish their State is irrevocable.

This right is the natural right of the Jewish people to be masters of their own fate, like all other nations, in their own sovereign State.

ACCORDINGLY WE, MEMBERS OF THE PEOPLE'S COUNCIL, REPRESENTATIVES OF THE JEWISH COMMUNITY OF ERETZ-ISRAEL AND OF THE ZIONIST MOVEMENT, ARE HERE ASSEMBLED ON THE DAY OF THE TERMINATION OF THE BRITISH MANDATE OVER ERETZ-ISRAEL AND, BY VIRTUE OF OUR NATURAL AND HISTORIC RIGHT AND ON THE STRENGTH OF THE RESOLUTION OF THE UNITED NATIONS GENERAL ASSEMBLY, HEREBY DECLARE THE ESTABLISHMENT OF A JEWISH STATE IN ERETZ-ISRAEL, TO BE KNOWN AS THE STATE OF ISRAEL.

WE DECLARE that, with effect from the moment of the termination of the Mandate being tonight, the eve of Sabbath, the 6th Iyar, 5708 (15th May, 1948), until the establishment of the elected, regular authorities of the State in accordance with the Constitution which shall be adopted by the Elected Constituent Assembly not later than the 1st October 1948, the People's Council shall act as a Provisional Council of State, and its executive organ, the People's Administration, shall be the Provisional Government of the Jewish State, to be called "Israel".

THE STATE OF ISRAEL will be open for Jewish immigration and for the Ingathering of the Exiles; it will foster the development of the country for the benefit of all its inhabitants; it will be based on freedom, justice and peace as envisaged by the prophets of Israel; it will ensure complete equality of social and political rights to all its inhabitants irrespective of religion, race or sex; it will guarantee freedom of religion, conscience, language, education and culture; it will safeguard the Holy Places of all religions; and it will be faithful to the principles of the Charter of the United Nations.

THE STATE OF ISRAEL is prepared to cooperate with the agencies and representatives of the United Nations in implementing the resolution of the General Assembly of the 29th November, 1947, and will take steps to bring about the economic union of the whole of Eretz-Israel.

WE APPEAL to the United Nations to assist the Jewish people in the building-up of its State and to receive the State of Israel into the comity of nations.

WE APPEAL—in the very midst of the onslaught launched against us now for months—to the Arab inhabitants of the State of Israel to preserve peace and participate in the upbuilding of the State on the basis of full and equal citizenship and due representation in all its provisional and permanent institutions.

WE EXTEND our hand to all neighbouring states and their peoples in an offer of peace and good neighbourliness, and appeal to them to establish bonds of cooperation and mutual help with the sovereign Jewish people settled in its own land. The State of Israel is prepared to do its share in a common effort for the advancement of the entire Middle East.

WE APPEAL to the Jewish people throughout the Diaspora to rally round the Jews of Eretz-Israel in the tasks of immigration and upbuilding and to stand by them in the great struggle for the realization of the age-old dream—the redemption of Israel.

PLACING OUR TRUST IN THE "ROCK OF ISRAEL", WE AFFIX OUR SIGNATURES TO THIS PROCLAMATION AT THIS SESSION OF THE PROVISIONAL COUNCIL OF STATE, ON THE SOIL OF THE HOMELAND, IN THE CITY OF TEL-AVIV, ON THIS SABBATH EVE, THE 5TH DAY OF IYAR, 5708 (14TH MAY, 1948).

David Ben-Gurion

Daniel Auster	*Rachel Cohen*	*David Zvi Pinkas*
Mordekhai Bentov	*Rabbi Kalman Kahana*	*Aharon Zisling*
Yitzchak Ben Zvi	*Saadia Kobashi*	*Moshe Kolodny*
Eliyahu Berligne	*Rabbi Yitzchak Meir Levin*	*Eliezer Kaplan*
Fritz Bernstein	*Meir David Loewenstein*	*Abraham Katznelson*
Rabbi Wolf Gold	*Zvi Luria*	*Felix Rosenblueth*
Meir Grabovsky	*Golda Myerson*	*David Remez*
Yitzchak Gruenbaum	*Nachum Nir*	*Berl Repetur*
Dr. Abraham Granovsky	*Zvi Segal*	*Mordekhai Shattner*
Eliyahu Dobkin	*Rabbi Yehuda Leib Hacohen*	*Ben Zion Sternberg*
Meir Wilner-Kovner	*Fishman*	*Bekhor Shitreet*
Zerach Wahrhaftig		*Moshe Shapira*
Herzl Vardi		*Moshe Shertok*

* Published in the *Official Gazette*, **No. 1 of the 5th, Iyar, 5708 (14th May, 1948).**

18 Creation of a Conciliation Commission, General Assembly Resolution 194 (III) (December 11, 1948)

The General Assembly,

Having considered further the situation in Palestine,

1. Expresses its deep appreciation of the progress achieved through the good offices of the late United Nations Mediator in promoting a peaceful adjustment of the future situation of Palestine, for which cause he sacrificed his life; and

Extends its thanks to the Acting Mediator and his staff for their continued efforts and devotion to duty in Palestine;

2. Establishes a Conciliation Commission consisting of three States Members of the United Nations . . .

3. Decides that a Committee of the Assembly, consisting of China, France, the Union of Soviet Socialist Republics, the United Kingdom and the United States of America, shall present, before the end of the first part of the present session of the General Assembly, for the approval of the Assembly, a proposal concerning the names of the three States which will constitute the Conciliation Commission;

4. Requests the Commission to begin its functions at once . . .

5. Calls upon the Governments and authorities concerned to extend the scope of the negotiations provided for in the Security Council's resolution of 16 November 1948 and to seek agreement by negotiations conducted either with the Conciliation Commission or directly with a view to the final settlement of all questions outstanding between them;

6. [. . .]

7. Resolves that the Holy Places—including Nazareth—religious buildings and sites in Palestine should be protected and free access to them assured, . . .

8. Resolves that, in view of its association with three world religions, the Jerusalem area . . . should be accorded special and separate treatment from the rest of Palestine and should be placed under effective United Nations control;

Requests the Security Council to take further steps to ensure the demilitarization of Jerusalem at the earliest possible date;

[. . .]

The Conciliation Commission is authorized to appoint a United Nations representative who shall cooperate with the local authorities with respect to the interim administration of the Jerusalem area;

9. Resolves that, pending agreement on more detailed arrangements among the Governments and authorities concerned, the freest possible access to Jerusalem by road, rail or air should be accorded to all inhabitants of Palestine;

[. . .]

10. Instructs the Conciliation Commission to seek arrangements among the Governments and authorities concerned which will facilitate the economic development of the area, including arrangements for access to ports and airfields and the use of transportation and communication facilities;

11. Resolves that the refugees wishing to return to their homes and live at peace with their neighbours should be permitted to do so at the earliest practicable date, and that compensation should be paid for the property of those choosing not to return and for loss of or damage to property which, under principles of international law or in equity, should be made good by the Governments or authorities responsible;

Instructs the Conciliation Commission to facilitate the repatriation, resettlement and economic and social rehabilitation of the refugees and the payment of compensation, and to maintain close relations with the Director of the United Nations Relief for Palestine Refugees and, through him, with the appropriate organs and agencies of the United Nations;

12. [. . .]

13. Instructs the Conciliation Commission to render progress reports periodically to the Secretary-General for transmission to the Security Council and to the Members of the United Nations;

14. Calls upon all Governments and authorities concerned to cooperate with the Conciliation Commission and to take all possible steps to assist in the implementation of the present resolution;

15. Requests the Secretary-General to provide the necessary staff and facilities and to make appropriate arrangements to provide the necessary funds required in carrying out the terms of the present resolution.

19 Admission of Israel to the United Nations, General Assembly Resolution 273 (May 11, 1949)

Text

Having received the report of the Security Council on the application of Israel for membership in the United Nations,

Noting that, in the judgment of the Security Council, Israel is a peace-loving State and is able and willing to carry out the obligations contained in the Charter,

Noting that the Security Council has recommended to the General Assembly that it admit Israel to membership in the United Nations,

Noting furthermore the declaration by the State of Israel that it "unreservedly accepts the obligations of the United Nations Charter and undertakes to honour them from the day when it becomes a Member of the United Nations",

Recalling its resolutions of 29 November 1947 and 11 December 1948 and taking note of the declarations and explanations made by the representatives of the Government of Israel before the *Ad Hoc* Political Committee in respect of the implementation of the said resolutions,

The General Assembly

Acting in discharge of its functions under Article 4 of the Charter and rule 125 of its rules of procedure,

1. Decides that Israel is a peace-loving State which accepts the obligations contained in the Charter and is able and willing to carry out those obligations;

2. Decides to admit Israel to membership in the United Nations.

Part III

From Recognition (1949) Through the Start of a Peace Process (1978)

20 General Assembly Resolution 303 (IV). Palestine: Question of an International Regime for the Jerusalem Area and the Protection of the Holy Places (December, 1949)

The General Assembly,

Having regard to its resolutions 181 (II) of 29 November 1947 and 194 (III) of 11 December 1948,

Having studied the reports of the United Nations Conciliation Commission for Palestine set up under the latter resolution,

I. *Decides*

In relation to Jerusalem,

Believing that the principles underlying its previous resolutions concerning this matter, and in particular its resolution of 29 November 1947, represent a just and equitable settlement of the question,

1. To restate, therefore, its intention that Jerusalem should be placed under a permanent international regime, which should envisage appropriate guarantees for the protection of the Holy Places, both within and outside Jerusalem, and to confirm specifically the following provisions of General Assembly Resolution 181 (II)

(1) the City of Jerusalem shall be established as a *corpus separatum* under a special international regime and shall be administered by the United Nations;

(2) the Trusteeship Council shall be designated to discharge the responsibilities of the Administering Authority . . . ; and

(3) the City of Jerusalem shall include the present municipality of Jerusalem plus the surrounding villages and towns, the most eastern of which shall be Abu Dis; the most southern, Bethlehem; the most western, Ein Karim (including also the built-up area of Motsa); and the most northern, Shu'fat . . .

II. *Calls upon* the States concerned to make formal undertakings, at an early date and in the light of their obligations as Members of the United Nations, that they will approach these matters with good will and be guided by the terms of the present resolution.

21 State of Israel: Law of Return (July, 1950)

Right of aliyah**

1. Every Jew has the right to come to this country as an oleh**.

Oleh's visa

2. (a) Aliyah shall be by oleh's visa.
(b) An oleh's visa shall be granted to every Jew who has expressed his desire to settle in Israel, unless the Minister of Immigration is satisfied that the applicant

(1) is engaged in an activity directed against the Jewish people; or
(2) is likely to endanger public health or the security of the State.

Oleh's certificate

3. (a) A Jew who has come to Israel and subsequent to his arrival has expressed his desire to settle in Israel may, while still in Israel, receive an oleh's certificate.
(b) The restrictions specified in section 2(b) shall apply also to the grant of an oleh's certificate, but a person shall not be regarded as endangering public health on account of an illness contracted after his arrival in Israel.

Residents and persons born in this country

4. Every Jew who has immigrated into this country before the coming into force of this Law, and every Jew who was born in this country, whether before or after the coming into force of this Law, shall be deemed to be a person who has come to this country as an oleh under this Law.

Implementation and regulations

5. The Minister of Immigration is charged with the implementation of this Law and may make regulations as to any matter relating to such implementation and also as to the grant of oleh's visas and oleh's certificates to minors up to the age of 18 years

DAVID BEN-GURION
Prime Minister

MOSHE SHAPIRA
Minister of Immigration

YOSEF SPRINZAK
Acting President of the State
Chairman of the Knesset

** Translation Note: Aliyah means immigration of Jews, and oleh (plural: olim) means a Jew immigrating, into Israel.

Note: The Law of Return has been amended on more than one occasion. In 1970 the Law of Return (Amendment No. 2) 5730–1970 focused on the rights of members of a family and added that

(a) The rights of a Jew under this Law and the rights of an oleh under the Nationality Law, 5712–1952, as well as the rights of an oleh under any other enactment, are also vested in a child and a grandchild of a Jew, the spouse of a Jew, the spouse of a child of a Jew and the spouse of a grandchild of a Jew, except for a person who has been a Jew and has voluntarily changed his religion.

(b) It shall be immaterial whether or not a Jew by whose right a right under sub-section (a) is claimed is still alive and whether or not he has immigrated to Israel.

(c) The restrictions and conditions prescribed in respect of a Jew or an oleh by or under this Law or by the enactments referred to in subsection (a) shall also apply to a person who claims a right under "Jew" means a person who was born of a Jewish mother or has become converted to Judaism and who is not a member of another religion.

22 U.N. Security Council: Resolution 95, Concerning . . . the Passage of Ships Through the Suez Canal (September 1, 1951)

The Security Council,

Recalling that in its resolution 73 (1949) of 11 August 1949 relating to the conclusion of Armistice Agreements between Israel and the neighbouring Arab States it drew attention to the pledges in these Agreements "against any further acts of hostility between the parties",

Recalling further that in its resolution 89 (1950) of 17 November 1950 it reminded the States concerned that the Armistice Agreements to which they were parties contemplated "the return of permanent peace in Palestine", and, therefore, urged them and the other States in the area to take all such steps as would lead to the settlement of the issues between them,

Noting the report of the Chief of Staff of the United Nations Truce Supervision Organization in Palestine to the Security Council of 12 June 1951,

Further noting that the Chief of Staff of the Truce Supervision Organization recalled the statement of the senior Egyptian delegate in Rhodes on 13 January 1949, to the effect that his delegation was "inspired with every spirit of co-operation, conciliation and a sincere desire to restore peace in Palestine", and that the Egyptian Government has not complied with the earnest plea of the Chief of Staff made to the Egyptian delegate on 12 June 1951, that it desist from the present practice of interfering with the passage through the Suez Canal of goods destined for Israel,

Considering that since the armistice regime, which has been in existence for nearly two and a half years, is of a permanent character, neither party can reasonably assert that it is actively a belligerent or requires to exercise the right of visit, search and seizure for any legitimate purpose of self-defence,

Finds that the maintenance of the practice mentioned in the fourth paragraph of the present resolution is inconsistent with the objectives of a peaceful settlement between the parties and the establishment of a permanent peace in Palestine set forth in the Armistice Agreement between Egypt and Israel;

Finds further that such practice is an abuse of the exercise of the right of visit, search and seizure;

Further finds that that practice cannot in the prevailing circumstances be justified on the ground that it is necessary for self-defence;

And further noting that the restrictions on the passage of goods through the Suez Canal to Israel ports are denying to nations at no time connected with the conflict in Palestine valuable supplies required for their economic reconstruction, and that these restrictions together with sanctions applied by Egypt to certain ships which have visited Israel ports represent unjustified interference with the rights of nations to navigate the seas and to trade freely with one another, including the Arab States and Israel,

Calls upon Egypt to terminate the restrictions on the passage of international commercial shipping and goods through the Suez Canal wherever bound and to cease all interference with such shipping beyond that essential to the safety of shipping in the Canal itself and to the observance of the international conventions in force.

Adopted at the 558th meeting by 8 votes to none, with 3 abstentions (China, India, Union of Soviet Socialist Republics).

23 Palestine National Authority: Palestine Liberation Organization Draft Constitution (December, 1963)

1. In accordance with this constitution, an organization known as "The Palestine Liberation Organization" shall be formed, and shall launch its responsibilities in accordance with the principles of the National Charter and clauses of this constitution.
2. All the Palestinians are natural members in the Liberation Organization exercising their duty in their liberation of their homeland in accordance with their abilities and efficiency.
3. The Palestinian people shall form the larger base for this Organization; and the Organization, after its creation, shall work closely and constantly with the Palestine people for the sake of their organization and mobilization so they may be able to assume their responsibility in the liberation of their country.
4. Until suitable conditions are available for holding free general elections among all the Palestinians and in all the countries in which they reside, the Liberation Organization shall be set up in accordance with the rules set in this constitution.
5. Measures listed in this constitution shall be taken for the convocation of a Palestinian General Assembly in which shall be represented all Palestinian factions, emigrants, and residents, including organizations, societies, unions, trade unions and representatives of (Palestinian) public opinions of various ideological trends; this assembly shall be called the National Assembly of the Palestine Liberation Organization.
6. In preparation and facilitation of work of the assembly, the Palestinian representative at the Arab league (i.e., Ahmed Shukairy), shall, after holding consultations with various Palestinian factors, form:
    *   A Preparatory Committee in every Arab country hosting a minimum of 10,000 Palestinians; the mission of each one of these committees is to prepare lists according to which Palestinian candidates in the respective Arab country will be chosen as members of the assembly; these committees shall also prepare studies and proposals which may help the assembly carry out its work; these studies and proposals shall be presented to the Coordination Committee listed below.
    *   A Coordination Committee, with headquarters in Jerusalem; the mission of this committee shall be to issue invitations to the assembly, adopt all necessary measures for the holdings of the assembly, and coordinate all proposals and studies as well as lists of candidates to the assembly, as specified

in the clause above; also the committee shall prepare a provisional agenda—or as a whole, undertake all that is required for the holding and success of the assembly in the execution of its mission.

7. The National Assembly shall be held once every two years; its venue rotates between Jerusalem and Gaza; the National Assembly shall meet for the first time on May 14, 1964, in the city of Jerusalem.

8. To facilitate its work, the Assembly shall form the following committees:

   a. The Political Committee: shall be in charge of studying the political sides of the Palestine question in the Arab and international fields.

   b. The Charter By-laws and Lists Committee: shall consider the National Charter as well as the various by-laws and lists required by the Organization in the execution of its duties.

   c. The Financial Committee: shall formulate a complete plan for the National Palestinian Fund required for financing the Organization.

   d. Information Committee: shall work out a complete scheme for information and offices to be established in various parts of the world.

   e. The Juridical Committee: shall study the various legal aspects of the Palestine question, be it in relation to principles of International Law, U.N. Charter, or international documents pertaining to the Palestinian question.

   f. Proposals and Nomination Committee: shall coordinate proposals and nominations submitted to the Assembly.

   g. Awakening Committee: Shall study ways and means for the upbringing of the new generations both ideologically and spiritually so they may serve their country and work for the liberation of their homeland.

   h. The National Organization Committee: Shall lay down general plans pertaining to trade unions, federations, sports organizations and scouts groups; this is in accordance with rules and laws in effect in Arab countries.

9. The National Assembly shall have a Presidency Office composed of the president, two vice presidents, a secretary, and a secretary general; these officers shall be elected by the National Assembly when it meets.

10. These (above-listed eight committees) shall submit their reports and recommendations to the National Assembly which, in turn, shall discuss them and issue necessary resolutions.

11. The National Assembly shall have an executive apparatus to be called "The Executive Committee of the Liberation Organization" which shall practice all responsibilities of the Liberation Organization in accordance with the general plans and resolutions issued by the National Assembly.

12. The Executive Committee shall be formed of fifteen members elected by the National Assembly; the Committee shall in its turn elect a President, two Vice Presidents and a Secretary General.

13. The Executive Committee can be called to a meeting in the time and place decided by the President, or by a proposal submitted by five members of the Committee.

14. The President of the Executive Committee shall represent the Palestinians at the Arab League; therefore, his office shall be in Cairo since the Arab League Headquarters is there.

15. The Executive Committee shall establish the following departments:
    a. Department of Political and Information Affairs.
    b. Department of National Fund.
    c. Department of General Affairs.
    Each one of these departments shall have a Director General and the needed number of employees. Duties of each one of these departments shall be defined by special by-laws prepared by the Executive Committee.

16. The Executive Committee has the right of calling the National Assembly to meet in a place and time it specifies; it has the right also to call to a meeting any committee of the National Assembly to study certain subjects.

17. The Executive Committee shall have a consultative council to be known as "The Shura (Consultative) Council," the Executive Committee shall select the president and members of this council from people of opinion and prestige among the Palestinians; prerogatives of the Consultative Council are in matters proposed to it by the Executive Committee.

18. The Arab states shall avail the sons of Palestine the opportunity of enlisting in their regular armies on the widest scale possible.

19. Private Palestinian contingents shall be formed in accordance with the military needs and plans decided by the Unified Arab Military Command in agreement and cooperation with the concerned Arab states.

20. A Fund, to be known as "The National Palestinian Fund", shall be established to finance operations of the Executive Committee: the Fund shall have a Board of Directors whose members shall be elected by the National Assembly.

21. Sources of the Fund are to be from:
    a. Fixed taxes levied on Palestinians and collected in accordance with special laws.
    b. Financial assistance offered by the Arab governments and people.
    c. A "Liberation Stamp" to be issued by the Arab states and be used in postal and other transactions.
    d. Donations on national occasions.
    e. Loans and assistance given by the Arabs or by friendly nations.

22. Committees, to be known as "Support Palestine Committees", shall be established in Arab and friendly countries to collect donations and to support the Liberation Organization.

23. The Executive Committee shall have the right to issue by-laws for fulfillment of provisions of this constitution.

24. This draft constitution shall be submitted to the National Assembly for consideration; what is ratified of it cannot be changed except by a two-thirds majority of the National Assembly.

24 Israeli Foreign Minister Abba Eban: Speech to the Security Council of the United Nations (June 6, 1967)

Mr. Eban (Israel)

I thank you, Mr. President, for giving me this opportunity to address the Council. I have just come from Jerusalem to tell the Security Council that Israel, by its independent effort and sacrifice, has passed from serious danger to successful resistance.

Two days ago Israel's condition caused much concern across the humane and friendly world. Israel had reached a sombre hour. Let me try to evoke the point at which our fortunes stood.

An army, greater than any force ever assembled in history in Sinai, had massed against Israel's southern frontier. Egypt had dismissed the United Nations forces which symbolized the international interest in the maintenance of peace in our region. Nasser had provocatively brought five infantry divisions and two armoured divisions up to our very gates; 80,000 men and 900 tanks were poised to move.

A special striking force, comprising an armoured division with at least 200 tanks, was concentrated against Eilat at the Negev's southern tip. Here was a clear design to cut the southern Negev off from the main body of our State. For Egypt had openly proclaimed that Eilat did not form part of Israel and had predicted that Israel itself would soon expire. The proclamation was empty; the prediction now lies in ruin. While the main brunt of the hostile threat was focussed on the southern front, an alarming plan of encirclement was under way. With Egypt's initiative and guidance, Israel was already being strangled in its maritime approaches to the whole eastern half of the world. For sixteen years, Israel had been illicitly denied passage in the Suez Canal, despite the Security Council's decision of 1 September 1951 [Resolution 95 (1951)]. And now the creative enterprise of ten patient years which had opened an international route across the Strait of Tiran and the Gulf of Aqaba had been suddenly and arbitrarily choked. Israel was and is breathing only with a single lung.

Jordan had been intimidated, against its better interest, into joining a defence pact. It is not a defence pact at all: it is an aggressive pact, of which I saw the consequences with my own eyes yesterday in the shells falling upon institutions of health and culture in the City of Jerusalem. Every house and street in Jerusalem now came into the range of fire as a result of Jordan's adherence to this pact; so also did the crowded and pathetically narrow coastal strip in which so much of Israel's life and population is concentrated.

Iraqi troops reinforced Jordanian units in areas immediately facing vital and vulnerable Israel communication centres. Expeditionary forces from Algeria and Kuwait had reached Egyptian territory. Nearly all the Egyptian forces which had been attempting the conquest of the Yemen had been transferred to the coming assault upon Israel. Syrian units, including artillery, overlooked the Israel villages in the Jordan Valley. Terrorist troops came regularly into our territory to kill, plunder and set off explosions; the most recent occasion was five days ago.

In short, there was peril for Israel wherever it looked. Its manpower had been hastily mobilized. Its economy and commerce were beating with feeble pulses. Its streets were dark and empty. There was an apocalyptic air of approaching peril. And Israel faced this danger alone.

We were buoyed up by an unforgettable surge of public sympathy across the world. The friendly Governments expressed the rather ominous hope that Israel would manage to live, but the dominant theme of our condition was danger and solitude. Now there could be no doubt about what was intended for us. With my very ears I heard President Nasser's speech on 26 May. He said:

"We intend to open a general assault against Israel. This will be total war. Our basic aim will be to destroy Israel."

[. . .]

The question then widely asked in Israel and across the world was whether we had not already gone beyond the utmost point of danger. Was there any precedent in world history, for example, for a nation passively to suffer the blockade of its only southern port, involving nearly all its vital fuel, when such acts of war, legally and internationally, have always invited resistance? This was a most unusual patience. It existed because we had acceded to the suggestion of some of the maritime States that we give them scope to concert their efforts in order to find an international solution which would ensure the maintenance of free passage in the Gulf of Aqaba for ships of all nations and of all flags.

As we pursued this avenue of international solution, we wished the world to have no doubt about our readiness to exhaust every prospect, however fragile, of a diplomatic solution—and some of the prospects that were suggested were very fragile indeed.

But as time went on, there was no doubt that our margin of general security was becoming smaller and smaller. Thus, on the morning of 5 June, when Egyptian forces engaged us by air and land, bombarding the villages of Kissufim, Nahal-Oz and Ein Hashelosha we knew that our limit of safety had been reached, and perhaps passed. In accordance with its inherent right of self-defence as formulated in Article 51 of the United Nations Charter, Israel responded defensively in full strength. Never in the history of nations has armed force been used in a more righteous or compelling cause.

Even when engaged with Egyptian forces, we still hoped to contain the conflict. Egypt was overtly bent on our destruction, but we still hoped that others would not join the aggression. Prime Minister Eshkol, who for weeks had carried the heavy burden of calculation and decision, published and conveyed a message to other neighbouring States proclaiming:

"We shall not attack any country unless it opens war on us. Even now, when the mortars speak, we have not given up our quest for peace. We strive to repel all menace of terrorism and any danger of aggression to ensure our security and our legitimate rights."

In accordance with this same policy of attempting to contain the conflict, yesterday I invited General Bull, the Chief of Staff of the Truce Supervision Organization, to inform the heads of the Jordanian State that Israel had no desire to expand the conflict beyond the unfortunate dimensions that it had already assumed and that if Israel were not attacked on the Jordan side, it would not attack and would act only in self-defence. It reached my ears that this message had been duly and faithfully conveyed and received. Nevertheless, Jordan decided to join the Egyptian posture against Israel and opened artillery attacks across the whole long frontier, including Jerusalem. Those attacks are still in progress.

To the appeal of Prime Minister Eshkol to avoid any further extension of the conflict, Syria answered at 12.25 yesterday morning by bombing Megiddo from the air and bombing Degania at 12.40 with artillery fire and kibbutz Ein Hammifrats and Kurdani with long-range guns. But Jordan embarked on a much more total assault by artillery and aircraft along the entire front, with special emphasis on Jerusalem, to whose dangerous and noble ordeal yesterday I come to bear personal witness.

There has been bombing of houses; there has been a hit on the great new National Museum of Art; there has been a hit on the University and on Shaare Zedek, the first hospital ever to have been established outside the ancient walls. Is this not an act of vandalism that deserves the condemnation of all mankind? And in the Knesset building, whose construction had been movingly celebrated by the entire democratic world ten months ago, the Israel Cabinet and Parliament met under heavy gunfire, whose echoes mingled at the end of our meeting with Hatikvah, the anthem of hope.

Thus throughout the day and night of 5 June, the Jordan which we had expressly invited to abstain from needless slaughter became, to our surprise, and still remains, the most intense of all the belligerents; and death and injury, as so often in history, stalk Jerusalem's streets.

When the approaching Egyptian aircraft appeared on our radar screens, soon to be followed by artillery attacks on our villages near the Gaza Strip, I instructed Mr. Rafael to inform the Security Council, in accordance with the provisions of Article 51 of the Charter. I know that that involved arousing you, Mr. President, at a most uncongenial hour of the night, but we felt that the Security Council should be most urgently seized.

I should, however, be less than frank if I were to conceal the fact that the Government and people of Israel have been disconcerted by some aspects of the United Nations role in this conflict. The sudden withdrawal of the United Nations Emergency Force was not accompanied, as it should have been, by due international consultations on the consequences of that withdrawal. Moreover, Israeli interests were affected; they were not adequately explored. No attempt was made, little time given, to help Israel to surmount grave prejudice to its vital interests consequent on that withdrawal. After all, a new confrontation of forces suddenly arose. It suddenly had to be met and at Sharm el-Sheikh at the entrance to the Gulf of Aqaba, the Strait of Tiran, legality walked out and blockade walked in. The peace of the world trembled.

And thus the United Nations had somehow been put into a position of leaving Sinai safe for belligerency.

[. . .]

The United Nations Emergency Force rendered distinguished service. Nothing became it less than the manner of its departure. All gratitude and appreciation are owed to the individuals who sustained its action. And if in the course of the recent combat United Nations personnel have fallen dead or wounded—as they have—then I join my voice in an expression of the most sincere regret.

The problem of the future role of a United Nations presence in conflicts such as these is being much debated. But we must ask ourselves a question that has arisen as a result of this experience. People in our country and in many countries ask: What is the use of a United Nations presence if it is in effect an umbrella which is taken away as soon as it begins to rain? Surely, then, future arrangements for peace-keeping must depend more on the agreement and the implementation of the parties themselves than on machinery which is totally at the mercy of the host country, so totally at its mercy as to be the instrument of its policies, whatever those policies may be.

We have lived through three dramatic weeks. Those weeks, I think, have brought into clear view the main elements of tension and also the chief promise of relaxed tension in the future. The first link in the chain was the series of sabotage acts emanating from Syria. In October of 1966, the Security Council was already seized of this problem, and a majority of its member States found it possible and necessary to draw attention to the Syrian Government's responsibility for altering that situation. Scarcely a day passed without a mine, a bomb, a hand-grenade or a mortar exploding on Israel's soil, sometimes with lethal or crippling effects, always with an unsettling psychological influence. In general, fourteen or fifteen such incidents would accumulate before a response was considered necessary, and this ceaseless accumulation of terrorist sabotage incidents in the name of what was called "popular war", together with responses which in the long run sometimes became inevitable, were for a long period the main focus of tension in the Middle East.

But then there came a graver source of tension in mid-May, when abnormal troop concentrations were observed in the Sinai Peninsula. For the ten years of relative stability beginning with March 1957 and ending with May 1967, the Sinai Desert had been free of Egyptian troops. In other words, a natural geographic barrier, a largely uninhabited space, separated the main forces of the two sides. It is true that in terms of sovereignty and law, any State has a right to put its armies in any part of its territory that it chooses. This, however, is not a legal question: it is a political and a security question.

Experience in many parts of the world, not least in our own, demonstrates that massive armies in close proximity to each other, against a background of a doctrine of belligerency and accompanying threats by one army to annihilate the other, constitute an inflammatory situation.

We were puzzled in Israel by the relative lack of preoccupation on the part of friendly Governments and international agencies with this intense concentration which found its reflection in precautionary concentrations on our side. My Government proposed, I think at least two weeks ago, the concept of a parallel and reciprocal reduction of forces on both sides of the frontier. We elicited no response, and certainly no action.

To these grave sources of tension—the sabotage and terrorist movement, emanating mostly from Syria, and the heavy troop concentrations accompanied by dire, apocalyptic threats in Sinai—there was added in the third week of May the most electric shock of all, namely the closure of the international waterway consisting of the Strait of Tiran and the Gulf of Aqaba. It is not difficult, I think, to understand why this incident had a more drastic impact than any other. In 1957 the maritime nations, within the framework of the United Nations General Assembly, correctly enunciated the doctrine of free and innocent passage through the Strait.

[. . .]

All this, then, had grown up as an effective usage under the United Nations flag. Does Mr. Nasser really think that he can come upon the scene in ten minutes and cancel the established legal usage and interests of ten years?

There was in this wanton act a quality of malice. For surely the closing of the Strait of Tiran gave no benefit whatever to Egypt except the perverse joy of inflicting injury on others. It was an anarchic act, because it showed a total disregard for the law of nations, the application of which in this specific case had not been challenged for ten years. And it was, in the literal sense, an act of arrogance, because there are other nations in Asia and East Africa, that trade with the Port of Eilat, as they have every right to do, through the Strait of Tiran and across the Gulf of Aqaba. Other sovereign States from Japan to Ethiopia, from Thailand to Uganda, from Cambodia to Madagascar, have a sovereign right to decide for themselves whether they wish or do not wish to trade with Israel. These countries are not colonies of Cairo. They can trade with Israel or not trade with Israel as they wish, and President Nasser is not the policeman of other African and Asian States.

Here then was a wanton intervention in the sovereign rights of other States in the eastern half of the world to decide for themselves whether or not they wish to establish trade relations with either or both of the two ports at the head of the Gulf of Aqaba.

When we examine, then, the implications of this act, we have no cause to wonder that the international shock was great. There was another reason too for that shock. Blockades have traditionally been regarded, in the pre-Charter parlance, as acts of war. To blockade, after all, is to attempt strangulation; and sovereign States are entitled not to have their trade strangled. To understand how the State of Israel felt, one has merely to look around this table and imagine, for example, a foreign Power forcibly closing New York or Montreal, Boston or Marseille, Toulon or Copenhagen, Rio or Tokyo or Bombay harbour. How would your Governments react? What would you do? How long would you wait?

But Israel waited because of its confidence that the other maritime Powers and countries interested in this new trading pattern would concert their influence in order to re-establish a legal situation and to liquidate this blockade. We concerted action with them not because Israel's national interest was here abdicated. There will not be, there cannot be, an Israel without Eilat. We cannot be expected to return to a dwarfed stature, with our face to the Mediterranean alone. In law and in history, peace and blockades have never co-existed. How could it be expected that the blockade of

Eilat and a relaxation of tension in the Middle East could ever be brought into harmony?

These then were the three main elements in the tension: the sabotage movement; the blockade of the port; and, perhaps more imminent than anything else, this vast and purposeful encirclement movement, against the background of an authorized presidential statement announcing that the objective of the encirclement was to bring about the destruction and the annihilation of a sovereign State.

These acts taken together—the blockade, the dismissal of the United Nations Emergency Force, and the heavy concentration in Sinai—effectively disrupted the status quo which had ensured a relative stability on the Egyptian-Israel frontier for ten years. I do not use the words "relative stability" lightly, for in fact while those elements in the Egyptian-Israel relationship existed there was not one single incident of violence between Egypt and Israel for ten years. But suddenly this status quo, this pattern of mutually accepted stability, was smashed to smithereens. It is now the task of the Governments concerned to elaborate the new conditions of their co-existence. I think that much of this work should be done directly by these Governments themselves. Surely, after what has happened we must have better assurance than before, for Israel and for the Middle East, of peaceful co-existence. The question is whether there is any reason to believe that such a new era may yet come to pass. If I am a little sanguine on this point, it is because of a conviction that men and nations do behave wisely once they have exhausted all other alternatives. Surely the other alternatives of war and belligerency have now been exhausted. And what has anybody gained from that? But in order that the new system of inter-State relationships may flourish in the Middle East, it is important that certain principles be applied above and beyond the cease-fire to which the Security Council has given its unanimous support.

Let me then say here that Israel welcomes the appeal for the cease-fire as formulated in this Resolution. But I must point out that the implementation depends on the absolute and sincere acceptance and co-operation of the other parties, which, in our view, are responsible for the present situation. And in conveying this Resolution to my colleagues, I must at this moment point out that these other Governments have not used the opportunity yet to clarify their intentions. I have said that the situation to be constructed after the cease-fire must depend on certain principles. The first of these principles surely must be the acceptance of Israel's statehood and the total elimination of the fiction of its non-existence. It would seem to me that after 3,000 years the time has arrived to accept Israel's nationhood as a fact, for here is the only State in the international community which has the same territory, speaks the same language and upholds the same faith as it did 3,000 years ago.

And if, as everybody knows to be the fact, the universal conscience was in the last week or two most violently shaken at the prospect of danger to Israel, it was not only because there seemed to be a danger to a State, but also, I think, because the State was Israel, with all that this ancient name evokes, teaches, symbolizes and inspires. How grotesque would be an international community which found room for 122 sovereign units and which did not acknowledge the sovereignty of that people which had given nationhood its deepest significance and its most enduring grace.

No wonder, then, that when danger threatened we could hear a roar of indignation sweep across the world, that men in progressive movements and members of the scientific and humanistic cultures joined together in sounding an alarm bell about an issue that vitally affected the human conscience. And no wonder, correspondingly, that a deep and universal sense of satisfaction and relief has accompanied the news of Israel's gallant and successful resistance.

But the central point remains the need to secure an authentic intellectual recognition by our neighbours of Israel's deep roots in the Middle Eastern reality. There is an intellectual tragedy in the failure of Arab leaders to come to grips, however reluctantly, with the depth and authenticity of Israel's roots in the life, the history, the spiritual experience and the culture of the Middle East.

This, then, is the first axiom. A much more conscious and uninhibited acceptance of Israel's statehood is an axiom requiring no demonstration, for there will never be a Middle East without an independent and sovereign State of Israel in its midst.

The second principle must be that of the peaceful settlement of disputes. The Resolution thus adopted falls within the concept of the peaceful settlement of disputes. I have already said that much could be done if the Governments of the area would embark much more on direct contacts. They must find their way to each other. After all, when there is conflict between them they come together face to face. Why should they not come together face to face to solve the conflict? And perhaps on some occasions it would not be a bad idea to have the solution before, and therefore instead of, the conflict.

When the Council discusses what is to happen after the cease-fire, we hear many formulas: back to 1956, back to 1948—I understand our neighbours would wish to turn the clock back to 1947. The fact is, however, that most clocks move forward and not backward, and this, I think, should be the case with the clock of Middle Eastern peace—not backward to belligerency, but forward to peace.

The point was well made this evening by the representative of Argentina, who said: the cease-fire should be followed immediately by the most intensive efforts to bring about a just and lasting peace in the Middle East. In a similar sense, the representative of Canada warned us against merely reproducing the old positions of conflict, without attempting to settle the underlying issues of Arab-Israel co-existence. After all, many things in recent days have been mixed up with each other. Few things are what they were. And in order to create harmonious combinations of relationships, it is inevitable that the States should come together in negotiation.

Another factor in the harmony that we would like to see in the Middle East relates to external Powers. From these, and especially from the greatest amongst them, the small States of the Middle East—and most of them are small—ask for a rigorous support, not for individual States, but for specific principles; not to be for one State against other States, but to be for peace against war, for free commerce against belligerency, for the pacific settlement of disputes against violent irredentist threats; in other words, to exercise an even-handed support for the integrity and independence of States and for the rights of States under the Charter of the United Nations and other sources of international law.

There are not two categories of States. The United Arab Republic, Iraq, Syria, Jordan, Lebanon—not one of these has a single ounce or milligram of statehood which does not adhere in equal measures to Israel itself.

It is important that States outside our region apply a balanced attitude, that they do not exploit temporary tensions and divergencies in the issues of global conflict, that they do not seek to win gains by inflaming fleeting passions, and that they strive to make a balanced distribution of their friendship amongst the States of the Middle East. Now whether all the speeches of all the Great Powers this evening meet this criterion, everybody, of course, can judge for himself. I do not propose to answer in detail all the observations of the representative of the Soviet Union. I had the advantage of hearing the same things in identical language a few days ago from his colleague, the Soviet Ambassador in Israel. I must confess that I was no more convinced this evening than I was the day before yesterday about the validity of this most vehement and one-sided denunciation. But surely world opinion, before whose tribunal this debate unrolls, can solve this question by posing certain problems to itself. Who was it that attempted to destroy a neighbouring State in 1948, Israel or its neighbours? Who now closes an international waterway to the port of a neighbouring State, Israel or the United Arab Republic? Does Israel refuse to negotiate a peace settlement with the Arab States, or do they refuse to do so with it? Who disrupted the 1957 pattern of stability, Israel or Egypt? Did troops of Egypt, Syria, Jordan, Iraq, Lebanon, Kuwait and Algeria surround Israel in this menacing confrontation, or has any distinguished representative seen some vast Israel colossus surrounding the area between Morocco and Kuwait?

I raise these points of elementary logic. Of course, a Great Power can take refuge in its power from the exigencies of logic. All of us in our youth presumably recounted La Fontaine's fable, "*La raison du plus fort est toujours la meilleure.*" But here, after all, there is nobody who is more or less strong than others; we sit here around the table on the concept of sovereign equality. But I think we have an equal duty to bring substantive proof for any denunciation that we make, each of the other.

I would say in conclusion that these are, of course, still grave times. And yet they may perhaps have a fortunate issue. This could be the case if those who for some reason decided so violently, three weeks ago, to disrupt the status quo would ask themselves what the results and benefits have been. As he looks around him at the arena of battle, at the wreckage of planes and tanks, at the collapse of intoxicated hopes, might not an Egyptian ruler ponder whether anything was achieved by that disruption? What has it brought but strife, conflict with other powerful interests, and the stem criticism of progressive men throughout the world?

I think that Israel has in recent days proved its steadfastness and vigour. It is now willing to demonstrate its instinct for peace. Let us build a new system of relationships from the wreckage of the old. Let us discern across the darkness the vision of a better and a brighter dawn.

25 Protection of Holy Places Law (June 27, 1967)

1. The Holy Places shall be protected from desecration and any other violation and from anything likely to violate the freedom of access of the members of the different religions to the places sacred to them or their feelings with regard to those places.
2. a. Whosoever desecrates or otherwise violates a Holy Place shall be liable to imprisonment for a term of seven years.
   b. Whosoever does anything likely to violate the freedom of access of the members of the different religions to the places sacred to them or their feelings with regard to those places shall be liable to imprisonment for a term of five years.
3. This Law shall add to, and not derogate from, any other law.
4. The Minister of Religious Affairs is charged with the implementation of this Law, and he may, after consultation with, or upon the proposal of, representatives of the religions concerned and with the consent of the Minister of Justice make regulations as to any matter relating to such implementation.
5. This Law shall come into force on the date of its adoption by the Knesset.

Levi Eshkol
Prime Minister

Zerach Warhaftig
Minister of Religious Affairs

Shneur Zalman Shazar
President of the State

26 The Khartoum Resolutions (September 1, 1967)

TEXT:

1. The conference has affirmed the unity of Arab ranks, the unity of joint action and the need for coordination and for the elimination of all differences. The Kings, Presidents and representatives of the other Arab Heads of State at the conference have affirmed their countries' stand by and implementation of the Arab Solidarity Charter which was signed at the third Arab summit conference in Casablanca.

2. The conference has agreed on the need to consolidate all efforts to eliminate the effects of the aggression on the basis that the occupied lands are Arab lands and that the burden of regaining these lands falls on all the Arab States.

3. The Arab Heads of State have agreed to unite their political efforts at the international and diplomatic level to eliminate the effects of the aggression and to ensure the withdrawal of the aggressive Israeli forces from the Arab lands which have been occupied since the aggression of June 5. This will be done within the framework of the main principles by which the Arab States abide, namely, no peace with Israel, no recognition of Israel, no negotiations with it, and insistence on the rights of the Palestinian people in their own country.

4. The conference of Arab Ministers of Finance, Economy and Oil recommended that suspension of oil pumping be used as a weapon in the battle. However, after thoroughly studying the matter, the summit conference has come to the conclusion that the oil pumping can itself be used as a positive weapon, since oil is an Arab resource which can be used to strengthen the economy of the Arab States directly affected by the aggression, so that these States will be able to stand firm in the battle . . .

5. The participants in the conference have approved the plan proposed by Kuwait to set up an Arab Economic and Social Development Fund on the basis of the recommendation of the Baghdad conference of Arab Ministers of Finance, Economy and Oil.

6. The participants have agreed on the need to adopt the necessary measures to strengthen military preparation to face all eventualities.

7. The conference has decided to expedite the elimination of foreign bases in the Arab States.

27 U.N. Security Council: Resolution 242 (November 22, 1967)

The Security Council,

Expressing its continuing concern with the grave situation in the Middle East,

Emphasizing the inadmissibility of the acquisition of territory by war and the need to work for a just and lasting peace in which every State in the area can live in security,

Emphasizing further that all Member States in their acceptance of the Charter of the United Nations have undertaken a commitment to act in accordance with Article 2 of the Charter,

1. Affirms that the fulfillment of Charter principles requires the establishment of a just and lasting peace in the Middle East which should include the application of both the following principles:
    - Withdrawal of Israeli armed forces from territories occupied in the recent conflict;
    - Termination of all claims or states of belligerency and respect for and acknowledgement of the sovereignty, territorial integrity and political independence of every State in the area and their right to live in peace within secure and recognized boundaries free from threats or acts of force;
2. Affirms further the necessity
    - For guaranteeing freedom of navigation through international waterways in the area;
    - For achieving a just settlement of the refugee problem;
    - For guaranteeing the territorial inviolability and political independence of every State in the area, through measures including the establishment of demilitarized zones;
3. Requests the Secretary General to designate a Special Representative to proceed to the Middle East to establish and maintain contacts with the States concerned in order to promote agreement and assist efforts to achieve a peaceful and accepted settlement in accordance with the provisions and principles in this resolution;
4. Requests the Secretary-General to report to the Security Council on the progress of the efforts of the Special Representative as soon as possible.

28 The Palestinian National Charter: Resolutions of the Palestine National Council (July 1–17, 1968)

Text of the 1968 Charter:

Article 1: Palestine is the homeland of the Arab Palestinian people; it is an indivisible part of the Arab homeland, and the Palestinian people are an integral part of the Arab nation.

Article 2: Palestine, with the boundaries it had during the British Mandate, is an indivisible territorial unit.

Article 3: The Palestinian Arab people possess the legal right to their homeland and have the right to determine their destiny after achieving the liberation of their country in accordance with their wishes and entirely of their own accord and will.

Article 4: The Palestinian identity is a genuine, essential, and inherent characteristic; it is transmitted from parents to children. The Zionist occupation and the dispersal of the Palestinian Arab people, through the disasters which befell them, do not make them lose their Palestinian identity and their membership in the Palestinian community, nor do they negate them.

Article 5: The Palestinians are those Arab nationals who, until 1947, normally resided in Palestine regardless of whether they were evicted from it or have stayed there. Anyone born, after that date, of a Palestinian father—whether inside Palestine or outside it—is also a Palestinian.

Article 6: The Jews who had normally resided in Palestine until the beginning of the Zionist invasion will be considered Palestinians.

Article 7: That there is a Palestinian community and that it has material, spiritual, and historical connection with Palestine are indisputable facts. It is a national duty to bring up individual Palestinians in an Arab revolutionary manner. All means of information and education must be adopted in order to acquaint the Palestinian with his country in the most profound manner, both spiritual and material, that is possible. He must be prepared for the armed struggle and ready to sacrifice his wealth and his life in order to win back his homeland and bring about its liberation.

Article 8: The phase in their history, through which the Palestinian people are now living, is that of national struggle for the liberation of Palestine. Thus the conflicts among the Palestinian national forces are secondary, and should be ended for the sake of the basic conflict that exists between the forces of Zionism and of imperialism on the one hand, and the Palestinian Arab people on the other. On this basis the Palestinian masses, regardless of whether they are residing in the national homeland or in diaspora constitute—both their organizations and the individuals—one national front working for the retrieval of Palestine and its liberation through armed struggle.

Article 9: Armed struggle is the only way to liberate Palestine. Thus it is the overall strategy, not merely a tactical phase. The Palestinian Arab people assert their absolute determination and firm resolution to continue their armed struggle and to work for an armed popular revolution for the liberation of their country and their return to it. They also assert their right to normal life in Palestine and to exercise their right to self-determination and sovereignty over it.

Article 10: Commando action constitutes the nucleus of the Palestinian popular liberation war. This requires its escalation, comprehensiveness, and the mobilization of all the Palestinian popular and educational efforts and their organization and involvement in the armed Palestinian revolution. It also requires the achieving of unity for the national struggle among the different groupings of the Palestinian people, and between the Palestinian people and the Arab masses, so as to secure the continuation of the revolution, its escalation, and victory.

Article 11: The Palestinians will have three mottoes: national unity, national mobilization, and liberation.

Article 12: The Palestinian people believe in Arab unity. In order to contribute their share toward the attainment of that objective, however, they must, at the present stage of their struggle, safeguard their Palestinian identity and develop their consciousness of that identity, and oppose any plan that may dissolve or impair it.

Article 13: Arab unity and the liberation of Palestine are two complementary objectives, the attainment of either of which facilitates the attainment of the other. Thus, Arab unity leads to the liberation of Palestine, the liberation of Palestine leads to Arab unity; and work toward the realization of one objective proceeds side by side with work toward the realization of the other.

Article 14: The destiny of the Arab nation, and indeed Arab existence itself, depend upon the destiny of the Palestine cause. From this interdependence springs the Arab nation's pursuit of, and striving for, the liberation of Palestine. The people of Palestine play the role of the vanguard in the realization of this sacred goal.

Article 15: The liberation of Palestine, from an Arab viewpoint, is a national duty and it attempts to repel the Zionist and imperialist aggression against the

Arab homeland, and aims at the elimination of Zionism in Palestine. Absolute responsibility for this falls upon the Arab nation—peoples and governments—with the Arab people of Palestine in the vanguard. Accordingly, the Arab nation must mobilize all its military, human, moral, and spiritual capabilities to partici-pate actively with the Palestinian people in the liberation of Palestine. It must, particularly in the phase of the armed Palestinian revolution, offer and furnish the Palestinian people with all possible help, and material and human support, and make available to them the means and opportunities that will enable them to continue to carry out their leading role in the armed revolution, until they liberate their homeland.

Article 16: The liberation of Palestine, from a spiritual point of view, will provide the Holy Land with an atmosphere of safety and tranquility, which in turn will safeguard the country's religious sanctuaries and guarantee freedom of worship and of visit to all, without discrimination of race, color, language, or religion. Accordingly, the people of Palestine look to all spiritual forces in the world for support.

Article 17: The liberation of Palestine, from a human point of view, will restore to the Palestinian individual his dignity, pride, and freedom. Accordingly the Palestinian Arab people look forward to the support of all those who believe in the dignity of man and his freedom in the world.

Article 18: The liberation of Palestine, from an international point of view, is a defensive action necessitated by the demands of self-defense. Accordingly the Palestinian people, desirous as they are of the friendship of all people, look to freedom-loving, and peace-loving states for support in order to restore their legitimate rights in Palestine, to re-establish peace and security in the country, and to enable its people to exercise national sovereignty and freedom.

Article 19: The partition of Palestine in 1947 and the establishment of the state of Israel are entirely illegal, regardless of the passage of time, because they were contrary to the will of the Palestinian people and to their natural right in their homeland, and inconsistent with the principles embodied in the Charter of the United Nations, particularly the right to self-determination.

Article 20: The Balfour Declaration, the Mandate for Palestine, and everything that has been based upon them, are deemed null and void. Claims of historical or religious ties of Jews with Palestine are incompatible with the facts of history and the true conception of what constitutes statehood. Judaism, being a religion, is not an independent nationality. Nor do Jews constitute a single nation with an identity of its own; they are citizens of the states to which they belong.

Article 21: The Arab Palestinian people, expressing themselves by the armed Palestinian revolution, reject all solutions which are substitutes for the total liberation of Palestine and reject all proposals aiming at the liquidation of the Palestinian problem, or its internationalization.

Article 22: Zionism is a political movement organically associated with international imperialism and antagonistic to all action for liberation and to progressive movements in the world. It is racist and fanatic in its nature, aggressive, expansionist, and colonial in its aims, and fascist in its methods. Israel is the instrument of the Zionist movement, and geographical base for world imperialism placed strategically in the midst of the Arab homeland to combat the hopes of the Arab nation for liberation, unity, and progress. Israel is a constant source of threat vis-a-vis peace in the Middle East and the whole world. Since the liberation of Palestine will destroy the Zionist and imperialist presence and will contribute to the establishment of peace in the Middle East, the Palestinian people look for the support of all the progressive and peaceful forces and urge them all, irrespective of their affiliations and beliefs, to offer the Palestinian people all aid and support in their just struggle for the liberation of their homeland.

Article 23: The demand of security and peace, as well as the demand of right and justice, require all states to consider Zionism an illegitimate movement, to outlaw its existence, and to ban its operations, in order that friendly relations among peoples may be preserved, and the loyalty of citizens to their respective homelands safeguarded.

Article 24: The Palestinian people believe in the principles of justice, freedom, sovereignty, self-determination, human dignity, and in the right of all peoples to exercise them.

Article 25: For the realization of the goals of this Charter and its principles, the Palestine Liberation Organization will perform its role in the liberation of Palestine in accordance with the Constitution of this Organization.

Article 26: The Palestine Liberation Organization, representative of the Palestinian revolutionary forces, is responsible for the Palestinian Arab people's movement in its struggle—to retrieve its homeland, liberate and return to it and exercise the right to self-determination in it—in all military, political, and financial fields and also for whatever may be required by the Palestine case on the inter-Arab and international levels.

Article 27: The Palestine Liberation Organization shall cooperate with all Arab states, each according to its potentialities; and will adopt a neutral policy among them in the light of the requirements of the war of liberation; and on this basis it shall not interfere in the internal affairs of any Arab state.

Article 28: The Palestinian Arab people assert the genuineness and independence of their national revolution and reject all forms of intervention, trusteeship, and subordination.

Article 29: The Palestinian people possess the fundamental and genuine legal right to liberate and retrieve their homeland. The Palestinian people determine their attitude toward all states and forces on the basis of the stands they adopt vis-a-vis to the Palestinian revolution to fulfill the aims of the Palestinian people.

Article 30: Fighters and carriers of arms in the war of liberation are the nucleus of the popular army which will be the protective force for the gains of the Palestinian Arab people.

Article 31: The Organization shall have a flag, an oath of allegiance, and an anthem. All this shall be decided upon in accordance with a special regulation.

Article 32: Regulations, which shall be known as the Constitution of the Palestinian Liberation Organization, shall be annexed to this Charter. It will lay down the manner in which the Organization, and its organs and institutions, shall be constituted; the respective competence of each; and the requirements of its obligation under the Charter.

Article 33: This Charter shall not be amended save by [vote of] a majority of two-thirds of the total membership of the National Congress of the Palestine Liberation Organization [taken] at a special session convened for that purpose.

* English rendition as published in Basic Political Documents of the Armed Palestinian Resistance Movement; Leila S. Kadi (ed.), Palestine Research Centre, Beirut, December 1969, pp.137–141.

29 The Seven Points of Fatah (January, 1969)

1. Fatah, the Palestine National Liberation Movement, is the expression of the Palestinian people and of its will to free its land from Zionist colonisation in order to recover its national identity.

2. Fatah, the Palestine National Liberation Movement, is not struggling against the Jews as an ethnic and religious community. It is struggling against Israel as the expression of colonisation based on a theocratic, racist and expansionist system and of Zionism and colonialism.

3. Fatah, the Palestine National Liberation Movement, rejects any solution that does not take account of the existence of the Palestinian people and its right to dispose of itself.

4. Fatah, the Palestine National Liberation Movement, categorically rejects the Security Council Resolution of 22 November 1967 and the Jarring Mission to which it gave rise.

This resolution ignores the national rights of the Palestinian people failing to mention its existence. Any solution claiming to be peaceful which ignores this basic factor, will thereby be doomed to failure. In any event, the acceptance of the resolution of 22 November 1967, or any pseudo-political solution, by whatsoever party, is in no way of binding upon the Palestinian people, which is determined to pursue mercilessly its struggle against foreign occupation and Zionist colonisation.

5. Fatah, the Palestine National Liberation Movement, solemnly proclaims that the final objective of its struggle is the restoration of the independent, democratic State of Palestine, all of whose citizens will enjoy equal rights irrespective of their religion.

6. Since Palestine forms part of the Arab fatherland, Fatah, the Palestine National Liberation Movement, will work for the State of Palestine to contribute actively towards the establishment of a progressive and united Arab society.

7. The struggle of the Palestinian People, like that of the Vietnamese people and other peoples of Asia, Africa, and Latin America, is part of the historic process of the liberation of the oppressed peoples from colonialism and imperialism.

30 U.N. Security Council: Resolution 338 (October 22, 1973)

The Security Council,

1. Calls upon all parties to present fighting to cease all firing and terminate all military activity immediately, no later than 12 hours after the moment of the adoption of this decision, in the positions after the moment of the adoption of this decision, in the positions they now occupy;
2. Calls upon all parties concerned to start immediately after the cease-fire the implementation of Security Council Resolution 242 (1967) in all of its parts;

Decides that, immediately and concurrently with the cease-fire, negotiations start between the parties concerned under appropriate auspices aimed at establishing a just and durable peace in the Middle East.

31 Palestine National Council: Resolutions at the 12th Session of the Palestine National Council (June, 1974)

Cairo, 8 June 1974

The Palestine National Council,

On the basis of the Palestine National Charter and the Political Program drawn up at the eleventh session, held from 6–12 January 1974; and from its belief that it is impossible for a permanent and just peace to be established in the area unless our Palestinian people recover from all their national rights and, first and foremost, their rights to return and to self-determination on the whole of the soil of their homeland; and in the light of a study of the new political circumstances that have come into existence in the period between the Council's last and present sessions, resolves the following:

1. To reaffirm the Palestine Liberation Organization's previous attitude to Resolution 242, which obliterates the national right of our people and deals with the cause of our people as a problem of refugees. The Council therefore refuses to have anything to do with this resolution at any level, Arab or international, including the Geneva Conference.

2. The Palestine Liberation Organization will employ all means, and first and foremost armed struggle, to liberate Palestinian territory and to establish the independent combatant national authority for the people over every part of Palestinian territory that is liberated. This will require further changes being effected in the balance of power in favor of our people and their struggle.

3. The Liberation Organization will struggle against any proposal for a Palestinian entity the price of which is recognition, peace, secure frontiers, renunciation of national rights, and the deprival of our people of their right to return and their right to self-determination on the soil of their homeland.

4. Any step taken towards liberation is a step towards the realization of the Liberation Organization's strategy of establishing the democratic Palestinian State specified in the resolutions of the previous Palestinian National Councils.

5. Struggle along with the Jordanian national forces to establish a Jordanian-Palestinian national front whose aim will be to set up in Jordan a democratic national authority in close contact with the Palestinian entity that is established through the struggle.

6. The Liberation Organization will struggle to establish unity in struggle between the two peoples and between all the forces of the Arab liberation movement that are in agreement on this program.

7. In the light of this program, the Liberation Organization will struggle to strengthen national unity and to raise it to the level where it will be able to perform its national duties and tasks.

8. Once it is established, the Palestinian national authority will strive to achieve a union of the confrontation countries, with the aim of completing the liberation of all Palestinian territory, and as a step along the road to comprehensive Arab unity.

9. The Liberation Organization will strive to strengthen its solidarity with the socialist countries, and with the forces of liberation and progress throughout the world, with the aim of frustrating all the schemes of Zionism, reaction and imperialism.

10. In light of this program, the leadership of the revolution will determine the tactics which will serve and make possible the realization of these objectives.

The Executive Committee of the Palestine Liberation Organization will make every effort to implement this program, and should a situation arise affecting the destiny and the future of the Palestinian people, the National Assembly will be convened in extraordinary session.

32 Interim Agreement Between Israel and Egypt (September 1, 1975)

AGREEMENT BETWEEN EGYPT AND ISRAEL

The Government of the Arab Republic of Egypt and the Government of Israel have agreed that:

Article I

The conflict between them and in the Middle East shall not be resolved by military force but by peaceful means.

The Agreement concluded by the parties on 18 January 1974, within the framework of the Geneva Peace Conference, constituted a first step towards a just and durable peace according to the provisions of Security Council Resolution 338 of 22 October 1973.

They are determined to reach a final and just peace settlement by means of negotiations called for by Security Council Resolution 338, this Agreement being a significant step towards that end.

Article II

The parties hereby undertake not to resort to the threat or use of force or military blockade against each other.

Article III

The parties shall continue scrupulously to observe the cease-fire on land, sea and air and to refrain from all military or para-military actions against each other. The parties also confirm that the obligations contained in the annex and, when concluded, the Protocol shall be an integral part of this Agreement.

Article IV

A. The military forces of the parties shall be deployed in accordance with [negotiated positions]: . . .

B. The details concerning the new lines, the redeployment of the forces and its timing, the limitation on armaments and forces, aerial reconnaissance, the operation of the early warning and surveillance installations and the use of the roads, the United Nations functions and other arrangements will all be in accordance with the provisions of the annex and map which are an integral part of this Agreement and of the protocol which is to result from negotiations pursuant to the annex and which, when concluded, shall become an integral part of this Agreement.

Article V
The United Nations Emergency Force is essential and shall continue its functions and its mandate shall be extended annually.

Article VI
The parties hereby establish a joint commission for the duration of this Agreement. It will function under the aegis of the chief co-ordinator of the United Nations peace-keeping missions in the Middle East in order to consider any problem arising from this Agreement and to assist the United Nations Emergency Force in the execution of its mandate. The joint commission shall function in accordance with procedures established in the Protocol.

Article VII
Non-military cargoes destined for or coming from Israel shall be permitted through the Suez Canal.

Article VIII
This Agreement is regarded by the parties as a significant step toward a just and lasting peace. It is not a final peace agreement.

The parties shall continue their efforts to negotiate a final peace agreement within the framework of the Geneva peace conference in accordance with Security Council Resolution 338.

Article IX
This Agreement shall enter into force upon signature of the Protocol and remain in force until superseded by a new agreement.

ANNEX TO THE EGYPT–ISRAEL AGREEMENT
Within five days after the signature of the Egypt-Israel Agreement, representatives of the two parties shall meet in the military working group of the Middle East peace conference at Geneva to begin preparation of a detailed Protocol for the implementation of the Agreement. The working group will complete the Protocol within two weeks. In order to facilitate preparation of the Protocol and implementation of the agreement, and to assist in maintaining the scrupulous observance of the cease-fire and other elements of the Agreement, the two parties have agreed on the following principles, which are an integral part of the Agreement, as guidelines for the working group.

1. DEFINITIONS OF LINES AND AREAS
The deployment lines, areas of limited forces and armaments, buffer zones, [and other areas] . . . shall be as indicated on the attached map (1:100,000—United States edition).

2. BUFFER ZONES

(A) Access to the buffer zones will be controlled by the United Nations Emergency Force, according to procedures to be worked out by the working group and the United Nations Emergency Force.

(B) Aircraft of either party will be permitted to fly freely up to the forward line of that party. Reconnaissance aircraft of either party may fly up to the middle line of the buffer zone. . . .

(C) In the buffer zone, . . . there will be established under article IV of the Agreement an early warning system entrusted to United States civilian personnel as detailed in a separate proposal, which is a part of this Agreement.

(D) Authorized personnel shall have access to the buffer zone for transit to and from the early warning system; the manner in which this is carried out shall be worked out by the working group and the United Nations Emergency Force.

3. AREA SOUTH OF LINE E AND WEST OF LINE M

(A) In this area, the United Nations Emergency Force will assure that there are no military or para-military forces of any kind, military fortifications and military installations; it will establish checkpoints and have the freedom of movement necessary to perform this function.

(B) Egyptian civilians and third country civilian oil field personnel shall have the right to enter, exit from, work and live in the above indicated area, . . . Egyptian civilian police shall be allowed in the area to perform normal civil police functions among the civilian population in such number and with such weapons and equipment as shall be provided for in the Protocol.

(C) Entry to and exit from the area, by land, by air or by sea, shall be only through United Nations Emergency Force checkpoints. The United Nations Emergency Force shall also establish checkpoints along the road, the dividing line and at either points, with the precise locations and number to be included in the Protocol.

(D) Access to the airspace and the coastal area shall be limited to unarmed Egyptian civilian vessels and unarmed civilian helicopters and transport planes involved in the civilian activities of the area as agreed by the working group.

(E) Israel undertakes to leave intact all currently existing civilian installations and infrastructures.

(F) Procedures for use of the common sections of the coastal road along the Gulf of Suez shall be determined by the working group and detailed in the Protocol.

4. AERIAL SURVEILLANCE

There shall be a continuation of aerial reconnaissance missions by the United States over the areas covered by the Agreement . . . following the same procedures already in practice. The missions will ordinarily be carried out at a frequency of one mission every 7–10 days, with either party or the United Nations Emergency Force empowered to request an earlier mission. The United States Government will make the mission results available expeditiously to Israel, Egypt and the chief coordinator of the United Nations peace-keeping missions in the Middle East.

5. LIMITATION OF FORCES AND ARMAMENTS [. . .]

6. PROCESS OF IMPLEMENTATION

The detailed implementation and timing of the redeployment of forces, turnover of oil fields, and other arrangements called for by the Agreement, annex and Protocol shall be determined by the working group, which will agree on the stages of this process, including the phased movement of Egyptian troops . . . and Israeli troops. . . . The first phase will be the transfer of the oil fields and installations to Egypt. This process will begin within two weeks from the signature of the Protocol with the introduction of the necessary technicians, and it will be completed no later than eight weeks after it begins. The details of the phasing will be worked out in the military working group.

Implementation of the redeployment shall be completed within five months after signature of the Protocol.

ATTACHED U.S. PROPOSAL FOR AN EARLY-WARNING SYSTEM IN SINAI
In connection with the early warning system referred to in article IV of the Agreement between Egypt and Israel concluded on this date and as an integral part of that Agreement (hereafter referred to as the basic Agreement), the United States proposes the following:

1. The early warning system to be established in accordance with article IV in the area shown on the map attached to the basic agreement will be entrusted to the United States. It shall have the following elements:

A. There shall be two surveillance stations to provide strategic early warning, one operated by Egyptian and one operated by Israeli personnel. Their locations are shown on the map attached to the basic Agreement. Each station shall be manned by not more than 250 technical and administrative personnel. They shall perform the functions of visual and electronic surveillance only within their stations.

B. In support of these stations, to provide tactical early warning and to verify access to them, three watch stations shall be established by the United States in the Mitla and Gidi Passes as will be shown on the map attached to the basic Agreement. These stations shall be operated by United States civilian personnel. In support of these stations, there shall be established three unmanned electronic sensor fields at both ends of each Pass and in the general vicinity of each station and the roads leading to and from those stations.

2. The United States civilian personnel shall perform the following duties in connection with the operation and maintenance of these stations.

A. At the two surveillance stations described in paragraph 1 A. above, United States civilian personnel will verify the nature of the operations of the stations and all movement into and out of each station and will immediately report any detected divergency from its authorized role of visual and electronic surveillance to the parties to the basic Agreement and to the United Nations Emergency Force.

B. At each watch station described in paragraph 1 B. above, the United States civilian personnel will immediately report to the parties to the basic Agreement and to the United Nations Emergency Force any movement of armed forces, other than the United Nations Emergency Force, into either Pass and any observed preparations for such movement.

C. The total number of United States civilian personnel assigned to functions under this proposal shall not exceed 200. Only civilian personnel shall be assigned to functions under this proposal.

3. No arms shall be maintained at the stations and other facilities covered by this proposal, except for small arms required for their protection.

4. The United States personnel serving the early warning system shall be allowed to move freely within the area of the system.

5. The United States and its personnel shall be entitled to have such support facilities as are reasonably necessary to perform their functions provided for in the United Nations Emergency Force Agreement of 13 February 1957.

6. The United States personnel shall be immune from local criminal, civil, tax and customs jurisdiction and may be accorded any other specific privileges and immunities provided for in the United Nations Emergency Force Agreement of 13 February 1957.

7. The United States affirms that it will continue to perform the functions described above for the duration of the basic Agreement.

8. Notwithstanding any other provision of this proposal, the United States may withdraw its personnel only if it concludes that their safety is jeopardized or that continuation of their role is no longer necessary. In the latter case the parties to the basic Agreement will be informed in advance in order to give them the opportunity to make alternative arrangements. If both parties to the basic Agreement request the United States to conclude its role under this proposal, the United States will consider such requests conclusive.

9. Technical problems including the location of the watch stations will be worked out through consultation with the United States.

33 Statement to the Knesset by Prime Minister Menahem Begin (November 20, 1977)

[Hebrew Translation]

Mr. Speaker, Honourable President of the State of Israel, Honourable President of the Arab Republic of Egypt, Worthy and Learned Knesset Members:

We send our greetings to the President and to all adherents of the Islamic faith, in our own country and wherever they may be, on the occasion of the Feast of Sacrifice, Id el-Adha.

[. . .]

I greet the President of Egypt on the occasion of his visit to our country and his participation in this session of the Knesset. The duration of the flight from Cairo to Jerusalem is short but, until last night, the distance between them was infinite. President Sadat showed courage in crossing this distance. We Jews can appreciate courage, as exhibited by our guest, because it is with courage that we arose, and with it we shall continue to exist.

Mr. Speaker, this small People, the surviving remnant of the Jewish People which returned to our historic Homeland, always sought peace. And, when the dawn of our freedom rose on the 14th of May, 1948, the 4th of Iyar, 5708, David Ben-Gurion said, in the Declaration of Independence, the charter of our national independence:

"We extend our hand to all neighbouring states and their peoples in an offer of peace and good neighbourliness, and appeal to them to establish bonds of cooperation and mutual help with the sovereign Jewish People settled in its own Land."

[. . .]

But it is my duty—my duty Mr. Speaker, and not only my privilege—to assert today in truth that our hand, extended in peace, was rejected. And, one day after our independence was renewed, in accordance with our eternal and indisputable right, we were attacked on three fronts, and we stood virtually without arms—few against many, weak against strong. One day after the declaration of our independence, an attempt was made to strangle it with enmity, and to extinguish the last hope of the Jewish People in the generation of Holocaust and Resurrection.

No, we do not believe in might, and we have never based our relations with the Arab Nation on force. On the contrary, force was exercised against us. Throughout all the years of this generation we have never ceased to be attacked with brute force in order to destroy our Nation, to demolish our independence, to annul our right. And we defended ourselves.

True, we defended our right, our existence, our honour, our women and our children against recurrent attempts to crush us by brute force, and not on one front alone. This, too, is true: with the help of God we overcame the forces of aggression and assured the survival of our nation, not only for this generation, but for all those to come.

We do not believe in might; we believe in right, only in right. And that is why our aspiration, from the depths of our hearts, from time immemorial until this very day, is peace.

[. . .]

Therefore, allow me today to define the meaning of peace as we understand it. We seek a true, full peace, with absolute reconciliation between the Jewish People and the Arab People. We must not permit memories of the past to stand in our way. There have been wars; blood has been shed; our wonderful sons have fallen in battle on both sides. We shall always cherish the memory of our heroes who gave their lives so that this day, yea even this day, might come. We respect the valour of an adversary, and we pay tribute to all members of the young generation of the Arab Nation who have fallen as well.

Let us not be daunted by memories of the past, even if they are bitter to us all. We must overcome them, and focus on what lies ahead: on our Peoples, on our children, on our common future. For, in this region, we shall all live together—the Great Arab Nation in its States and its countries, and the Jewish People in its Land, Eretz Israel—forever and ever. For this reason the meaning of peace must be defined.

[. . .]

I agree, Mr. President, that you have not come here and we did not invite you to our country in order, as has been suggested in recent days, to drive a wedge between the Arab Peoples, or, expressed more cleverly in accord with the ancient saying, "divide et impera." Israel has no desire to rule and does not wish to divide. We want peace with all our neighbours—with Egypt and with Jordan, with Syria and with Lebanon.

There is no need to differentiate between a peace treaty and the termination of the state of war. We neither propose this, nor do we seek it. On the contrary, the first article of a peace treaty determines the end of the state of war, forever. We wish to establish normal relations between us, as exist among all nations after all wars. We have learned from history, Mr. President, that war is avoidable. It is peace that is inevitable.

Many nations have waged war against one another, and sometimes they have made use of the foolish term "eternal enemy." There are no eternal enemies. After all wars comes the inevitable—peace. Therefore, in the context of a peace treaty, we seek to stipulate the establishment of diplomatic relations, as is customary among civilized nations.

Today, Jerusalem is bedecked with two flags—the Egyptian and the Israeli. Together, Mr. President, we have seen our little children waving both flags. Let us sign a peace treaty and establish such a situation forever, both in Jerusalem and in Cairo. I hope the day will come when Egyptian children will wave Israeli and Egyptian flags together, just as the Israeli children are waving both of these flags together in Jerusalem; when you, Mr. President, will be represented by a loyal Ambassador in Jerusalem, and we, by an Ambassador in Cairo and, should differences of opinion arise between us, we will clarify them, like civilized peoples, through our authorized emissaries.

We propose economic cooperation for the development of our countries. God created marvelous lands in the Middle East—virtual oases in the desert—but there are also deserts, and these can be made fertile. Let us join hands in facing this challenge, and cooperate in developing our countries, in abolishing poverty, hunger and homelessness. Let us raise our nations to the status of developed countries, so that we may no longer be called developing states.

[. . .]

Therefore, I renew my invitation to the President of Syria to follow in your footsteps, Mr. President, and to come to our country to begin negotiations on the establishment of peace between Israel and Syria and on the signing of a peace treaty between us. I am sorry to say, there is no justification for the mourning that has been decreed on the other side of our northern border. On the contrary, such visits, such contacts and discussions, can and should be a cause of happiness, a cause of elation for all peoples.

I invite King Hussein to come here and we shall discuss with him all the problems that exist between us. I also invite genuine spokesmen of the Palestinian Arabs to come and to hold talks with us on our common future, on guaranteeing human freedom, social justice, peace and mutual respect.

And, if they should invite us to come to their capitals, we shall respond to their invitation. Should they invite us to begin negotiations in Damascus, Amman or Beirut, we shall go to those capitals in order to negotiate there. We do not wish to divide. We seek true peace with all our neighbours, to be expressed in peace treaties, the context of which shall be as I have already clarified.

Mr. Speaker, it is my duty today to tell our guests and all the nations who are watching us and listening to our words about the bond between our People and this Land. The President mentioned the Balfour Declaration. No, sir, we took no foreign land. We returned to our Homeland. The bond between our People and this Land is eternal. It was created at the dawn of human history. It was never severed. In this Land we established our civilization; here our prophets spoke those holy words you cited this very day; here the Kings of Judah and Israel prostrated themselves; here we became a nation; here we established our Kingdom and, when we were exiled from our country by the force that was exercised against us, even when we were far away, we did not forget this Land, not even for a single day. We prayed for it; we longed for it; we have believed in our return to it ever since the day these words were spoken:

"When the Lord brought back the captivity of Zion we were like those who dream. Then our mouth was filled with laughter and our tongue with joyful shouting."

[. . .]

This, our right, has been recognized. The Balfour Declaration was included in the Mandate which was recognized by the nations of the world, including the United States of America. And the preamble to that authoritative international document states:

"Whereas recognition has thereby been given to the historical connection of the Jewish People with Palestine (or, in Hebrew, 'Eretz Israel') and to the grounds for reconstituting their National Home in that country (that is, in 'Eretz Israel') . . ."

In 1919, we also gained recognition of this right from the spokesman of the Arab People. The agreement of 3 January 1919, signed by Emir Feisal and Chaim Weizmann, states:

"Mindful of the racial kinship and ancient bonds existing between the Arabs and the Jewish People, and realizing that the surest means of working out the consummation of their national aspirations is through the closest possible collaboration in the development of the Arab State and of Palestine . . ."

Afterwards, follow all the articles on cooperation between the Arab State and Eretz Israel. That is our right; its fulfilment—the truth.

What happened to us when our Homeland was taken from us? I accompanied you this morning, Mr. President, to Yad Vashem. With your own eyes you saw what the fate of our People was when this Homeland was taken from it. It is an incredible story. We both agreed, Mr. President, that whoever has not himself seen what is found in Yad Vashem cannot understand what befell this People when it was homeless, robbed of its own Homeland. And we both read a document dated 30 January 1939, in which the word "vernichtung" appears—"if war breaks out the Jewish race in Europe will be annihilated." Then, too, we were told to pay no heed to such words. The whole world heard. No one came to our rescue; not during the nine critical, fateful months following this announcement—the likes of which had never been heard since God created man and man created Satan—and not during those six years when millions of our people, among them a million and a half small Jewish children were slaughtered in every possible way.

No one came to our rescue, not from the East and not from the West. And therefore we, this entire generation, the generation of Holocaust and Resurrection, swore an oath of allegiance: never again shall we endanger our People; never again will our wives and our children—whom it is our duty to defend, if need be even at the cost of our own lives—be put in the devastating range of enemy fire.

[. . .]

President Sadat knows, as he knew from us before he came to Jerusalem, that our position concerning permanent borders between us and our neighbours differs from his. However, I call upon the President of Egypt and upon all our neighbours: do not rule out negotiations on any subject whatsoever. I propose, in the name of the overwhelming majority of this Parliament, that everything will be negotiable. Anybody who says that, in the relationship between the Arab People—or the Arab Nations in the area—and the State of Israel there are subjects that should be excluded from negotiations, is assuming an awesome responsibility. Everything is negotiable. No side shall say the contrary. No side shall present prior conditions. We will conduct the negotiations with respect.

If there are differences of opinion between us, that is not exceptional. Anyone who has studied the history of wars and the annals of peace treaties knows that all negotiations for peace treaties have begun with differences of opinion between the parties concerned, and that, in the course of the negotiations, they have reached solutions which have made possible the signing of agreements or peace treaties. That is the path we propose to follow.

We shall conduct the negotiations as equals. There are no vanquished and there are no victors. All the Peoples of the region are equal, and all will relate to each other with respect. In this spirit of openness, of readiness of each to listen to the other—to facts, reasons, explanations—with every reasonable attempt at mutual persuasion—let us conduct the negotiations as I have asked and propose to open them, to conduct them, to continue them persistently until we succeed, in good time, in signing a peace treaty between us.

We are prepared, not only, to sit with representatives of Egypt and with representatives of Jordan, Syria and Lebanon—if it so desires—at a Peace Conference in Geneva. We proposed that the Geneva Conference be renewed on the basis of Resolutions 242 and 338 of the Security Council. However, should problems arise between us prior to the convening of the Geneva Conference, we will clarify them today and tomorrow and, if the President of Egypt will be interested in continuing to clarify them in Cairo—all the better; if on neutral ground—no opposition. Anywhere. Let us clarify—even before the Geneva Conference convenes—the problems that should be made clear before it meets, with open eyes and a readiness to listen to all suggestions.

Allow me to say a word about Jerusalem. Mr. President, today you prayed in a house of worship sacred to the Islamic faith, and from there you went to the Church of the Holy Sepulchre. You witnessed the fact, known to all who come from throughout the world, that, ever since this city was joined together, there is absolutely free access, without any interference or obstacle, for the members of all religions to their holy places. This positive phenomenon did not exist for 19 years. It has existed now for about 11 years, and we can assure the Moslem world and the Christian world—all the nations—that there will always be free access to the holy places of every faith. We shall defend this right of free access, for it is something in which we believe—in the equality of rights for every man and every citizen, and in respect for every faith.

Mr. Speaker, this is a special day for our Parliament, and it will undoubtedly be remembered for many years in the annals of our Nation, in the history of the Egyptian People, and perhaps, also, in the history of nations.

And on this day, with your permission, worthy and learned Members of the Knesset, I wish to offer a prayer that the God of our common ancestors will grant us the requisite wisdom of heart in order to overcome the difficulties and obstacles, the calumnies and slanders. With the help of God, may we arrive at the longed-for day for which all our people pray—the day of peace.

For indeed, as the Psalmist of Israel said, "Righteousness and peace have kissed," and, as the prophet Zecharia said, "Love truth and peace."

34 Statement to the Knesset by President Anwar al Sadat (November 20, 1977)

In the name of God, the Gracious and Merciful.

Mr. Speaker, Ladies and Gentlemen:

[. . .]

I come to you today on solid ground, to shape a new life, to establish peace. We all, on this land, the land of God; we all, Muslims, Christians and Jews, worship God and no one but God. God's teachings and commandments are love, sincerity, purity and peace.

I do not blame all those who received my decision—when I announced it to the entire world before the Egyptian People's Assembly—with surprise and amazement. Some, gripped by the violent surprise, believed that my decision was no more than verbal juggling to cater for world public opinion. Others, still, interpreted it as political tactics to camouflage my intention of launching a new war. . . .

I can see the point of all those who were astounded by my decision or those who had any doubts as to the sincerity of the intentions behind the declaration of my decision. No one would have ever conceived that the President of the biggest Arab State, which bears the heaviest burden and the top responsibility pertaining to the cause of war and peace in the Middle East, could declare his readiness to go to the land of the adversary while we were still in a state of war. Rather, we all are still bearing the consequences of four fierce wars waged within thirty years. The families of the 1973 October War are still moaning under the cruel pains of widowhood and bereavement of sons, fathers and brothers.

[. . .]

But, to be absolutely frank with you, I took this decision after long thinking, knowing that it constitutes a grave risk for, if God Almighty has made it my fate to assume the responsibility on behalf of the Egyptian People and to share in the fate-determining responsibility of the Arab Nation and the Palestinian People, the main duty dictated by this responsibility is to exhaust all and every means in a bid to save my Egyptian Arab People and the entire Arab Nation the horrors of new, shocking and destructive wars, the dimensions of which are foreseen by no other than God himself.

[. . .]

If I said that I wanted to save all the Arab People the horrors of shocking and destructive wars, I most sincerely declare before you that I have the same feelings and bear the same responsibility towards all and every man on earth, and certainly towards the Israeli People.

Any life lost in war is a human life, irrespective of its being that of an Israeli or an Arab. A wife who becomes a widow is a human being entitled to a happy family life, whether she be an Arab or an Israeli. Innocent children who are deprived of the care and compassion of their parents are ours, be they living on Arab or Israeli land. They command our top responsibility to afford them a comfortable life today and tomorrow.

[. . .]

I have shouldered the prerequisites of the historical responsibility and, therefore, I declared—on 4 February 1971, to be precise—that I was willing to sign a peace agreement with Israel. This was the first declaration made by a responsible Arab official since the outbreak of the Arab-Israeli conflict.

Motivated by all these factors dictated by the responsibilities of leadership, I called, on 16 October 1973, before the Egyptian People's Assembly, for an international conference to establish permanent peace based on justice. I was not heard. I was in the position of he who was pleading for peace or asking for a ceasefire.

Motivated by all these factors dictated by duties of history and leadership, we signed the first disengagement agreement, followed by the second disengagement agreement in Sinai. Then we proceeded trying both open and closed doors in a bid to find a certain path leading to a durable and just peace. We opened our hearts to the peoples of the entire world to make them understand our motivations and objectives, and to leave them actually convinced of the fact that we are advocates of justice and peace-makers.

[. . .]

Ladies and Gentlemen, let us be frank with each other, using straight-forward words and a clear conception, with no ambiguity. Let us be frank with each other today while the entire world, both East and West, follows these unparalleled moments which could prove to be a radical turning point in the history of this part of the world, if not in the history of the world as a whole. Let us be frank with each other as we answer this important question: how can we achieve permanent peace based on justice?

I have come to you carrying my clear and frank answer to this big question, so that the people in Israel as well as the whole world might hear it, and so that all those whose devoted prayers ring in my ears, pleading to God Almighty that this historic meeting may eventually lead to the results aspired to by millions, might also hear it.

Before I proclaim my answer, I wish to assure you that, in my clear and frank answer, I am basing myself on a number of facts which no one can deny.

The first fact: no one can build his happiness at the expense of the misery of others.

The second fact: never have I spoken or will ever speak in two languages. Never have I adopted or will adopt two policies. I never deal with anyone except in one language, one policy, and with one face.

The third fact: direct confrontation and a straight line are the nearest and most successful methods to reach a clear objective.

The fourth fact: the call for permanent and just peace, based on respect for the United Nations resolutions, has now become the call of the whole world. It has become a clear expression of the will of the international community, whether in official capitals, where policies are made and decisions taken, or at the level of world public opinion which influences policy-making and decision-taking.

The fifth fact: and this is probably the clearest and most prominent, is that the Arab Nation, in its drive for permanent peace based on justice, does not proceed from a position of weakness or hesitation, but it has the potential of power and stability which tells of a sincere will for peace.

[. . .]

In the light of these facts which I meant to place before you the way I see them, I would also wish to warn you in all sincerity; I warn you against some thoughts that could cross your minds; frankness makes it incumbent upon me to tell you the following:

First: I have not come here for a separate agreement between Egypt and Israel. This is not part of the policy of Egypt. The problem is not that of Egypt and Israel. Any separate peace between Egypt and Israel, or between any Arab confrontation State and Israel, will not bring permanent peace based on justice in the entire region. Rather, even if peace between all the confrontation States and Israel were achieved, in the absence of a just solution to the Palestinian problem, never will there be that durable and just peace upon which the entire world insists today.

Second: I have not come to you to seek a partial peace, namely to terminate the state of belligerency at this stage, and put off the entire problem to a subsequent stage. This is not the radical solution that would steer us to permanent peace.

Equally, I have not come to you for a third disengagement agreement in Sinai, or in the Golan and the West Bank. For this would mean that we are merely delaying the ignition of the fuse; it would mean that we are lacking the courage to confront peace, that we are too weak to shoulder the burdens and responsibilities of a durable peace based on justice.

I have come to you so that together we might build a durable peace based on justice, to avoid the shedding of one single drop of blood from an Arab or an Israeli. It is for this reason that I have proclaimed my readiness to go to the farthest corner of the world.

Here, I would go back to the answer to the big question: how can we achieve a durable peace based on justice?

[. . .]

We used to reject you. We had our reasons and our claims, yes. We used to brand you as "so-called" Israel, yes. We were together in international conferences and organizations and our representatives did not, and still do not, exchange greetings, yes. This has happened and is still happening.

It is also true that we used to set, as a precondition for any negotiations with you, a mediator who would meet separately with each party. Through this procedure, the talks of the first and second disengagement agreements took place.

Our delegates met in the first Geneva Conference without exchanging a direct word. Yes, this has happened.

[. . .]

As we really and truly seek peace, we really and truly welcome you to live among us in peace and security.

There was a huge wall between us which you tried to build up over a quarter of a century, but it was destroyed in 1973. It was a wall of a continuously inflammable and escalating psychological warfare. It was a wall of fear of the force that could sweep the entire Arab Nation. It was a wall of propaganda, that we were a Nation reduced to a motionless corpse. Rather, some of you had gone as far as to say that, even after 50 years, the Arabs would not regain any strength. It was a wall that threatened always with the long arm that could reach and strike anywhere. It was a wall that warned us against extermination and annihilation if we tried to use our legitimate right to liberate the occupied territories. Together we have to admit that that wall fell and collapsed in 1973.

Yet, there remained another wall. This wall constitutes a psychological barrier between us. A barrier of suspicion. A barrier of rejection. A barrier of fear of deception. A barrier of hallucinations around any action, deed or decision. A barrier of cautious and erroneous interpretations of all and every event or statement. It is this psychological barrier which I described in official statements as representing 70 percent of the whole problem.

Today, through my visit to you, I ask you: why don't we stretch our hands with faith and sincerity so that, together, we might destroy this barrier? Why shouldn't our and your will meet with faith and sincerity, so that together we might remove all suspicion of fear, betrayal and ill intentions? . . .

To tell you the truth, peace cannot be worth its name unless it is based on justice, and not on the occupation of the land of others. It would not be appropriate for you to demand for yourselves what you deny others. With all frankness, and with the spirit that has prompted me to come to you today, I tell you: you have to give up, once and for all, the dreams of conquest, and give up the belief that force is the best method for dealing with the Arabs. You should clearly understand and assimilate the lesson of confrontation between you and us.

[. . .]

What is peace for Israel? It means that Israel lives in the region with her Arab neighbours, in security and safety. To such logic, I say yes. It means that Israel lives within her borders, secure against any aggression. To such logic, I say yes. It means that Israel obtains all kinds of guarantees that ensure those two factors. To this demand, I say yes. More than that: we declare that we accept all the international guarantees you envisage and accept. We declare that we accept all the guarantees you want from the two super powers or from either of them, or from the Big Five, or some of them.

Once again, I declare clearly and unequivocally that we agree to any guarantees you accept because, in return, we shall obtain the same guarantees.

In short, then, when we ask: what is peace for Israel, the answer would be: it is that Israel live within her borders with her Arab neighbours, in safety and security within the framework of all the guarantees she accepts and which are offered to the other party. But how can this be achieved? How can we reach this conclusion which would lead us to permanent peace based on justice?

There are facts that should be faced with all courage and clarity. There are Arab territories which Israel has occupied by armed force. We insist on complete withdrawal from these territories, including Arab Jerusalem.

I have come to Jerusalem, as the City of Peace, which will always remain as a living embodiment of coexistence among believers of the three religions. It is inadmissible that anyone should conceive the special status of the City of Jerusalem within the framework of annexation or expansionism, but it should be a free and open city for all believers.

Above all, the city should not be severed from those who have made it their abode for centuries. Instead of awakening the prejudices of the Crusaders, we should revive the spirit of Ornar ibn el-Khattab and Saladdin, namely the spirit of tolerance and respect for rights. The holy shrines of Islam and Christianity are not only places of worship, but a living testimony of our uninterrupted presence here politically, spiritually and intellectually. Let us make no mistake about the importance and reverence we Christians and Muslims attach to Jerusalem.

Let me tell you, without the slightest hesitation, that I did not come to you under this dome to make a request that your troops evacuate the occupied territories. Complete withdrawal from the Arab territories occupied in 1967 is a logical and undisputed fact. Nobody should plead for that. Any talk about permanent peace based on justice, and any move to ensure our coexistence in peace and security in this part of the world, would become meaningless, while you occupy Arab territories by force of arms. For there is no peace that could be in consonance with, or be built on, the occupation of the land of others. Otherwise, it would not be a serious peace.

Yes, this is a foregone conclusion which is not open to discussion or debate—if intentions are sincere and if endeavours to establish a just and durable peace for ours and the generations to come are genuine.

As for the Palestinians' cause, nobody could deny that it is the crux of the entire problem. Nobody in the world could accept, today, slogans propagated here in Israel, ignoring the existence of the Palestinian People, and questioning their whereabouts. The cause of the Palestinian People and their legitimate rights are no longer ignored or denied today by anybody. Rather, nobody who has the ability of judgement can deny or ignore it.

It is an acknowledged fact received by the world community, both in the East and in the West, with support and recognition in international documents and official statements. It is of no use to anybody to turn deaf ears to its resounding voice which is being heard day and night, or to overlook its historical reality. Even the United States, your first ally which is absolutely committed to safeguard Israel's security and existence, and which offered and still offers Israel every moral, material and military support— I say—even the United States has opted to face up to reality and facts, and admit that the Palestinian People are entitled to legitimate rights and that the Palestinian problem is the core and essence of the conflict and that, so long as it continues to be unresolved, the conflict will continue to aggravate, reaching new dimensions. In all sincerity, I tell you that there can be no peace without the Palestinians. It is a grave error of unpredictable consequences to overlook or brush aside this cause.

[. . .]

I hail the Israeli voices that called for the recognition of the Palestinian People's rights to achieve and safeguard peace. Here I tell you, ladies and gentlemen, that it is no use to refrain from recognizing the Palestinian People and their rights to statehood and rights of return.

We, the Arabs, have faced this experience before, with you and with the reality of Israeli existence. The struggle took us from war to war, from victims to more victims, until you and we have today reached the edge of a horrifying abyss and a terrifying disaster, unless, together, we seize the opportunity, today, of a durable peace based on justice.

[. . .]

Conceive with me a peace agreement in Geneva that we would herald to a world thirsty for peace, a peace agreement based on the following points:

First: ending the Israeli occupation of the Arab territories occupied in 1967.

Second: achievement of the fundamental rights of the Palestinian People and their right to self-determination, including their right to establish their own state.

Third: the right of all states in the area to live in peace within their boundaries, which will be secure and guaranteed through procedures to be agreed upon, which provide appropriate security to international boundaries, in addition to appropriate international guarantees.

Fourth: commitment of all states in the region to administer the relations among them in accordance with the objectives and principles of the United Nations Charter, particularly the principles concerning the non-resort to force and the solution of differences among them by peaceful means.

Fifth: ending the state of belligerency in the region.

[. . .]

From the Egyptian People who bless this sacred mission of peace, I convey to you the message of peace, the message of the Egyptian People who do not know fanaticism, and whose sons, Muslims, Christians, and Jews, live together in a spirit of cordiality, love and tolerance. . . . To every man, woman and child in Israel, I say: encourage your leadership to struggle for peace. Let all endeavours be channelled towards building a huge edifice for peace, instead of strongholds and hideouts defended by destructive rockets. Introduce to the entire world the image of the new man in this area, so that he might set an example to the man of our age, the man of peace everywhere.

Be the heralds to your sons. Tell them that past wars were the last of wars and the end of sorrows. Tell them that we are in for a new beginning to a new life—the life of love, prosperity, freedom and peace.

You, bewailing mother; you, widowed wife; you, the son who lost a brother or a father; you, all victims of wars—fill the earth and space with recitals of peace. Fill bosoms and hearts with the aspirations of peace. Turn the song into a reality that blossoms and lives. Make hope a code of conduct and endeavour. The will of peoples is part of the will of God . . .

I repeat with Zechariah, "Love right and justice."

I quote the following verses from the holy Koran:

"We believe in God and in what has been revealed to us and what was revealed to Abraham, Ismail, Isaac, Jacob, and the tribes and in the books given to Moses, Jesus, and the prophets from their lord. We make no distinction between one and another among them and to God we submit."

35 Six-Point Program of the Palestine Liberation Organization (December 4, 1977)

We, all factions of the PLO, announce the following:

FIRST: We call for the formation of a "Steadfastness and Confrontation Front" composed of Libya, Algeria, Iraq, Democratic Yemen, Syria and the PLO, to oppose all confrontationist solutions planned by imperialism, Zionism and their Arab tools.

SECOND: We fully condemn any Arab party in the Tripoli Summit which rejects the formation of this Front, and we announce this.

THIRD: We reaffirm our rejection of Security Council resolutions 242 and 338.

FOURTH: We reaffirm our rejection of all international conferences based on these two resolutions, including the Geneva Conference.

FIFTH: To strive for the realization of the Palestinian people's rights to return and self-determination within the context of an independent Palestinian national state on any part of Palestinian land, without reconciliation, recognition or negotiations, as an interim aim of the Palestinian Revolution.

SIXTH: To apply the measures related to the political boycott of the Sadat regime.

[. . .]

The conference pledges to the Arab nation that it will continue the march of struggle, steadfastness, combat and adherence to the objectives of the Arab struggle. The conference also expresses its deep faith and absolute confidence that the Arab nation, which has staged revolutions, overcome difficulties and defeated plots during its long history of struggle—a struggle which abounds with heroism is today capable of replying with force to those who have harmed its dignity, squandered its rights, split its solidarity and departed from the principles of its struggle. It is confident of its own capabilities in liberation, progress and victory, thanks to God.

The conference records with satisfaction the national Palestinian unity within the framework of the PLO.

36 The Camp David Accords (September 17, 1978)

The Framework for Peace in the Middle East

Preamble

The search for peace in the Middle East must be guided by the following:

- The agreed basis for a peaceful settlement of the conflict between Israel and its neighbors is United Nations Security Council Resolution 242, in all its parts.
- After four wars during 30 years, despite intensive human efforts, the Middle East, which is the cradle of civilization and the birthplace of three great religions, does not enjoy the blessings of peace. . . .
- The historic initiative of President Sadat in visiting Jerusalem and the reception accorded to him by the parliament, government and people of Israel, and the reciprocal visit of Prime Minister Begin to Ismailia, the peace proposals made by both leaders, as well as the warm reception of these missions by the peoples of both countries, have created an unprecedented opportunity for peace which must not be lost if this generation and future generations are to be spared the tragedies of war.
- The provisions of the Charter of the United Nations and the other accepted norms of international law and legitimacy now provide accepted standards for the conduct of relations among all states.
- To achieve a relationship of peace, in the spirit of Article 2 of the United Nations Charter, future negotiations between Israel and any neighbor prepared to negotiate peace and security with it are necessary for the purpose of carrying out all the provisions and principles of Resolutions 242 and 338.
- Peace requires respect for the sovereignty, territorial integrity and political independence of every state in the area and their right to live in peace within secure and recognized boundaries free from threats or acts of force.
- Security is enhanced by a relationship of peace and by cooperation between nations which enjoy normal relations. . . .

Framework

Taking these factors into account, the parties are determined to reach a just, comprehensive, and durable settlement of the Middle East conflict through the conclusion of peace treaties based on Security Council resolutions 242 and 338 in all their parts. Their purpose is to achieve peace and good neighborly relations. They recognize that for peace to endure, it must involve all those who have been most deeply affected by the conflict. They therefore agree that this framework, as appropriate, is intended by them to constitute a basis for peace not only between Egypt and Israel, but also between Israel and each of its other neighbors which is prepared to negotiate peace with Israel on this basis. With that objective in mind, they have agreed to proceed as follows:

A. **West Bank and Gaza**
   1. Egypt, Israel, Jordan and the representatives of the Palestinian people should participate in negotiations on the resolution of the Palestinian problem in all its aspects. To achieve that objective, negotiations relating to the West Bank and Gaza should proceed in three stages:
      a. Egypt and Israel agree that, in order to ensure a peaceful and orderly transfer of authority, and taking into account the security concerns of all the parties, there should be transitional arrangements for the West Bank and Gaza for a period not exceeding five years. In order to provide full autonomy to the inhabitants, under these arrangements the Israeli military government and its civilian administration will be withdrawn as soon as a self-governing authority has been freely elected by the inhabitants of these areas to replace the existing military government. To negotiate the details of a transitional arrangement, Jordan will be invited to join the negotiations on the basis of this framework. These new arrangements should give due consideration both to the principle of self-government by the inhabitants of these territories and to the legitimate security concerns of the parties involved.
      b. Egypt, Israel, and Jordan will agree on the modalities for establishing elected self-governing authority in the West Bank and Gaza. . . . A withdrawal of Israeli armed forces will take place and there will be a redeployment of the remaining Israeli forces into specified security locations. . . . A strong local police force will be established, which may include Jordanian citizens. In addition, Israeli and Jordanian forces will participate in joint patrols and in the manning of control posts to assure the security of the borders.
      c. When the self-governing authority (administrative council) in the West Bank and Gaza is established and inaugurated, the transitional period of five years will begin. As soon as possible, but not later than the third year after the beginning of the transitional period, negotiations will take place to determine the final status of the West Bank and Gaza and its relationship with its neighbors and to conclude a peace treaty between Israel and Jordan by the end of the transitional period. . . . The negotiations shall be based on all the provisions and principles of UN Security Council Resolution 242. The negotiations will resolve, among other matters, the location of the boundaries and the nature of the security arrangements. The solution from the negotiations must also recognize the legitimate right of the Palestinian peoples and their just requirements. In this way, the Palestinians will participate in the determination of their own future through:

      i.   The negotiations among Egypt, Israel, Jordan and the representatives of the inhabitants of the West Bank and Gaza to agree on the final status of the West Bank and Gaza and other outstanding issues by the end of the transitional period.

      ii. Submitting their agreements to a vote by the elected representatives of the inhabitants of the West Bank and Gaza.

      iii. Providing for the elected representatives of the inhabitants of the West Bank and Gaza to decide how they shall govern themselves consistent with the provisions of their agreement.

      iv. Participating as stated above in the work of the committee negotiating the peace treaty between Israel and Jordan.

  d. All necessary measures will be taken and provisions made to assure the security of Israel and its neighbors during the transitional period and beyond. To assist in providing such security, a strong local police force will be constituted by the self-governing authority. . . .

  e. During the transitional period, representatives of Egypt, Israel, Jordan, and the self-governing authority will constitute a continuing committee to decide by agreement on the modalities of admission of persons displaced from the West Bank and Gaza in 1967, together with necessary measures to prevent disruption and disorder. Other matters of common concern may also be dealt with by this committee.

  f. Egypt and Israel will work with each other and with other interested parties to establish agreed procedures for a prompt, just and permanent implementation of the resolution of the refugee problem.

B. Egypt-Israel

1. Egypt-Israel undertake not to resort to the threat or the use of force to settle disputes. Any disputes shall be settled by peaceful means in accordance with the provisions of Article 33 of the U.N. Charter.

2. In order to achieve peace between them, the parties agree to negotiate in good faith with a goal of concluding within three months from the signing of the Framework a peace treaty between them while inviting the other parties to the conflict to proceed simultaneously to negotiate and conclude similar peace treaties with a view the achieving a comprehensive peace in the area. The Framework for the Conclusion of a Peace Treaty between Egypt and Israel will govern the peace negotiations between them. The parties will agree on the modalities and the timetable for the implementation of their obligations under the treaty.

C. Associated Principles

1. Egypt and Israel state that the principles and provisions described below should apply to peace treaties between Israel and each of its neighbors—Egypt, Jordan, Syria and Lebanon.

2. Signatories shall establish among themselves relationships normal to states at peace with one another. To this end, they should undertake to abide by all the provisions of the U.N. Charter. Steps to be taken in this respect include:

a. full recognition;

b. abolishing economic boycotts;

c. guaranteeing that under their jurisdiction the citizens of the other parties shall enjoy the protection of the due process of law.

3. Signatories should explore possibilities for economic development in the context of final peace treaties, with the objective of contributing to the atmosphere of peace, cooperation and friendship which is their common goal.

4. Claims commissions may be established for the mutual settlement of all financial claims.

5. The United States shall be invited to participate in the talks on matters related to the modalities of the implementation of the agreements and working out the timetable for the carrying out of the obligations of the parties.

6. The United Nations Security Council shall be requested to endorse the peace treaties and ensure that their provisions shall not be violated. The permanent members of the Security Council shall be requested to underwrite the peace treaties and ensure respect or the provisions. They shall be requested to conform their policies and actions with the undertaking contained in this Framework.

For the Government of Israel:
Menachem Begin

For the Government of
the Arab Republic of Egypt
Muhammed Anwar al-Sadat

Witnessed by
Jimmy Carter,
President of the United States of America

Framework for the Conclusion of a Peace Treaty between Egypt and Israel
In order to achieve peace between them, Israel and Egypt agree to negotiate in good faith with a goal of concluding within three months of the signing of this framework a peace treaty between them:

It is agreed that:
• The site of the negotiations will be under a United Nations flag at a location or locations to be mutually agreed.
• All of the principles of U.N. Resolution 242 will apply in this resolution of the dispute between Israel and Egypt.
• Unless otherwise mutually agreed, terms of the peace treaty will be implemented between two and three years after the peace treaty is signed.

The following matters are agreed between the parties:
1. the full exercise of Egyptian sovereignty up to the internationally recognized border between Egypt and mandated Palestine;

2. the withdrawal of Israeli armed forces from the Sinai;
3. the use of airfields left by the Israelis near al-Arish, Rafah, Ras en-Naqb, and Sharm el-Sheikh for civilian purposes only, including possible commercial use only by all nations;
4. the right of free passage by ships of Israel through the Gulf of Suez and the Suez Canal on the basis of the Constantinople Convention of 1888 applying to all nations; the Strait of Tiran and Gulf of Aqaba are international waterways to be open to all nations for unimpeded and nonsuspendable freedom of navigation and overflight;
5. the construction of a highway between the Sinai and Jordan near Eilat with guaranteed free and peaceful passage by Egypt and Jordan; and
6. the stationing of military forces listed below.

Stationing of Forces
No more than one division (mechanized or infantry) of Egyptian armed forces will be stationed within an area lying approximately 50 km. (30 miles) east of the Gulf of Suez and the Suez Canal.

[. . .]

The exact demarcation of the above areas will be as decided during the peace negotiations.

Early warning stations may exist to insure compliance with the terms of the agreement.

United Nations forces will be stationed [in areas to be negotiated] . . .

After a peace treaty is signed, and after the interim withdrawal is complete, normal relations will be established between Egypt and Israel, including full recognition, including diplomatic, economic and cultural relations; termination of economic boycotts and barriers to the free movement of goods and people; and mutual protection of citizens by the due process of law.

Interim Withdrawal
Between three months and nine months after the signing of the peace treaty, all Israeli forces will withdraw east of a line extending from a point east of El-Arish to Ras Muhammad, the exact location of this line to be determined by mutual agreement.

For the Government of
the Arab Republic of Egypt:
Muhammed Anwar al-Sadat

For the Government of Israel:
Menachem Begin

Witnessed by:
Jimmy Carter,
President of the United States of America

Part IV

From a Peace Treaty (1979)
to the Nobel Peace Prize (1994)

37 Peace Treaty Between Israel and Egypt (March 26, 1979)

Text:

The Government of the Arab Republic of Egypt and the Government of the State of Israel;

PREAMBLE

Convinced of the urgent necessity of the establishment of a just, comprehensive and lasting peace in the Middle East in accordance with Security Council Resolutions 242 and 338;

Reaffirming their adherence to the "Framework for Peace in the Middle East Agreed at Camp David," dated September 17, 1978;

Noting that the aforementioned Framework as appropriate is intended to constitute a basis for peace not only between Egypt and Israel but also between Israel and each of its other Arab neighbors which is prepared to negotiate peace with it on this basis;

Desiring to bring to an end the state of war between them and to establish a peace in which every state in the area can live in security;

Convinced that the conclusion of a Treaty of Peace between Egypt and Israel is an important step in the search for comprehensive peace in the area and for the attainment of settlement of the Arab-Israeli conflict in all its aspects;

Inviting the other Arab parties to this dispute to join the peace process with Israel guided by and based on the principles of the aforementioned Framework;

Desiring as well to develop friendly relations and cooperation between themselves in accordance with the United Nations Charter and the principles of international law governing international relations in times of peace;

Agree to the following provisions in the free exercise of their sovereignty, in order to implement the "Framework for the Conclusion of a Peace Treaty Between Egypt and Israel";

Article I

1. The state of war between the Parties will be terminated and peace will be established between them upon the exchange of instruments of ratification of this Treaty.
2. Israel will withdraw all its armed forces and civilians from the Sinai behind the international boundary between Egypt and mandated Palestine, as provided in the annexed protocol . . . , and Egypt will resume the exercise of its full sovereignty over the Sinai.
3. Upon completion of the interim withdrawal . . . the parties will establish normal and friendly relations . . .

Article II

The permanent boundary between Egypt and Israel is the recognized international boundary between Egypt and the former mandated territory of Palestine, as shown on the map at Annex II, without prejudice to the issue of the status of the Gaza Strip. The Parties recognize this boundary as inviolable. Each will respect the territorial integrity of the other, including their territorial waters and airspace.

Article III

1. The Parties will apply between them the provisions of the Charter of the United Nations and the principles of international law governing relations among states in times of peace. In particular:
   a. They recognize and will respect each other's sovereignty, territorial integrity and political independence;
   b. They recognize and will respect each other's right to live in peace within their secure and recognized boundaries;
   c. They will refrain from the threat or use of force, directly or indirectly, against each other and will settle all disputes between them by peaceful means.
2. Each Party undertakes to ensure that acts or threats of belligerency, hostility, or violence do not originate from and are not committed from within its territory, or by any forces subject to its control or by any other forces stationed on its territory against the population, citizens or property of the other Party. Each Party also undertakes to refrain from organizing, instigating, inciting, assisting or participating in acts or threats of belligerency, hostility, subversion or violence against the other Party, anywhere, and undertakes to ensure that perpetrators of such acts are brought to justice.
3. The Parties agree that the normal relationship established between them will include full recognition, diplomatic, economic and cultural relations, termination of economic boycotts and discriminatory barriers to the free movement of people and goods, and will guarantee the mutual enjoyment by citizens of the due process of law . . .

Article IV [Stationing of security arrangements] [. . .]

Article V [Israeli shipping through the Strait of Tiran and Gulf of Aqaba] [. . .]

Article VI [Obligations under this agreement] [. . .]

Article VII [Dispute resolution] [. . .]

Article VIII [Claims Commission] [. . .]

Article IX [Treaty effectiveness] [. . .]

Annex I, Protocol Concerning Israeli Withdrawal and Security Agreements . . .

Article I, Concept of Withdrawal

1. Israel will complete withdrawal of all its armed forces and civilians from the Sinai not later than three years from the date of exchange of instruments of ratification of this Treaty.
2. [. . .]
3. The withdrawal from the Sinai will be accomplished in two phases:
   a.   The interim withdrawal behind the line from east of El-Arish to Ras Mohammed as delineated on Map 2 within nine months from the date of exchange of instruments of ratification of this Treaty.
   b.   The final withdrawal from the Sinai behind the international boundary not later than three years from the date of exchange of instruments of ratification of this Treaty.
4. A Joint Commission will be formed immediately after the exchange of instruments of ratification of this Treaty in order to supervise and coordinate movements and schedules during the withdrawal, and to adjust plans and timetables as necessary within the limits established by paragraph 3, above . . .

Article II, Determination of Final Lines and Zones [. . .]

Article III, Aerial Military Regime

1. Flights of combat aircraft and reconnaissance flights of Egypt and Israel shall take place only over [specific negotiated areas], respectively.
2. Only unarmed, non-combat aircraft of Egypt and Israel will be stationed in [specific negotiated areas], respectively.
3. Only Egyptian unarmed transport aircraft will take off and land in Zone B and up to eight such aircraft may be maintained in Zone B. The Egyptian border unit . . . may be equipped with unarmed helicopters to perform their functions in Zone B.

4. The Egyptian civil police may be equipped with unarmed police helicopters to perform normal police functions in Zone C.
5. Only civilian airfields maybe built in the Zones.
6. Without prejudice to the provisions of this Treaty, only those military aerial activities specifically permitted by this Annex shall be allowed in the Zones and the airspace above their territorial waters.

Article IV, Naval Regime

1. Egypt and Israel may base and operate naval vessels along the coasts of Zones A and D, respectively.
2. Egyptian coast guard boats, lightly armed, may be stationed and operate in the territorial waters of Zone B to assist the border units in performing their functions in this Zone.
3. Egyptian civil police equipped with light boats, lightly armed, shall perform normal police functions within the territorial waters of Zone C.
4. Nothing in this Annex shall be considered as derogating from the right of innocent passage of the naval vessels of either party.
5. Only civilian maritime ports and installations may be built in the Zones.
6. Without prejudice to the provisions of this Treaty, only those naval activities specifically permitted by this Annex shall be allowed in the Zones and in their territorial waters.

Article V, Early Warning Systems

Egypt and Israel may establish and operate early warning systems only in Zones A and D respectively.

Article VI, United Nations Operations

1. The Parties will request the United Nations to provide forces and observers to supervise the implementation of this Annex and employ their best efforts to prevent any violation of its terms.
2. With respect to these United Nations forces and observers, as appropriate, . . .
3. The arrangements described in this article for each zone will be implemented in Zones A, B, and C by the United Nations Force and in Zone D by the United Nations Observers.
4. United Nations verification teams shall be accompanied by liaison officers of the respective Party.
5. The United Nations Force and observers will report their findings to both Parties.
6. The United Nations Force and Observers operating in the Zones will enjoy freedom of movement and other facilities necessary for the performance of their tasks.
7. The United Nations Force and Observers are not empowered to authorize the crossing of the international boundary.
8. The Parties shall agree on the nations from which the United Nations Force and Observers will be drawn. They will be drawn from nations other than those which are permanent members of the United Nations Security Council.

9. The Parties agree that the United Nations should make those command arrangements that will best assure the effective implementation of its responsibilities.

Article VII, Liaison System

1. Upon dissolution of the Joint Commission, a liaison system between the Parties will be established. This liaison system is intended to provide an effective method to assess progress in the implementation of obligations under the present Annex and to resolve any problem that may arise in the course of implementation, . . .

Article VIII, Respect for War Memorials

Each Party undertakes to preserve in good condition the War Memorials erected in the memory of soldiers of the other Party, namely those erected by Egypt in Israel, and shall permit access to such monuments.

Article IX, Interim Arrangements [. . .]

Appendix to Annex I, Organization of Movements in the Sinai [. . .]

Article I, Principles of Withdrawal [. . .]

Article II, Subphases of the Withdrawal to the Interim Withdrawal Line [. . .]

Article III, United Nations Forces [. . .]

Article IV, Joint Commission and Liaison [. . .]

Article V, Definition of the Interim Buffer Zone and Its Activities [. . .]

Article VI, Disposition of Installations and Military Barriers [. . .]

Article VII, Surveillance Activities [. . .]

Article VIII, Exercise of Egyptian Sovereignty

Egypt will resume the exercise of its full sovereignty over evacuated parts of the Sinai upon Israeli withdrawal as provided for in Article I of this Treaty.

ANNEX II, Map of Israel-Egypt International Boundary [. . .]

ANNEX III, Protocol Concerning Relations of the Parties

Article 1, Diplomatic and Consular Relations

The Parties agree to establish diplomatic and consular relations and to exchange ambassadors upon completion of the interim withdrawal.

Article 2, Economic and Trade Relations

1. The Parties agree to remove all discriminatory barriers to normal economic relations and to terminate economic boycotts of each other upon completion of the interim withdrawal.
2. As soon as possible, and not later than six months after the completion of the interim withdrawal, the Parties will enter negotiations with a view to concluding an agreement on trade and commerce for the purpose of promoting beneficial economic relations.

Article 3, Cultural Relations

1. The Parties agree to establish normal cultural relations following completion of the interim withdrawal.
2. They agree on the desirability of cultural exchanges in all fields, and shall, as soon as possible and not later than six months after completion of the interim withdrawal, enter into negotiations with a view to concluding a cultural agreement for this purpose.

Article 4, Freedom of Movement

1. Upon completion of the interim withdrawal, each Party will permit the free movement of the nationals and vehicles of the other into and within its territory according to the general rules applicable to nationals and vehicles of other states. Neither Party will impose discriminatory restrictions on the free movement of persons and vehicles from its territory to the territory of the other.
2. Mutual unimpeded access to places of religious and historical significance will be provided on a non-discriminatory basis.

Article 5, Cooperation for Development and Good Neighborly Relations

1. The Parties recognize a mutuality of interest in good neighbourly relations and agree to consider means to promote such relations.
2. The Parties will cooperate in promoting peace, stability and development in their region. Each agrees to consider proposals the other may wish to make to this end.
3. The Parties shall seek to foster mutual understanding and tolerance and will, accordingly, abstain from hostile propaganda against each other.

Article 6, Transportation and Telecommunications [. . .]

Article 7, Enjoyment of Human Rights

The Parties affirm their commitment to respect and observe human rights and fundamental freedoms for all, and they will promote these rights and freedoms in accordance with the United Nations Charter.

Article 8, Territorial Seas

Without prejudice to the provisions of Article 5 of the Treaty of Peace each Party recognizes the right of the vessels of the other Party to innocent passage through its territorial sea in accordance with the rules of international law.

AGREED MINUTES

Article I

Egypt's resumption of the exercise of full sovereignty over the Sinai provided for in paragraph 2 of Article I shall occur with regard to each area upon Israel's withdrawal from the area. . . .

Article VI (5)

It is agreed by the Parties that there is no assertion that this Treaty prevails over other Treaties or agreements or that other Treaties or agreements prevail over this Treaty . . .

*For the Government
of Israel*

*For the Government of the
Arab Republic of Egypt*

*Witnessed by:
Jimmy Carter
President of the United States of America*

38 Basic Law: Jerusalem, Capital of Israel (July, 1980)

1. Jerusalem, complete and united, is the capital of Israel.

2. Jerusalem is the seat of the President of the State, the Knesset, the Government and the Supreme Court.

3. The Holy Places shall be protected from desecration and any other violation and from anything likely to violate the freedom of access of the members of the different religions to the places sacred to them or their feelings towards those places.

4. (a) The Government shall provide for the development and prosperity of Jerusalem and the well-being of its inhabitants by allocating special funds, including a special annual grant to the Municipality of Jerusalem (Capital City Grant) with the approval of the Finance Committee of the Knesset.

   (b) Jerusalem shall be given special priority in the activities of the authorities of the State so as to further its development in economic and other matters.

   (c) The Government shall set up a special body or special bodies for the implementation of this section.

MENAHEM BEGIN
Prime Minister

YITZCHAK NAVON
President of the State

* Passed by the Knesset on the 17th Av, 5740 (30th July, 1980) and published in Sefer Ha-Chukkim No. 980 of the 23rd Av, 5740 (5th August, 1980), p. 186; the Bill and an Explanatory Note were published in Hatza'ot Chok No. 1464 of 5740, p. 287.

39 Saudi Crown Prince Fahd ibn Abd al-Aziz: The Fahd Plan (August 7, 1981)

[Hebrew Translation]

The Fahd Plan consists of eight points calling for:

1. Israeli withdrawal from all Arab territories taken in the Six Day War, including Arab (East) Jerusalem.

2. The dismantling of Israeli settlements in the territories captured in 1967.

3. The assurance of the freedom of worship for all religions in the holy sites.

4. The emphasis of the rights of the Palestinian nation, including compensation for those who do not wish to return.

5. A brief transition period for Gaza and the West Bank under the auspices of the United Nations.

6. The establishment of an independent Palestinian state with Jerusalem as its capital.

7. The right for all nations in the area to live in peace.

8. The U.N. or some of its members to guarantee the implementation of the above-mentioned principles.

40 Golan Heights Law (December 14, 1981)

[Text:]

1. The Law, jurisdiction and administration of the state shall apply to the Golan Heights. . . .
2. This Law shall become valid on the day of its passage in the Knesset.
3. The Minister of the Interior shall be charged with the implementation of this Law, and he is entitled, in consultation with the Minister of Justice, to enact regulations for its implementation and to formulate in regulations transitional provisions concerning the continued application of regulations, orders, administrative orders, rights and duties which were in force on the Golan Heights prior to the application of this Law.

41 Prime Minister Menachem Begin: The Wars of No Alternative and Operation Peace for the Galilee (August 8, 1982)

Address by Prime Minister Begin at the National Defense College, 8 August 1982.
[...]

Operation Peace for Galilee is not a military operation resulting from the lack of an alternative. The terrorists did not threaten the existence of the State of Israel; they "only" threatened the lives of Israel's citizens and members of the Jewish people. There are those who find fault with the second part of that sentence. If there was no danger to the existence of the state, why did you go to war?

I will explain why. We had three wars which we fought without alternative. The first was the War of Independence, which began on November 30, 1947, and lasted until January 1949. It is worthwhile remembering these dates, because there are also those who try to deceive concerning the nine weeks which have already passed since the beginning of Operation Peace for Galilee. This was a war without alternative, after the Arab armies invaded Eretz Israel. If not for our ability, none of us would have remained alive.

What happened in that war, which we went off to fight with no alternative?

Six thousand of our fighters were killed. We were then 650,000 Jews in Eretz Israel, and the number of fallen amounted to about 1 percent of the Jewish population. [...]

We carried on our lives then by a miracle, with a clear recognition of life's imperative: to win, to establish a state, a government, a parliament, a democracy, an army—a force to defend Israel and the entire Jewish people.

The second war of no alternative was the Yom Kippur War and the War of Attrition that preceded it. What was the situation on that Yom Kippur day [October 6, 1973]? We had 177 tanks deployed on the Golan Heights against 1,400 Soviet Syrian tanks; and fewer than 500 of our soldiers manned positions along the Suez Canal against five divisions sent to the front by the Egyptians.

Is it any wonder that the first days of that war were hard to bear? I remember Aluf Avraham Yaffe came to us, to the Knesset Foreign Affairs and Defence Committee, and said: "Oy, it's so hard! Our boys, 18- and 19-year-olds, are falling like flies and are defending our nation with their very bodies."

In the Golan Heights there was a moment when the O/C Northern Command—today our chief of staff—heard his deputy say, "This is it." What that meant was "We've lost; we have to come down off the Golan Heights." And the then OIC said, "Give me another five minutes".

Sometimes five minutes can decide a nation's fate. During those five minutes, several dozen tanks arrived, which changed the entire situation on the Golan Heights.

If this had not happened, if the Syrian enemy had come down from the heights to the valley, he would have reached Haifa—for there was not a single tank to obstruct his armoured column's route to Haifa. Yes, we would even have fought with knives—as one of our esteemed wives has said—with knives against tanks. Many more would have fallen, and in every settlement there would have been the kind of slaughter at which the Syrians are experts.

[. . .]

Our total casualties in that war of no alternative were 2,297 killed, 6,067 wounded. Together with the War of Attrition—which was also a war of no alternative—2,659 killed, 7,251 wounded. The terrible total: almost 10,000 casualties.

Our other wars were not without an alternative. In November 1956 we had a choice. The reason for going to war then was the need to destroy the fedayeen, who did not represent a danger to the existence of the state.

However, the political leadership of the time thought it was necessary to do this. As one who served in the parliamentary opposition, I was summoned to David Ben-Gurion before the cabinet received information of the plan, and he found it necessary to give my colleagues and myself these details: We are going to meet the enemy before it absorbs the Soviet weapons which began to flow to it from Czechoslovakia in 1955.

[. . .]

In June 1967 we again had a choice. The Egyptian army concentrations in the Sinai approaches do not prove that Nasser was really about to attack us. We must be honest with ourselves. We decided to attack him.

This was a war of self-defence in the noblest sense of the term. The government of national unity then established decided unanimously: We will take the initiative and attack the enemy, drive him back, and thus assure the security of Israel and the future of the nation.

We did not do this for lack of an alternative. We could have gone on waiting. We could have sent the army home. Who knows if there would have been an attack against us? There is no proof of it. There are several arguments to the contrary. While it is indeed true that the closing of the Straits of Tiran was an act of aggression, a *causus belli*, there is always room for a great deal of consideration as to whether it is necessary to make a *causus* into a *bellum*.

And so there were three wars with no alternative—the War of Independence, the War of Attrition and the Yom Kippur War—and it is our misfortunate that our wars have been so. If in the two other wars, the wars of choice—the Sinai Campaign and the Six Day War—we had losses like those in the no alternative wars, we would have been left today with few of our best youth, without the strength to withstand the Arab world.

As for Operation Peace for Galilee, it does not really belong to the category of wars of no alternative. We could have gone on seeing our civilians injured in Metulla or Kiryat Shmona or Nahariya. We could have gone on counting those killed by explosive charges left in a Jerusalem supermarket, or a Petah Tikva bus stop.

All the orders to carry out these acts of murder and sabotage came from Beirut. Should we have reconciled ourselves to the ceaseless killing of civilians, even after the agreement ending hostilities reached last summer, which the terrorists interpreted as an agreement permitting them to strike at us from every side, besides southern Lebanon? They tried to infiltrate gangs of murderers via Syria and Jordan, and by a miracle we captured them. We might also not have captured them. There was a gang of four terrorists which infiltrated from Jordan, whose members admitted they had been about to commandeer a bus (and we remember the bus on the coastal road).

And in the Diaspora? Even Philip Habib interpreted the agreement ending acts of hostility as giving them freedom to attack targets beyond Israel's borders. We have never accepted this interpretation. Shall we permit Jewish blood to be spilled in the Diaspora? Shall we permit bombs to be planted against Jews in Paris, Rome, Athens or London? Shall we permit our ambassadors to be attacked?

There are slanderers who say that a full year of quiet has passed between us and the terrorists. Nonsense. There was not even one month of quiet. The newspapers and communications media, including *The New York Times* and *The Washington Post*, did not publish even one line about our capturing the gang of murderers that crossed the Jordan in order to commandeer a bus and murder its passengers.

True, such actions were not a threat to the existence of the state. But they did threaten the lives of civilians, whose number we cannot estimate, day after day, week after week, month after month.

During the past nine weeks, we have in effect destroyed the combat potential of 20,000 terrorists. We hold 9,000 in a prison camp. Between 2,000 and 3,000 were killed and between 7,000 and 9,000 have been captured and cut off in Beirut. They have decided to leave there only because they have no possibility of remaining there. They will leave soon. We made a second condition: after the exit of most of the terrorists, an integrated multi-national force will enter. But if the minority refuse to leave, you—the U.S., Italy and France—must promise us in writing that you, together with the Lebanese army, will force them, the terrorists, to leave Beirut and Lebanon. They have the possibility of forcing 2,000–2,500 terrorists who will remain after the majority leaves.

And one more condition: if you aren't willing to force them, then, please, leave Beirut and Lebanon, and the I.D.F. will solve the problem.

This is what I wrote the Secretary of State today, and I want you and all the citizens of Israel and the U.S. to know it.

The problem will be solved. We can already now look beyond the fighting. It will end, as we hope, shortly. And then, as I believe, recognize and logically assume, we will have a protracted period of peace. There is no other country around us that is capable of attacking us.

We have destroyed the best tanks and planes the Syrians had. We have destroyed 24 of their ground-to-air missile batteries. After everything that happened, Syria did not go to war against us, not in Lebanon and not in the Golan Heights.

Jordan cannot attack us. We have learned that Jordan is sending telegrams to the Americans, warning that Israel is about to invade across the Jordan and capture Amman.

For our part, we will not initiate any attack against any Arab country. We have proved that we do not want wars. We made many painful sacrifices for a peace treaty with Egypt. That treaty stood the test of the fighting in Lebanon; in other words, it stood the test.

The demilitarized zone of 150 kilometres in Sinai exists and no Egyptian soldier has been placed there. From the experience of the 1930s, I have to say that if ever the other side violated the agreement about the demilitarized zone, Israel would be obliged to introduce, without delay, a force stronger than that violating the international commitment; not in order to wage war, but to achieve one of two results: restoration of the previous situation, i.e., resumed demilitarization, and the removal of both armies from the demilitarized zone; or attainment of strategic depth, in case the other side has taken the first step towards a war of aggression, as happened in Europe only three years after the abrogation of the demilitarized zone in the Rhineland.

Because the other Arab countries are completely incapable of attacking the State of Israel, there is reason to expect that we are facing a historic period of peace. It is obviously impossible to set a date.

It may well be that "The land shall be still for 40 years." Perhaps less, perhaps more. But from the facts before us, it is clear that, with the end of the fighting in Lebanon, we have ahead of us many years of establishing peace treaties and peaceful relations with the various Arab countries.

The conclusion—both on the basis of the relations between states and on the basis of our national experience—is that there is no divine mandate to go to war only if there is no alternative. There is no moral imperative that a nation must, or is entitled to, fight only when its back is to the sea, or to the abyss. Such a war may avert tragedy, if not a Holocaust, for any nation; but it causes it terrible loss of life.

Quite the opposite. A free, sovereign nation, which hates war and loves peace, and which is concerned about its security, must create the conditions under which war, if there is a need for it, will not be for lack of alternative. The conditions must be such—and their creation depends upon man's reason and his actions—that the price of victory will be few casualties, not many.

42 Agreement Between Israel and Lebanon (May 17, 1983)

AGREEMENT BETWEEN THE GOVERNMENT OF THE STATE OF ISRAEL AND THE GOVERNMENT OF THE REPUBLIC OF LEBANON, 17 May 1983

The Government of the State of Israel and the Government of the Republic of Lebanon:

Bearing in mind the importance of maintaining and strengthening international peace based on freedom, equality, justice, and respect for fundamental human rights;

Reaffirming their faith in the aims and principles of the Charter of the United Nations and recognizing their right and obligation to live in peace with each other as well as with all states, within secure and recognized boundaries;

Having agreed to declare the termination of the state of war between them;

Desiring to ensure lasting security for both their States and to avoid threats and the use of force between them;

Desiring to establish their mutual relations in the manner provided for in this Agreement;

[. . .]

Having agreed to the following provisions:

ARTICLE I

1. The Parties agree and undertake to respect the sovereignty, political independence and territorial integrity of each other. They consider the existing international boundary between Israel and Lebanon inviolable.

2. The Parties confirm that the state of war between Israel and Lebanon has been terminated and no longer exists.

3. Taking into account the provisions of paragraphs 1 and 2, Israel undertakes to withdraw all its armed forces from Lebanon in accordance with the Annex of the present Agreement.

ARTICLE 2

The Parties, being guided by the principles of the Charter of the United Nations and of international law, undertake to settle their disputes by peaceful means in such a manner as to promote international peace and security, and justice.

ARTICLE 3

In order to provide maximum security for Israel and Lebanon, the Parties agree to establish and implement security arrangements, including the creation of a Security Region, as provided for in the Annex of the present Agreement.

ARTICLE 4

1. The territory of each Party will not be used as a base for hostile or terrorist activity against the other Party, its territory, or its people.

2. Each Party will prevent the existence or organization of irregular forces, armed bands, organizations, bases, offices or infrastructure, the aims and purposes of which include incursions or any act of terrorism into the territory of the other Party, or any other activity aimed at threatening or endangering the security of the other Party and safety of its people. . . .

3. Without prejudice to the inherent right of self-defense in accordance with international law, each Party will refrain:

a. from organizing, instigating, assisting, or participating in threats or acts of belligerency, subversion, or incitement or any aggression directed against the other Party, its population or property, both within its territory and originating therefrom, or in the territory of the other Party.

b. from using the territory of the other Party for conducting a military attack against the territory of a third state.

c. from intervening in the internal or external affairs of the other Party . . .

ARTICLE 5

Consistent with the termination of the state of war and within the framework of their constitutional provisions, the Parties will abstain from any form of hostile propaganda against each other.

ARTICLE 6

Each Party will prevent entry into, deployment in, or passage through its territory, its air space and, subject to the right of innocent passage in accordance with international law, its territorial sea, by military forces, armament, or military equipment of any state hostile to the other Party.

ARTICLE 7

Except as provided in the present Agreement, nothing will preclude the deployment on Lebanese territory of international forces requested and accepted by the Government of Lebanon to assist in maintaining its authority. New contributors to such forces shall be selected from among states having diplomatic relations with both Parties to the present Agreement.

ARTICLE 8

1. a. Upon entry into force of the present Agreement, a Joint Liaison Committee will be established by the parties, in which the United States of America will be a participant, and will commence its functions. [. . .]

ARTICLE 9

[. . .] The Parties undertake not to apply existing obligations, enter into any obligations, or adopt laws or regulations in conflict with the present Agreement.

ARTICLE 10

1. The present Agreement shall be ratified by both Parties in conformity with their respective constitutional procedures [. . .]

ARTICLE 11

1. Disputes between the Parties arising out of the interpretation or application of the present Agreement will be settled by negotiation in the Joint Liaison Committee. [. . .]

ARTICLE 12

The present Agreement shall be communicated to the Secretariat of the United Nations for registration in conformity with the provisions of Article 102 of the Charter of the United Nations.

Done at Kiryat Shmona and Khaldeh this seventeenth day of May, 1983, in triplicate in four authentic texts in the Hebrew, Arabic, English, and French languages. In case of any divergence of interpretation, the English and French texts will be equally authoritative.

For the Government of the State of Israel

For the Government of the Republic of Lebanon

Witnessed by:
For the Government of the United States of America

43 Palestine National Council: Declaration of Independence (November 15, 1988)

In the name of God, the Compassionate, the Merciful

Palestine, the land of the three monotheistic faiths, is where the Palestinian Arab people was born, on which it grew, developed and excelled. The Palestinian people was never separated from or diminished in its integral bonds with Palestine. Thus the Palestinian Arab people ensured for itself an everlasting union between itself, its land, and its history.

Resolute throughout that history, the Palestinian Arab people forged its national identity, rising even to unimagined levels in its defense, as invasion, the design of others, and the appeal special to Palestine's ancient and luminous place on the eminence where powers and civilizations are joined. All this intervened thereby to deprive the people of its political independence. Yet the undying connection between Palestine and its people secured for the land its character, and for the people its national genius.

Nourished by an unfolding series of civilizations and cultures, inspired by a heritage rich in variety and kind, the Palestinian Arab people added to its stature by consolidating a union between itself and its patrimonial Land. The call went out from Temple, Church, and Mosque that to praise the Creator, to celebrate compassion and peace was indeed the message of Palestine. And in generation after generation, the Palestinian Arab people gave of itself unsparingly in the valiant battle for liberation and homeland. For what has been the unbroken chain of our people's rebellions but the heroic embodiment of our will for national independence. And so the people was sustained in the struggle to stay and to prevail.

When in the course of modern times a new order of values was declared with norms and values fair for all, it was the Palestinian Arab people that had been excluded from the destiny of all other peoples by a hostile array of local and foreign powers. Yet again had unaided justice been revealed as insufficient to drive the world's history along its preferred course.

And it was the Palestinian people, already wounded in its body, that was submitted to yet another type of occupation over which floated that falsehood that "Palestine was a land without people." This notion was foisted upon some in the world, whereas in Article 22 of the Covenant of the League of Nations (1919) and in the Treaty of Lausanne (1923), the community of nations had recognized that all the Arab territories, including Palestine, of the formerly Ottoman provinces, were to have granted to them their freedom as provisionally independent nations.

Despite the historical injustice inflicted on the Palestinian Arab people resulting in their dispersion and depriving them of their right to self-determination, following upon U.N. General Assembly Resolution 181 (1947), which partitioned Palestine into two states, one Arab, one Jewish, yet it is this Resolution that still provides those conditions of international legitimacy that ensure the right of the Palestinian Arab people to sovereignty.

By stages, the occupation of Palestine and parts of other Arab territories by Israeli forces, the willed dispossession and expulsion from their ancestral homes of the majority of Palestine's civilian inhabitants, was achieved by organized terror; those Palestinians who remained, as a vestige subjugated in its homeland, were persecuted and forced to endure the destruction of their national life.

Thus were principles of international legitimacy violated. Thus were the Charter of the United Nations and its Resolutions disfigured, for they had recognized the Palestinian Arab people's national rights, including the right of Return, the right to independence, the right to sovereignty over territory and homeland.

In Palestine and on its perimeters, in exile distant and near, the Palestinian Arab people never faltered and never abandoned its conviction in its rights of Return and independence. Occupation, massacres and dispersion achieved no gain in the unabated Palestinian consciousness of self and political identity, as Palestinians went forward with their destiny, undeterred and unbowed. And from out of the long years of trial in ever-mounting struggle, the Palestinian political identity emerged further consolidated and confirmed. And the collective Palestinian national will forged for itself a political embodiment, the Palestine Liberation Organization, its sole, legitimate representative recognized by the world community as a whole, as well as by related regional and international institutions. Standing on the very rock of conviction in the Palestinian people's inalienable rights, and on the ground of Arab national consensus and of international legitimacy, the PLO led the campaigns of its great people, molded into unity and powerful resolve, one and indivisible in its triumphs, even as it suffered massacres and confinement within and without its home. And so Palestinian resistance was clarified and raised into the forefront of Arab and world awareness, as the struggle of the Palestinian Arab people achieved unique prominence among the world's liberation movements in the modern era.

The massive national uprising, the intifada, now intensifying in cumulative scope and power on occupied Palestinian territories, as well as the unflinching resistance of the refugee camps outside the homeland, have elevated awareness of the Palestinian truth and right into still higher realms of comprehension and actuality. Now at last the curtain has been dropped around a whole epoch of prevarication and negation. The intifada has set siege to the mind of official Israel, which has for too long relied exclusively upon myth and terror to deny Palestinian existence altogether. Because of the intifada and its revolutionary irreversible impulse, the history of Palestine has therefore arrived at a decisive juncture.

Whereas the Palestinian people reaffirms most definitively its inalienable rights in the land of its patrimony:

Now by virtue of natural, historical and legal rights, and the sacrifices of successive generations who gave of themselves in defense of the freedom and independence of their homeland;

In pursuance of Resolutions adopted by Arab Summit Conferences and relying on the authority bestowed by international legitimacy as embodied in the Resolutions of the United Nations Organization since 1947;

And in exercise by the Palestinian Arab people of its rights to self-determination, political independence and sovereignty over its territory,

The Palestine National Council, in the name of God, and in the name of the Palestinian Arab people, hereby proclaims the establishment of the State of Palestine on our Palestinian territory with its capital Jerusalem (Al-Quds Ash-Sharif).

The State of Palestine is the state of Palestinians wherever they may be. The state is for them to enjoy in it their collective national and cultural identity, theirs to pursue in it a complete equality of rights. In it will be safeguarded their political and religious convictions and their human dignity by means of a parliamentary democratic system of governance, itself based on freedom of expression and the freedom to form parties. The rights of minorities will duly be respected by the majority, as minorities must abide by decisions of the majority. Governance will be based on principles of social justice, equality and non-discrimination in public rights of men or women, on grounds of race, religion, color or sex, and the aegis of a constitution which ensures the rule of law and an independent judiciary. Thus shall these principles allow no departure from Palestine's age-old spiritual and civilizational heritage of tolerance and religious coexistence.

The State of Palestine is an Arab state, an integral and indivisible part of the Arab nation, at one with that nation in heritage and civilization, with it also in its aspiration for liberation, progress, democracy and unity. The State of Palestine affirms its obligation to abide by the Charter of the League of Arab States, whereby the coordination of the Arab states with each other shall be strengthened. It calls upon Arab compatriots to consolidate and enhance the emergence in reality of our state, to mobilize potential, and to intensify efforts whose goal is to end Israeli occupation.

The State of Palestine proclaims its commitment to the principles and purposes of the United Nations, and to the Universal Declaration of Human Rights. It proclaims its commitment as well to the principles and policies of the Non-Aligned Movement.

It further announces itself to be a peace-loving State, in adherence to the principles of peaceful co-existence. It will join with all states and peoples in order to assure a permanent peace based upon justice and the respect of rights so that humanity's potential for well-being may be assured, an earnest competition for excellence may be maintained, and in which confidence in the future will eliminate fear for those who are just and for whom justice is the only recourse.

In the context of its struggle for peace in the land of Love and Peace, the State of Palestine calls upon the United Nations to bear special responsibility for the

Palestinian Arab people and its homeland. It calls upon all peace- and freedom-loving peoples and states to assist it in the attainment of its objectives, to provide it with security, to alleviate the tragedy of its people, and to help it terminate Israel's occupation of the Palestinian territories.

The State of Palestine herewith declares that it believes in the settlement of regional and international disputes by peaceful means, in accordance with the U.N. Charter and resolutions. With prejudice to its natural right to defend its territorial integrity and independence, it therefore rejects the threat or use of force, violence and terrorism against its territorial integrity or political independence, as it also rejects their use against territorial integrity of other states.

Therefore, on this day unlike all others, November 15, 1988, as we stand at the threshold of a new dawn, in all honor and modesty we humbly bow to the sacred spirits of our fallen ones, Palestinian and Arab, by the purity of whose sacrifice for the homeland our sky has been illuminated and our Land given life. Our hearts are lifted up and irradiated by the light emanating from the much blessed intifada, from those who have endured and have fought the fight of the camps, of dispersion, of exile, from those who have borne the standard for freedom, our children, our aged, our youth, our prisoners, detainees and wounded, all those ties to our sacred soil are confirmed in camp, village, and town. We render special tribute to that brave Palestinian Woman, guardian of sustenance and Life, keeper of our people's perennial flame. To the souls of our sainted martyrs, the whole of our Palestinian Arab people that our struggle shall be continued until the occupation ends, and the foundation of our sovereignty and independence shall be fortified accordingly.

Therefore, we call upon our great people to rally to the banner of Palestine, to cherish and defend it, so that it may forever be the symbol of our freedom and dignity in that homeland, which is a homeland for the free, now and always.

In the name of God, the Compassionate, the Merciful:

"Say: 'O God, Master of the Kingdom,
Thou givest the Kingdom to whom Thou wilt,
and seizes the Kingdom from whom Thou wilt,
Thou exalted whom Thou wilt, and Thou
abasest whom Thou wilt; in Thy hand
is the good; Thou are powerful over everything.'"

44 Israel's Peace Initiative (May 14, 1989)

TEXT:

GENERAL:

1. This document presents the principles of a political initiative of the Government of Israel which deals with the continuation of the peace process; the termination of the state of war with the Arab states; a solution for the Arabs of Judea, Samaria and the Gaza district; peace with Jordan; and a resolution of the problem of the residents of the refugee camps in Judea, Samaria and the Gaza district.

2. The document includes:
   a. The principles upon which the initiative is based.
   b. Details of the processes for its implementation.
   c. Reference to the subject of the elections under consideration. Further details relating to the elections as well as other subjects of the initiative will be dealt with separately.

BASIC PREMISES:

3. The initiative is founded upon the assumption that there is a national consensus for it on the basis of the basic guidelines of the Government of Israel, including the following points:
   a. Israel yearns for peace and the continuation of the political process by means of direct negotiations based on the principles of the Camp David Accords.
   b. Israel opposes the establishment of an additional Palestinian state in the Gaza district and in the area between Israel and Jordan.
   c. Israel will not conduct negotiations with the PLO.
   d. There will be no change in the status of Judea, Samaria and Gaza other than in accordance with the basic guidelines of the Government.

SUBJECTS TO BE DEALT WITH IN THE PEACE PROCESS:

4. a. Israel views as important that the peace between Israel and Egypt, based on the Camp David Accords, will serve as a cornerstone for enlarging the circle

of peace in the region, and calls for a common endeavor for the strengthening of the peace and its extension, through continued consultation.

b. Israel calls for the establishment of peaceful relations between it and those Arab states which still maintain a state of war with it for the purpose of promoting a comprehensive settlement for the Arab-Israel conflict, including recognition, direct negotiation, ending the boycott, diplomatic relations, cessation of hostile activity in international institutions or forums and regional and bilateral cooperation.

c. Israel calls for an international endeavour to resolve the problem of the residents of the Arab refugee camps in Judea. Samaria and the Gaza district in order to improve their living conditions and to rehabilitate them. Israel is prepared to be a partner in this endeavour.

d. In order to advance the political negotiation process leading to peace, Israel proposes free and democratic elections among the Palestinian Arab inhabitants of Judea, Samaria and the Gaza district in an atmosphere devoid of violence, threats and terror.

In these elections a representation will be chosen to conduct negotiations for a transitional period of self-rule. This period will constitute a test for co-existence and cooperation. At a later stage, negotiations will be conducted for a permanent solution during which all the proposed options for an agreed settlement will be examined, and peace between Israel and Jordan will be achieved.

e. All the above-mentioned steps should be dealt with simultaneously.

f. The details of what has been mentioned in (d) above will be given below.

THE PRINCIPLES CONSTITUTING THE INITIATIVE:

STAGES:

5. The initiative is based on two stages:
   a. Stage A—A transitional period for an interim agreement.
   b. Stage B—Permanent Solution.
6. The interlock between the stages is a timetable on which the Plan is built: the peace process delineated by the initiative is based on Resolutions 242 and 338 upon which the Camp David Accords are founded.

TIMETABLE:

7. The transitional period will continue for 5 years.
8. As soon as possible, but not later than the third year after the beginning of the transitional period, negotiations for achieving a permanent solution will begin.

PARTIES PARTICIPATING IN THE NEGOTIATIONS IN BOTH STAGES:

9. The parties participating in the negotiations for the First Stage (the interim agreement) shall include Israel and the elected representation of the Palestinian

Arab inhabitants of Judea, Samaria and the Gaza district. Jordan and Egypt will be invited to participate in these negotiations if they so desire.

10. The parties participating in the negotiations for the Second Stage (Permanent Solution) shall include Israel and the elected representation of the Palestinian Arab inhabitants of Judea, Samaria and the Gaza district, as well as Jordan; furthermore, Egypt may participate in these negotiations. In negotiations between Israel and Jordan, in which the elected representation of the Palestinian Arab inhabitants of Judea, Samaria and the Gaza district will participate, the peace treaty between Israel and Jordan will be concluded.

SUBSTANCE OF TRANSITIONAL PERIOD

11. During the transitional period the Palestinian Arab inhabitants of Judea, Samaria and the Gaza district will be accorded self-rule by means of which they will, themselves, conduct their affairs of daily life. Israel will continue to be responsible for security, foreign affairs and all matters concerning Israeli citizens in Judea, Samaria and the Gaza district. Topics involving the implementation of the plan for self-rule will be considered and decided within the framework of the negotiations for an interim agreement.

SUBSTANCE OF PERMANENT SOLUTION

12. In the negotiations for a permanent solution every party shall be entitled to present for discussion all the subjects it may wish to raise.

13. The aim of the negotiations should be:
    a. The achievement of a permanent solution acceptable to the negotiating parties.
    b. The arrangements for peace and borders between Israel and Jordan.

45 U.S. Secretary of State James Baker's Five-Point Plan (October 10, 1989)

1. The United States understands that because Egypt and Israel have been working hard on the peace process; there is agreement that an Israel delegation should conduct a dialogue with a Palestinian delegation in Cairo.

2. The United States understands that Egypt cannot substitute itself for the Palestinians and Egypt will consult with Palestinians on all aspects of that dialogue. Egypt will also consult with Israel and the United States.

3. The United States understands that Israel will attend the dialogue only after a satisfactory list of Palestinians has been worked out.

4. The United States understands that the Government of Israel will come to the dialogue on the basis of the Israeli Government's Initiative. The United States further understands that Palestinians will come to the dialogue prepared to discuss elections and the negotiating process in accordance with Israel's initiative. The United States understands, therefore, that Palestinians would be free to raise issues that relate to their opinions on how to make elections and the negotiating process succeed.

5. In order to facilitate this process, the United States proposes that the Foreign Ministers of Israel, Egypt, and the United States meet in Washington within two weeks.

46 Letter of Invitation to the Madrid Peace Conference (October 30, 1991), jointly issued by the United States and the Soviet Union

TEXT:

After extensive consultations with Arab states, Israel and the Palestinians, the United States and the Soviet Union believe that an historic opportunity exists to advance the prospects for genuine peace throughout the region. The United States and the Soviet Union are prepared to assist the parties to achieve a just, lasting and comprehensive peace settlement, through direct negotiations along two tracks, between Israel and the Arab states, and between Israel and the Palestinians, based on United Nations Security Council Resolutions 242 and 338. The objective of this process is real peace.

Toward that end, the president of the U.S. and the president of the USSR invite you to a peace conference, which their countries will co-sponsor, followed immediately by direct negotiations. The conference will be convened in Madrid on October 30, 1991.

President Bush and President Gorbachev request your acceptance of this invitation no later than 6 P.M. Washington time, October 23, 1991, in order to ensure proper organization and preparation of the conference.

Direct bilateral negotiations will begin four days after the opening of the conference. Those parties who wish to attend multilateral negotiations will convene two weeks after the opening of the conference to organize those negotiations. The co-sponsors believe that those negotiations should focus on region-wide issues of water, refugee issues, environment, economic development, and other subjects of mutual interest.

The co-sponsors will chair the conference which will be held at ministerial level. Governments to be invited include Israel, Syria, Lebanon and Jordan. Palestinians will be invited and attend as part of a joint Jordanian-Palestinian delegation. Egypt will be invited to the conference as a participant. The European Community will be a participant in the conference, alongside the United States and the Soviet Union and will be represented by its presidency. The Gulf Cooperation Council will be invited to send its secretary-general to the conference as an observer, and GCC member states will be invited to participate in organizing the negotiations on multilateral issues. The United Nations will be invited to send an observer, representing the secretary-general.

The conference will have no power to impose solutions on the parties or veto agreements reached by them. It will have no authority to make decisions for the parties and no ability to vote on issues of results. The conference can reconvene only with the consent of all the parties.

With respect to negotiations between Israel and Palestinians who are part of the joint Jordanian-Palestinian delegation, negotiations will be conducted in phases, beginning with talks on interim self-government arrangements. These talks will be conducted with the objective of reaching agreement within one year. Once agreed, the interim self-government arrangements will last for a period of five years; beginning the third year of the period of interim self-government arrangements, negotiations will take place on permanent status. These permanent status negotiations, and the negotiations between Israel and the Arab states, will take place on the basis of Resolutions 242 and 338.

It is understood that the co-sponsors are committed to making this process succeed. It is their intention to convene the conference and negotiations with those parties who agree to attend.

The co-sponsors believe that this process offers the promise of ending decades of confrontation and conflict and the hope of a lasting peace. Thus, the co-sponsors hope that the parties will approach these negotiations in a spirit of good will and mutual respect. In this way, the peace process can begin to break down the mutual suspicions and mistrust that perpetuate the conflict and allow the parties to begin to resolve their differences. Indeed, only through such a process can real peace and reconciliation among the Arab states, Israel and the Palestinians be achieved. And only through this process can the peoples of the Middle East attain the peace and security they richly deserve.

47 Israel-PLO Recognition: Exchange of Letters Between Prime Minister Rabin and Chairman Arafat (September 9, 1993)

1. LETTER FROM YASSER ARAFAT TO PRIME MINISTER RABIN:

September 9, 1993

Yitzhak Rabin
Prime Minister of Israel

Mr. Prime Minister,

The signing of the Declaration of Principles marks a new era in the history of the Middle East. In firm conviction thereof, I would like to confirm the following PLO commitments:

The PLO recognizes the right of the State of Israel to exist in peace and security.

The PLO accepts United Nations Security Council Resolutions 242 and 338.

The PLO commits itself to the Middle East peace process, and to a peaceful resolution of the conflict between the two sides and declares that all outstanding issues relating to permanent status will be resolved through negotiations.

The PLO considers that the signing of the Declaration of Principles constitutes a historic event, inaugurating a new epoch of peaceful coexistence, free from violence and all other acts which endanger peace and stability. Accordingly, the PLO renounces the use of terrorism and other acts of violence and will assume responsibility over all PLO elements and personnel in order to assure their compliance, prevent violations and discipline violators.

In view of the promise of a new era and the signing of the Declaration of Principles and based on Palestinian acceptance of Security Council Resolutions 242 and 338, the PLO affirms that those articles of the Palestinian Covenant which deny Israel's right to exist, and the provisions of the Covenant which are inconsistent with the commitments of this letter are now inoperative and no longer valid. Consequently, the PLO undertakes to submit to the Palestinian National Council for formal approval the necessary changes in regard to the Palestinian Covenant.

Sincerely,

Yasser Arafat
Chairman
The Palestine Liberation Organization

2. LETTER FROM YASSER ARAFAT TO NORWEGIAN FOREIGN MINISTER:

September 9, 1993

His Excellency
Johan Jorgen Holst
Foreign Minister of Norway

Dear Minister Holst,

I would like to confirm to you that, upon the signing of the Declaration of Principles, the PLO encourages and calls upon the Palestinian people in the West Bank and Gaza Strip to take part in the steps leading to the normalization of life, rejecting violence and terrorism, contributing to peace and stability and participating actively in shaping reconstruction, economic development and cooperation.

Sincerely,

Yasser Arafat
Chairman
The Palestine Liberation Organization

3. LETTER FROM PRIME MINISTER RABIN TO YASSER ARAFAT:

September 9, 1993

Yasser Arafat
Chairman

The Palestinian Liberation Organization

Mr. Chairman,

In response to your letter of September 9, 1993, I wish to confirm to you that, in light of the PLO commitments included in your letter, the Government of Israel has decided to recognize the PLO as the representative of the Palestinian people and commence negotiations with the PLO within the Middle East peace process.

Yitzhak Rabin
Prime Minister of Israel

48 Declaration of Principles on Interim Self-Government Arrangements ["Oslo Agreement"] (September 13, 1993)

September 13, 1993

The Government of the State of Israel and the P.L.O. team (in the Jordanian-Palestinian delegation to the Middle East Peace Conference) (the "Palestinian Delegation"), representing the Palestinian people, agree that it is time to put an end to decades of confrontation and conflict, recognize their mutual legitimate and political rights, and strive to live in peaceful coexistence and mutual dignity and security and achieve a just, lasting and comprehensive peace settlement and historic reconciliation through the agreed political process. Accordingly, the, two sides agree to the following principles:

ARTICLE I: AIM OF THE NEGOTIATIONS

The aim of the Israeli-Palestinian negotiations within the current Middle East peace process is, among other things, to establish a Palestinian Interim Self-Government Authority, the elected Council (the "Council"), for the Palestinian people in the West Bank and the Gaza Strip, for a transitional period not exceeding five years, leading to a permanent settlement based on Security Council Resolutions 242 and 338.

It is understood that the interim arrangements are an integral part of the whole peace process and that the negotiations on the permanent status will lead to the implementation of Security Council Resolutions 242 and 338.

ARTICLE II: FRAMEWORK FOR THE INTERIM PERIOD

The agreed framework for the interim period is set forth in this Declaration of Principles.

ARTICLE III: ELECTIONS

1. In order that the Palestinian people in the West Bank and Gaza Strip may govern themselves according to democratic principles, direct, free and general political elections will be held for the Council under agreed supervision and international observation, while the Palestinian police will ensure public order.
2. An agreement will be concluded on the exact mode and conditions of the

elections in accordance with the protocol attached as Annex I, with the goal of holding the elections not later than nine months after the entry into force of this Declaration of Principles. . . .

ARTICLE IV: JURISDICTION

Jurisdiction of the Council will cover West Bank and Gaza Strip territory, except for issues that will be negotiated in the permanent status negotiations. The two sides view the West Bank and the Gaza Strip as a single territorial unit, whose integrity will be preserved during the interim period.

ARTICLE V: TRANSITIONAL PERIOD AND PERMANENT STATUS NEGOTIATIONS

1. The five-year transitional period will begin upon the withdrawal from the Gaza Strip and Jericho area.
2. Permanent status negotiations will commence as soon as possible, but not later than the beginning of the third year of the interim period, between the Government of Israel and the Palestinian people representatives.
3. It is understood that these negotiations shall cover remaining issues, including: Jerusalem, refugees, settlements, security arrangements, borders, relations and cooperation with other neighbors, and other issues of common interest. . . .

ARTICLE VI: PREPARATORY TRANSFER OF POWERS AND RESPONSIBILITIES

1. Upon the entry into force of this Declaration of Principles and the withdrawal from the Gaza Strip and the Jericho area, a transfer of authority from the Israeli military government and its Civil Administration to the authorised Palestinians for this task, as detailed herein, will commence. This transfer of authority will be of a preparatory nature until the inauguration of the Council.
2. Immediately after the entry into force of this Declaration of Principles and the withdrawal from the Gaza Strip and Jericho area, with the view to promoting economic development in the West Bank and Gaza Strip, authority will be transferred to the Palestinians on the following spheres: education and culture, health, social welfare, direct taxation, and tourism. The Palestinian side will commence in building the Palestinian police force, as agreed upon. Pending the inauguration of the Council, the two parties may negotiate the transfer of additional powers and responsibilities, as agreed upon.

ARTICLE VII: INTERIM AGREEMENT

1. The Israeli and Palestinian delegations will negotiate an agreement on the interim period (the "Interim Agreement").
2. The Interim Agreement shall specify, among other things, the structure of the Council, the number of its members, and the transfer of powers and responsi-

bilities from the Israeli military government and its Civil Administration to the Council. The Interim Agreement shall also specify the Council's executive authority, legislative authority in accordance with Article IX below, and the independent Palestinian judicial organs. . . .

ARTICLE VIII: PUBLIC ORDER AND SECURITY

In order to guarantee public order and internal security for the Palestinians of the West Bank and the Gaza Strip, the Council will establish a strong police force, while Israel will continue to carry the responsibility for defending against external threats, as well as the responsibility for overall security of Israelis for the purpose of safeguarding their internal security and public order.

ARTICLE IX: LAWS AND MILITARY ORDERS

1. The Council will be empowered to legislate, in accordance with the Interim Agreement, within all authorities transferred to it.
2. Both parties will review jointly laws and military orders presently in force in remaining spheres.

ARTICLE X: JOINT ISRAELI–PALESTINIAN LIAISON COMMITTEE

In order to provide for a smooth implementation of this Declaration of Principles and any subsequent agreements pertaining to the interim period, upon the entry into force of this Declaration of Principles, a Joint Israeli-Palestinian Liaison Committee will be established in order to deal with issues requiring coordination, other issues of common interest, and disputes.

ARTICLE XI: ISRAELI–PALESTINIAN COOPERATION IN ECONOMIC FIELDS

Recognizing the mutual benefit of cooperation in promoting the development of the West Bank, the Gaza Strip and Israel, upon the entry into force of this Declaration of Principles, an Israeli-Palestinian Economic Cooperation Committee will be established [. . .]

ARTICLE XII: LIAISON AND COOPERATION WITH JORDAN AND EGYPT

The two parties will invite the Governments of Jordan and Egypt to participate in establishing further liaison and cooperation arrangements between the Government of Israel and the Palestinian representatives, on the one hand, and the Governments of Jordan and Egypt, on the other hand, to promote cooperation between them. . . .

ARTICLE XIII: REDEPLOYMENT OF ISRAELI FORCES

1. After the entry into force of this Declaration of Principles, and not later than the eve of elections for the Council, a redeployment of Israeli military forces in the West Bank and the Gaza Strip will take place, . . .
2. In redeploying its military forces, Israel will be guided by the principle that its military forces should be redeployed outside populated areas.
3. Further redeployments to specified locations will be gradually implemented commensurate with the assumption of responsibility for public order and internal security by the Palestinian police force pursuant to Article VIII above.

ARTICLE XIV: ISRAELI WITHDRAWAL FROM THE GAZA STRIP AND JERICHO AREA

Israel will withdraw from the Gaza Strip and Jericho area . . .

ARTICLE XV: RESOLUTION OF DISPUTES

1. Disputes arising out of the application or interpretation of this Declaration of Principles, or any subsequent agreements pertaining to the interim period, shall be resolved by negotiations through the Joint Liaison Committee . . .

ARTICLE XVI: ISRAELI–PALESTINIAN COOPERATION CONCERNING REGIONAL PROGRAMS

Both parties view the multilateral working groups as an appropriate instrument for promoting a "Marshall Plan", the regional programs and other programs, including special programs for the West Bank and Gaza Strip, . . .

ARTICLE XVII: MISCELLANEOUS PROVISIONS

1. This Declaration of Principles will enter into force one month after its signing.
2. All protocols annexed to this Declaration of Principles and Agreed Minutes pertaining thereto shall be regarded as an integral part hereof.

Done at Washington, D.C., this thirteenth day of September, 1993.

For the Government of Israel
For the P.L.O.

Witnessed By:
The United States of America
The Russian Federation

[Annexes attached]

49 Israel–Jordan Common Agenda (September 14, 1993)

Goal:

The achievement of just, lasting and comprehensive peace between the Arab States, the Palestinians and Israel as per the Madrid invitation.

Components of Israel–Jordan Peace Negotiations:

1. Searching for steps to arrive at a state of peace based on Security Council Resolutions 242 and 338 in all their aspects.
2. Security:
   a. Refraining from actions or activities by either side that may adversely affect the security of the other or may prejudge the final outcome of negotiations.
   b. Threats to security resulting from all kinds of terrorism.
      i. Mutual commitment not to threaten each other by any use of force and not to use weapons by one side against the other including conventional and non-conventional mass destruction weapons.
      ii. Mutual commitment, as a matter of priority and as soon as possible, to work towards a Middle East free from weapons of mass destruction, conventional and non-conventional weapons; this goal is to be achieved in the context of a comprehensive, lasting and stable peace characterized by the renunciation of the use of force, reconciliation and openness.
      Note: The above (items i-ii) may be revised in accordance with relevant agreements to be reached in the Multilateral Working Group on Arms Control and Regional Security.
   c. Mutually agreed upon security arrangements and security confidence building measures.
3. Water:
   a. Securing the rightful water shares of the two sides.
   b. Searching for ways to alleviate water shortage.
4. Refugees and Displaced Persons:
   Achieving an agreed just solution to the bilateral aspects of the problem of refugees and displaced persons in accordance with international law.
5. Borders and Territorial Matters:
   Settlement of territorial matters and agreed definitive delimitation and demarcation of the international boundary between Israel and Jordan with reference to

the boundary definition under the Mandate, without prejudice to the status of any territories that came under Israeli Military Government control in 1967. Both parties will respect and comply with the above international boundary.

6. Exploring the potentials of future bilateral cooperation, within a regional context where appropriate, in the following:

   a. Natural Resources:
      • Water, energy and environment
      • Rift Valley development
   b. Human Resources:
      • Demography
      • Labor
      • Health
      • Education
      • Drug Control
   c. Infrastructure:
      • Transportation: land and air
      • Communication
   d. Economic areas including tourism.

7. Phasing the discussion, agreement and implementation of the items above including appropriate mechanisms for negotiations in specific fields.

8. Discussion on matters related to both tracks to be decided upon in common by the two tracks.

It is anticipated that the above endeavor will ultimately, following the attainment of mutually satisfactory solutions to the elements of this agenda, culminate in a peace treaty.

50 Agreement on the Gaza Strip and the Jericho Area (May 4, 1994)

May 4, 1994

The Government of the State of Israel and the Palestine Liberation Organization (hereinafter "the PLO"), the representative of the Palestinian people;

PREAMBLE

WITHIN the framework of the Middle East peace process initiated at Madrid in October 1991;

REAFFIRMING their determination to live in peaceful coexistence, mutual dignity and security, while recognizing their mutual legitimate and political rights;

REAFFIRMING their desire to achieve a just, lasting and comprehensive peace settlement through the agreed political process;

REAFFIRMING their adherence to the mutual recognition and commitments expressed in the letters dated September 9, 1993 , signed by and exchanged between the Prime Minister of Israel and the Chairman of the PLO;

REAFFIRMING their understanding that the interim self-government arrangements, including the arrangements to apply in the Gaza Strip and the Jericho Area contained in this Agreement, are an integral part of the whole peace process and that the negotiations on the permanent status will lead to the implementation of Security Council Resolutions 242 and 338;

DESIROUS of putting into effect the Declaration of Principles on Interim Self-Government Arrangements signed at Washington, D.C. on September 13, 1993, and the Agreed Minutes thereto (hereinafter "the Declaration of Principles"), and in particular the Protocol on withdrawal of Israeli forces from the Gaza Strip and the Jericho Area;

HEREBY AGREE to the following arrangements regarding the Gaza Strip and the Jericho Area:

ARTICLE I: DEFINITIONS

For the purpose of this Agreement:

a. the Gaza Strip and the Jericho Area are delineated on map No. 1 and map No. 2 attached to this Agreement;
b. "the Settlements" means the Gush Katif and Erez settlement areas, as well as the other settlements in the Gaza Strip, as shown on attached map No. 1;
c. "the Military Installation Area" means the Israeli military installation area along the Egyptian border in the Gaza Strip, as shown on map No. 1; and
d. the term "Israelis" shall also include Israeli statutory agencies and corporations registered in Israel.
    [Maps are not included here.]

ARTICLE II: SCHEDULED WITHDRAWAL OF ISRAELI MILITARY FORCES

1. Israel shall implement an accelerated and scheduled withdrawal of Israeli military forces from the Gaza Strip and from the Jericho Area to begin immediately with the signing of this Agreement. Israel shall complete such withdrawal within three weeks from this date.
2. Subject to the arrangements included in the Protocol Concerning Withdrawal of Israeli Military Forces and Security Arrangements . . . , the Israeli withdrawal shall include evacuating all military bases and other fixed installations to be handed over to the Palestinian Police, to be established pursuant to Article IX below (hereinafter "the Palestinian Police"). . . .

ARTICLE III: TRANSFER OF AUTHORITY

1. Israel shall transfer authority as specified in this Agreement from the Israeli military government and its Civil Administration to the Palestinian Authority, hereby established, in accordance with Article V of this Agreement, except for the authority that Israel shall continue to exercise as specified in this Agreement.
2. [. . .]
3. [. . .]
4. Upon the completion of the Israeli withdrawal and the transfer of powers and responsibilities as detailed in paragraphs 1 and 2 above and in Annex II, the Civil Administration in the Gaza Strip and the Jericho Area will be dissolved and the Israeli military government will be withdrawn. The withdrawal of the military government shall not prevent it from continuing to exercise the powers and responsibilities specified in this Agreement.
5. [. . .]
6. [. . .]

ARTICLE IV: STRUCTURE AND COMPOSITION OF THE PALESTINIAN AUTHORITY

1. The Palestinian Authority will consist of one body of 24 members which shall carry out and be responsible for all the legislative and executive powers and responsibilities transferred to it under this Agreement, in accordance with this Article, and shall be responsible for the exercise of judicial functions in accordance with Article VI, subparagraph 1.b. of this Agreement.
2. The Palestinian Authority shall administer the departments transferred to it and may establish, within its jurisdiction, other departments and subordinate administrative units as necessary for the fulfillment of its responsibilities. It shall determine its own internal procedures.
3. [. . .]
4. [. . .]

ARTICLE V: JURISDICTION

1. The authority of the Palestinian Authority encompasses all matters that fall within its territorial, functional and personal jurisdiction . . .
2. The Palestinian Authority has, within its authority, legislative, executive and judicial powers and responsibilities, as provided for in this Agreement.
3. Israel has authority over the Settlements, the Military Installation Area, Israelis, external security, internal security and public order of Settlements, the Military Installation Area and Israelis, and those agreed powers and responsibilities specified in this Agreement. Israel shall exercise its authority through its military government, which, for that end, shall continue to have the necessary legislative, judicial and executive powers and responsibilities, in accordance with international law. This provision shall not derogate from Israel's applicable legislation over Israelis in personam.
4. [. . .]
5. [. . .]
6. [. . .]

ARTICLE VI: POWERS AND RESPONSIBILITIES OF THE PALESTINIAN AUTHORITY

1. Subject to the provisions of this Agreement, the Palestinian Authority, within its jurisdiction:
   a. has legislative powers as set out in Article VII of this Agreement, as well as executive powers;
   b. will administer justice through an independent judiciary;
   c. will have, inter alia, power to formulate policies, supervise their implementation, employ staff, establish departments, authorities and institutions, sue and be sued and conclude contracts; and
   d. will have, inter alia, the power to keep and administer registers and records of the population, and issue certificates, licenses and documents.
   e. In accordance with the Declaration of Principles, the Palestinian Authority will not have powers and responsibilities in the sphere of foreign relations, which

sphere includes the establishment abroad of embassies, consulates or other types of foreign missions and posts or permitting their establishment in the Gaza Strip or the Jericho Area, the appointment of or admission of diplomatic and consular staff, and the exercise of diplomatic functions.

ARTICLE VII: LEGISLATIVE POWERS OF THE PALESTINIAN AUTHORITY [. . .]

ARTICLE VIII: ARRANGEMENTS FOR SECURITY AND PUBLIC ORDER

1. In order to guarantee public order and internal security for the Palestinians of the Gaza Strip and the Jericho Area, the Palestinian Authority shall establish a strong police force . . . Israel shall continue to carry the responsibility for defense against external threats, including the responsibility for protecting the Egyptian border and the Jordanian line, and for defense against external threats from the sea and from the air, as well as the responsibility for overall security of Israelis and Settlements, for the purpose of safeguarding their internal security and public order, and will have all the powers to take the steps necessary to meet this responsibility. . . .

ARTICLE IX: THE PALESTINIAN DIRECTORATE OF POLICE FORCE [. . .]

ARTICLE X: PASSAGES [. . .]

ARTICLE XI: SAFE PASSAGE BETWEEN THE GAZA STRIP AND THE JERICHO AREA [. . .]

ARTICLE XII: RELATIONS BETWEEN ISRAEL AND THE PALESTINIAN AUTHORITY

1. Israel and the Palestinian Authority shall seek to foster mutual understanding and tolerance and shall accordingly abstain from incitement, including hostile propaganda, against each other and, without derogating from the principle of freedom of expression, shall take legal measures to prevent such incitement by any organizations, groups or individuals within their jurisdiction.
2. Without derogating from the other provisions of this Agreement, Israel and the Palestinian Authority shall cooperate in combatting criminal activity which may affect both sides, including offenses related to trafficking in illegal drugs and psychotropic substances, smuggling, and offenses against property, including offenses related to vehicles.

ARTICLE XIII: ECONOMIC RELATIONS [. . .]

ARTICLE XIV: HUMAN RIGHTS AND THE RULE OF LAW [. . .]

ARTICLE XV: THE JOINT ISRAELI-PALESTINIAN LIAISON COMMITTEE [. . .]

ARTICLE XVI: LIAISON AND COOPERATION WITH JORDAN AND EGYPT [. . .]

ARTICLE XVII: SETTLEMENT OF DIFFERENCES AND DISPUTES [. . .]

ARTICLE XVIII: PREVENTION OF HOSTILE ACTS [. . .]

ARTICLE XIX: MISSING PERSONS [. . .]

ARTICLE XX: CONFIDENCE BUILDING MEASURES

With a view to creating a positive and supportive public atmosphere to accompany the implementation of this Agreement, and to establish a solid basis of mutual trust and good faith, both Parties agree to carry out confidence building measures as detailed herewith:

1. Upon the signing of this Agreement, Israel will release, or turn over, to the Palestinian Authority within a period of 5 weeks, about 5,000 Palestinian detainees and prisoners, residents of the West Bank and the Gaza Strip. Those released will be free to return to their homes anywhere in the West Bank or the Gaza Strip. Prisoners turned over to the Palestinian Authority shall be obliged to remain in the Gaza Strip or the Jericho Area for the remainder of their sentence.
2. After the signing of this Agreement, the two Parties shall continue to negotiate the release of additional Palestinian prisoners and detainees, building on agreed principles.
3. The implementation of the above measures will be subject to the fulfillment of the procedures determined by Israeli law for the release and transfer of detainees and prisoners.
4. With the assumption of Palestinian authority, the Palestinian side commits itself to solving the problem of those Palestinians who were in contact with the Israeli authorities. Until an agreed solution is found, the Palestinian side undertakes not to prosecute these Palestinians or to harm them in any way.
5. Palestinians from abroad whose entry into the Gaza Strip and the Jericho Area is approved pursuant to this Agreement, and to whom the provisions of this Article are applicable, will not be prosecuted for offenses committed prior to September 13, 1993.

ARTICLE XXI: TEMPORARY INTERNATIONAL PRESENCE

1. The Parties agree to a temporary international or foreign presence in the Gaza Strip and the Jericho Area (hereinafter "the TIP"), in accordance with the provisions of this Article.

2. The TIP shall consist of 400 qualified personnel, including observers, instructors and other experts, from 5 or 6 of the donor countries.
3. The two Parties shall request the donor countries to establish a special fund to provide finance for the TIP.
4. The TIP will function for a period of 6 months. The TIP may extend this period, or change the scope of its operation, with the agreement of the two Parties.
5. The TIP shall be stationed and operate within the following cities and villages: Gaza, Khan Yunis, Rafah, Deir El Ballah, Jabaliya, Absan, Beit Hanun and Jericho.
6. Israel and the Palestinian Authority shall agree on a special Protocol to implement this Article, with the goal of concluding negotiations with the donor countries contributing personnel within two months.

ARTICLE XXII: RIGHTS, LIABILITIES AND OBLIGATIONS [. . .]

ARTICLE XXIII: FINAL CLAUSES [. . .]

51 The Washington Declaration (July 25, 1994)

A. After generations of hostility, blood and tears and in the wake of years of pain and wars, His Majesty King Hussein and Prime Minister Yitzhak Rabin are determined to bring an end to bloodshed and sorrow. It is in this spirit that His Majesty King Hussein of the Hashemite Kingdom of Jordan and Prime Minister and Minister of Defense, Mr. Yitzhak Rabin of Israel, met in Washington today at the invitation of President William J. Clinton of the United States of America. This initiative of President William J. Clinton constitutes an historic landmark in the United States' untiring efforts in promoting peace and stability in the Middle East. The personal involvement of the President has made it possible to realise agreement on the content of this historic declaration.

The signing of this declaration bears testimony to the President's vision and devotion to the cause of peace.

B. In their meeting, His Majesty King Hussein and Prime Minister Yitzhak Rabin have jointly reaffirmed the five underlying principles of their understanding on an Agreed Common Agenda designed to reach the goal of a just, lasting and comprehensive peace between the Arab States and the Palestinians, with Israel.
   1. Jordan and Israel aim at the achievement of just, lasting and comprehensive peace between Israel and its neighbours and at the conclusion of a Treaty of Peace between both countries.
   2. The two countries will vigorously continue their negotiations to arrive at a state of peace, based on Security Council Resolutions 242 and 338 in all their aspects, and founded on freedom, equality and justice.
   3. Israel respects the present special role of the Hashemite Kingdom of Jordan in Muslim Holy shrines in Jerusalem. When negotiations on the permanent status will take place, Israel will give high priority to the Jordanian historic role in these shrines. In addition the two sides have agreed to act together to promote interfaith relations among the three monotheistic religions.
   4. The two countries recognise their right and obligation to live in peace with each other as well as with all states within secure and recognised boundaries. The two states affirmed their respect for and acknowledgment of the sovereignty, territorial integrity and political independence of every state in the area.

5. The two countries desire to develop good neighbourly relations of cooperation between them to ensure lasting security and to avoid threats and the use of force between them.

C. The long conflict between the two states is now coming to an end. In this spirit the state of belligerency between Jordan and Israel has been terminated.

D. Following this declaration and in keeping with the Agreed Common Agenda, both countries will refrain from actions or activities by either side that may adversely affect the security of the other or may prejudice the final outcome of negotiations. Neither side will threaten the other by use of force, weapons, or any other means, against each other, and both sides will thwart threats to security resulting from all kinds of terrorism.

E. His Majesty King Hussein and Prime Minister Yitzhak Rabin took note of the progress made in the bilateral negotiations within the Jordan-Israel track last week on the steps decided to implement the sub-agendas on borders, territorial matters, security, water, energy, environment and the Jordan Rift Valley.

In this framework, mindful of items of the Agreed Common Agenda (borders and territorial matters) they noted that the boundary sub-commission has reached agreement in July 1994 in fulfillment of part of the role entrusted to it in the sub-agenda. They also noted that the sub-commission for water, environment and energy agreed to mutually recognise, as the role of their negotiations, the rightful allocations of the two sides in Jordan River and Yarmouk River waters and to fully respect and comply with the negotiated rightful allocations, in accordance with agreed acceptable principles with mutually acceptable quality. Similarly, His Majesty King Hussein and Prime Minister Yitzhak Rabin expressed their deep satisfaction and pride in the work of the trilateral commission in its meeting held in Jordan on Wednesday, July 20th 1994, hosted by the Jordanian Prime Minister, Dr. Abdessalam al-Majali, and attended by Secretary of State Warren Christopher and Foreign Minister Shimon Peres. They voiced their pleasure at the association and commitment of the United States in this endeavour.

F. His Majesty King Hussein and Prime Minister Yitzhak Rabin believe that steps must be taken both to overcome psychological barriers and to break with the legacy of war. By working with optimism towards the dividends of peace for all the people in the region, Jordan and Israel are determined to shoulder their responsibilities towards the human dimension of peace making. They recognise imbalances and disparities are a root cause of extremism which thrives on poverty and unemployment and the degradation of human dignity. In this spirit His Majesty King Hussein and Prime Minister Yitzhak Rabin have today approved a series of steps to symbolise the new era which is now at hand:

1. Direct telephone links will be opened between Jordan and Israel.
2. The electricity grids of Jordan and Israel will be linked as part of a regional concept.
3. Two new border crossings will be opened between Jordan and Israel—one at the southern tip of Aqaba-Eilat and the other at a mutually agreed point in the north.
4. In principle free access will be given to third country tourists traveling between Jordan and Israel.

5. Negotiations will be accelerated on opening an international air corridor between both countries.

6. The police forces of Jordan and Israel will cooperate in combating crime with emphasis on smuggling and particularly drug smuggling. The United States will be invited to participate in this joint endeavour.

7. Negotiations on economic matters will continue in order to prepare for future bilateral cooperation including the abolition of all economic boycotts.

All these steps are being implemented within the framework of regional infrastructural development plans and in conjunction with the Jordan-Israel bilaterals on boundaries, security, water and related issues and without prejudice to the final outcome of the negotiations on the items included in the Agreed Common Agenda between Jordan and Israel.

G. His Majesty King Hussein and Prime Minister Yitzhak Rabin have agreed to meet periodically or whenever they feel necessary to review the progress of the negotiations and express their firm intention to shepherd and direct the process in its entirety.

H. In conclusion, His Majesty King Hussein and Prime Minister Yitzhak Rabin wish to express once again their profound thanks and appreciation to President William J. Clinton and his Administration for their untiring efforts in furthering the cause of peace, justice and prosperity for all the peoples of the region. They wish to thank the President personally for his warm welcome and hospitality. In recognition of their appreciation to the President, His Majesty King Hussein and Prime Minister Yitzhak Rabin have asked President William J. Clinton to sign this document as a witness and as a host to their meeting.

His Majesty King Hussein
Prime Minister Yitzhak Rabin
President William J. Clinton

52 Treaty of Peace Between the Hashemite Kingdom of Jordan and the State of Israel (October 26, 1994)

PREAMBLE

The Government of the State of Israel and the Government of the Hashemite Kingdom of Jordan:

Bearing in mind the *Washington Declaration*, signed by them on 25th July, 1994, and which they are both committed to honour;

Aiming at the achievement of a just, lasting and comprehensive peace in the Middle East based on Security Council resolutions 242 and 338 in all their aspects;

Bearing in mind the importance of maintaining and strengthening peace based on freedom, equality, justice and respect for fundamental human rights, thereby overcoming psychological barriers and promoting human dignity;

Reaffirming their faith in the purposes and principles of the Charter of the United Nations and recognising their right and obligation to live in peace with each other as well as with all states, within secure and recognised boundaries;

Desiring to develop friendly relations and co-operation between them in accordance with the principles of international law governing international relations in time of peace;

Desiring as well to ensure lasting security for both their States and in particular to avoid threats and the use of force between them;

Bearing in mind that in their Washington Declaration of 25th July, 1994, they declared the termination of the state of belligerency between them;

Deciding to establish peace between them in accordance with this Treaty of Peace;

Have agreed as follows:

ARTICLE 1: ESTABLISHMENT OF PEACE

Peace is hereby established between the State of Israel and the Hashemite Kingdom of Jordan (the "Parties") effective from the exchange of the instruments of ratification of this Treaty.

ARTICLE 2: GENERAL PRINCIPLES

The Parties will apply between them the provisions of the Charter of the United Nations and the principles of international law governing relations among states in times of peace. In particular:

1. They recognise and will respect each other's sovereignty, territorial integrity and political independence;
2. They recognise and will respect each other's right to live in peace within secure and recognised boundaries;
3. They will develop good neighbourly relations of co-operation between them to ensure lasting security, will refrain from the threat or use of force against each other and will settle all disputes between them by peaceful means;
4. They respect and recognise the sovereignty, territorial integrity and political independence of every state in the region;
5. They respect and recognise the pivotal role of human development and dignity in regional and bilateral relationships;
6. They further believe that within their control, involuntary movements of persons in such a way as to adversely prejudice the security of either Party should not be permitted.

ARTICLE 3: INTERNATIONAL BOUNDARY

1. The international boundary between Israel and Jordan is delimited with reference to the boundary definition under the Mandate as is shown in Annex I (a), on the mapping materials attached thereto and co-ordinates specified therein.
2. The boundary, as set out in Annex I (a), is the permanent, secure and recognised international boundary between Israel and Jordan, without prejudice to the status of any territories that came under Israeli military government control in 1967.
3. The parties recognise the international boundary, as well as each other's territory, territorial waters and airspace, as inviolable, and will respect and comply with them.
4. The demarcation of the boundary will take place as set forth in Appendix (I) to Annex I and will be concluded not later than nine months after the signing of the Treaty.
5. It is agreed that where the boundary follows a river, in the event of natural changes in the course of the flow of the river as described in Annex I (a), the boundary

shall follow the new course of the flow. In the event of any other changes the boundary shall not be affected unless otherwise agreed.

6. Immediately upon the exchange of the instruments of ratification of this Treaty, each Party will deploy on its side of the international boundary as defined in Annex I (a).

7. The Parties shall, upon the signature of the Treaty, enter into negotiations to conclude, within 9 months, an agreement on the delimitation of their maritime boundary in the Gulf of Aqaba . . .

ARTICLE 4: SECURITY

1. a. Both Parties, acknowledging that mutual understanding and co-operation in security-related matters will form a significant part of their relations and will further enhance the security of the region, take upon themselves to base their security relations on mutual trust, advancement of joint interests and co-operation, and to aim towards a regional framework of partnership in peace . . .

2. The obligations referred to in this Article are without prejudice to the inherent right of self-defence in accordance with the United Nations Charter.

3. The Parties undertake, in accordance with the provisions of this Article, the following:
   a. to refrain from the threat or use of force or weapons, conventional, non-conventional or of any other kind, against each other, or of other actions or activities that adversely affect the security of the other Party;
   b. to refrain from organising, instigating, inciting, assisting or participating in acts or threats of belligerency, hostility, subversion or violence against the other Party;
   c. to take necessary and effective measures to ensure that acts or threats of belligerency, hostility, subversion or violence against the other Party do not originate from, and are not committed within, through or over their territory (hereinafter the term "territory" includes the airspace and territorial waters).

4. Consistent with the era of peace and with the efforts to build regional security and to avoid and prevent aggression and violence, the Parties further agree to refrain from the following:
   a. joining or in any way assisting, promoting or co-operating with any coalition, organisation or alliance with a military or security character with a third party, the objectives or activities of which include launching aggression or other acts of military hostility against the other Party, in contravention of the provisions of the present Treaty.
   b. allowing the entry, stationing and operating on their territory, or through it, of military forces, personnel or materiel of a third party, in circumstances which may adversely prejudice the security of the other Party.

5. Both Parties will take necessary and effective measures, and will co-operate in combating terrorism of all kinds. The Parties undertake:
   a. to take necessary and effective measures to prevent acts of terrorism, subversion

or violence from being carried out from their territory or through it and to take necessary and effective measures to combat such activities and all their perpetrators.

b. [. . .]

c. to co-operate in preventing and combating cross-boundary infiltrations.

ARTICLE 5: DIPLOMATIC AND OTHER BILATERAL RELATIONS

1. The Parties agree to establish full diplomatic and consular relations and to exchange resident ambassadors within one month of the exchange of the instruments of ratification of this Treaty.
2. The Parties agree that the normal relationship between them will further include economic and cultural relations.

ARTICLE 6: WATER

With the view to achieving a comprehensive and lasting settlement of all the water problems between them:

1. The Parties agree mutually to recognise the rightful allocations of both of them in Jordan River and Yarmouk River waters and Araba/Arava ground water in accordance with the agreed acceptable principles, quantities and quality as set out in Annex II , which shall be fully respected and complied with.
2. The Parties, recognising the necessity to find a practical, just and agreed solution to their water problems and with the view that the subject of water can form the basis for the advancement of co-operation between them, jointly undertake to ensure that the management and development of their water resources do not, in any way, harm the water resources of the other Party.
3. The Parties recognise that their water resources are not sufficient to meet their needs. More water should be supplied for their use through various methods, including projects of regional and international co-operation . . .

ARTICLE 7: ECONOMIC RELATIONS

1. Viewing economic development and prosperity as pillars of peace, security and harmonious relations between states, peoples and individual human beings, the Parties, taking note of understandings reached between them, affirm their mutual desire to promote economic co-operation between them, as well as within the framework of wider regional economic co-operation.
2. In order to accomplish this goal, the Parties agree to the following:
   a. to remove all discriminatory barriers to normal economic relations, to terminate economic boycotts directed at each other, and to co-operate in terminating boycotts against either Party by third parties;
   b. recognising that the principle of free and unimpeded flow of goods and services should guide their relations, the Parties will enter into negotiations with a view to concluding agreements on economic co-operation, including trade and the

establishment of a free trade area, investment, banking, industrial co-operation and labour, for the purpose of promoting beneficial economic relations, based on principles to be agreed upon, as well as on human development considerations on a regional basis. These negotiations will be concluded no later than 6 months from the exchange of the instruments of ratification of this Treaty.

c. to co-operate bilaterally, as well as in multilateral forums, towards the promotion of their respective economies and of their neighbourly economic relations with other regional parties.

ARTICLE 8: REFUGEES AND DISPLACED PERSONS

1. Recognising the massive human problems caused to both Parties by the conflict in the Middle East, as well as the contribution made by them towards the alleviation of human suffering, the Parties will seek to further alleviate those problems arising on a bilateral level. . . .

ARTICLE 9: PLACES OF HISTORICAL AND RELIGIOUS SIGNIFICANCE

1. Each party will provide freedom of access to places of religious and historical significance.
2. In this regard, in accordance with the Washington Declaration, Israel respects the present special role of the Hashemite Kingdom of Jordan in Muslim Holy shrines in Jerusalem. When negotiations on the permanent status will take place, Israel will give high priority to the Jordanian historic role in these shrines.
3. The Parties will act together to promote interfaith relations among the three monotheistic religions, with the aim of working towards religious understanding, moral commitment, freedom of religious worship, and tolerance and peace.

ARTICLE 10: CULTURAL AND SCIENTIFIC EXCHANGES

The Parties, wishing to remove biases developed through periods of conflict, recognise the desirability of cultural and scientific exchanges in all fields, and agree to establish normal cultural relations between them. Thus, they shall, as soon as possible and not later than 9 months from the exchange of the instruments of ratification of this Treaty, conclude the negotiations on cultural and scientific agreements.

ARTICLE 11: MUTUAL UNDERSTANDING AND GOOD NEIGHBOURLY RELATIONS [. . .]

ARTICLE 12: COMBATING CRIME AND DRUGS [. . .]

ARTICLE 13: TRANSPORTATION AND ROADS

Taking note of the progress already made in the area of transportation, the Parties recognise the mutuality of interest in good neighbourly relations in the area of transportation and agree to the following means to promote relations between them in this sphere:

1. Each party will permit the free movement of nationals and vehicles of the other into and within its territory according to the general rules applicable to nationals and vehicles of other states. Neither party will impose discriminatory taxes or restrictions on the free movement of persons and vehicles from its territory to the territory of the other.
2. The Parties will open and maintain roads and border-crossings between their countries and will consider further road and rail links between them.
3. The Parties will continue their negotiations concerning mutual transportation agreements in the above and other areas, such as joint projects, traffic safety, transport standards and norms, licensing of vehicles, land passages, shipment of goods and cargo, and meteorology, to be concluded not later than 6 months from the exchange of the instruments of ratification of this Treaty.
4. The Parties agree to continue their negotiations for a highway to be constructed and maintained between Egypt, Israel and Jordan near Eilat.

ARTICLE 14: FREEDOM OF NAVIGATION AND ACCESS TO PORTS

1. [. . .]
2. The Parties consider the Strait of Tiran and the Gulf of Aqaba to be international waterways open to all nations for unimpeded and non-suspendable freedom of navigation and overflight. The Parties will respect each other's right to navigation and overflight for access to either Party through the Strait of Tiran and the Gulf of Aqaba.

ARTICLE 15: CIVIL AVIATION [. . .]

ARTICLE 16: POSTS AND TELECOMMUNICATIONS [. . .]

ARTICLE 17: TOURISM [. . .]

ARTICLE 18: ENVIRONMENT

The Parties will co-operate in matters relating to the environment, a sphere to which they attach great importance, including conservation of nature and prevention of pollution, as set forth in Annex IV. They will negotiate an agreement on the above, to be concluded not later than 6 months from the exchange of the instruments of ratification of this Treaty.

ARTICLE 19: ENERGY [. . .]

ARTICLE 20: RIFT VALLEY DEVELOPMENT [. . .]

ARTICLE 21: HEALTH [. . .]

ARTICLE 22: AGRICULTURE [. . .]

ARTICLE 23: AQABA AND EILAT [. . .]

ARTICLE 24: CLAIMS [. . .]

ARTICLE 25: RIGHTS AND OBLIGATIONS [. . .]

ARTICLE 26: LEGISLATION [. . .]

ARTICLE 27: RATIFICATION [. . .]

ARTICLE 28: INTERIM MEASURES [. . .]

ARTICLE 29: SETTLEMENT OF DISPUTES [. . .]

ARTICLE 30: REGISTRATION

This Treaty shall be transmitted to the Secretary General of the United Nations for registration in accordance with the provisions of Article 102 of the Charter of the United Nations.

Done at the Arava/Araba Crossing Point this day Heshvan 21st, 5775, Jumada Al-Ula 21st, 1415 which corresponds to 26th October, 1994 in the Hebrew, English and Arabic languages, all texts being equally authentic. In case of divergence of interpretation the English text shall prevail.

For the State of Israel
Yitzhak Rabin, Prime Minister

For the Hashemite Kingdom of Jordan
Abdul Salam Majali, Prime Minister

Witnessed by:
William J. Clinton
President of the United States of America

53 Nobel Lecture by Yasser Arafat (December 10, 1994)

Your Majesty King Harald,
Your Majesty Queen Sonja,
Professor Sejersted—Chairman of the Nobel Peace Prize Committee,
Your Excellencies,
Ladies and Gentlemen,

A quote from the Holy Koran, "Then if they should be inclined to make peace, do thou incline towards it also, and put thy trust in Allah." The Holy Koran, 8:62.

Ever since I was entrusted by my people to undertake the arduous task of seeking our lost home, I have been filled with a warm faith that all those in exile who bore the keys to their homes with them as they bore their limbs, an inseparable part of them, and those in the homeland, who bore their wounds as they bear their names . . . would, one day, for all their sacrifices, be granted the rewards of returning and freedom. And that, the difficult journey on that long pain-filled path would end in their own hallways.

Now, as we celebrate together the first sighting of the crescent moon of peace, I stare into the eyes of those martyrs whose look has seared into my consciousness as I stand here on this podium and who ask me about the homeland, about their vacant places. I hide my tears from them and tell them: "How right you were. Your generous sacrifice has enabled us to behold the Holy land, to tread our first steps on it in a difficult battle, the battle for peace, the peace of the brave."

Now, as we celebrate the reawakening of creative forces within us and restore the war-torn home that overlooks the neighbors' where our children shall play together and compete to pick flowers, now, I feel national and human pride in my Palestinian Arab People whose powers of patience and giving, of retaining a never-ending bond between homeland, history and people, have added a new chapter to the homelands' ancient legends, that of The Epic of Hope.

To them, to the sons and daughters of that kind enduring nation, that nation of Yew and dew, of fire and sweat, I dedicate this Nobel Prize. I shall bear it to those children who have been promised freedom, safety and security in a homeland free of the threats of external occupation or internal exploitation.

I know, I know full well, Mr. Chairman, that this supreme and greatly significant prize was not awarded to me and to my partners: Mr. Yitzhak Rabin, the Israeli Prime Minister, and Mr. Shimon Peres, the Foreign Minister, to crown an achievement:

but as an encouragement to pursue a route with greater steps and deeper awareness, with truer intentions so that we may transform the peace option, the peace of the brave, from words into practice and reality and for us to be worthy of carrying forward the message entrusted to us by our peoples, as well as humanity and a universal moral duty.

The Palestinians, whose national cause guards the gates of Arab-Israeli peace, look forward like their Arab brethren, to that comprehensive, just and lasting peace, based on "land for peace" and compliance with international legitimacy and resolutions. Peace, for us, is an asset and in our interest. It is an absolute human asset that allows an individual to freely develop his individuality unbound by any regional, religious or ethnic fetters. It restores to Arab-Israeli relations their innocent nature, and enables the Arab spirit to reflect through unrestrained human expression its profound understanding of the Jewish-European tragedy, just as it allows the tortured Jewish spirit to express its unfettered empathy for the suffering endured by the Palestinian people over their ruptured history. Only the tortured can understand those who have endured torture.

Peace is in our interest: as only in an atmosphere of just peace shall the Palestinian people achieve their legitimate ambition for independence and sovereignty, and be able to develop their national and cultural identity, as well as enjoy sound neighborly relations, mutual respect and cooperation with the Israeli people. They, in return, will be able to articulate their Middle Eastern identity, and to open up economically and culturally towards their Arab neighbors. The Arabs are looking forward to developing their region which the long years of war had prevented from finding its true place in today's world, in an atmosphere of democracy, pluralism and prosperity.

Just as war is a great adventure, peace is a challenge and wager. If we fail to endow peace with the wherewithal to withstand the tempest amid the storm, if we fail to nurture peace so that it may gain in strength, if we fail to give it scope to grow and gain in strength, the wager could be wasted and lost. So, from this rostrum I call upon my partners in peace to speed up the peace process, to bring about an early withdrawal, to allow elections to be held and to move on rapidly to the next stage, so that peace may become entrenched and grow, become an established reality.

We started the peace process on the basis of land for peace, and on the basis of UN resolution 242 and 338, as well as other international decisions on achieving the legitimate rights of the Palestinian people. Even though the peace process has not reached its full scope, the new environment of trust as well as the modest steps implemented during the first and second years of the peace agreement are very promising and call for the lifting of reservations, for procedures to be simplified. We must fulfill what remains, especially the transfer of power and taking further steps in Israeli withdrawal from the West Bank and the settlements to achieve full withdrawal. This would provide our society with the opportunity to rebuild its infrastructure and to contribute from its location, with its own heritage, knowledge and know-how in forging our new world.

In this context I call on Russia and the United States of America, the cosponsors of the peace conference, to help the peace process take bigger steps, by contributing to the process and helping to overcome all obstacles. I also call on Norway and Egypt as the first countries to have nurtured the Israeli-Palestinian peace to pursue this worthy initiative that took off from Oslo, to Washington to Cairo. Oslo shall remain the bright name that accompanies the process of peace, the peace of the brave, as will the name of those countries sponsoring the multilateral talks.

Here I call on all the countries of the world especially the donor countries to speed up their contributions so that the Palestinian people may overcome their economic and social problems and proceed with reconstruction and the rebuilding of infrastructures. Peace cannot thrive, and the peace process cannot be consolidated in the absence of the necessary material conditions.

I call on my partners in peace to reinforce the peace process with the necessary comprehensive and strategic vision.

Confidence alone does not make peace. But acknowledging rights and confidence do. Failure to recognize these rights creates a sense of injustice, it keeps the embers burning under the ashes. It moves peace towards the quicksands of danger and rekindles a fuse that is ready to explode.

We view peace as a historic strategic option, not a tactical one directed by current calculations of gain or loss. The peace process is not only a political process, it is an integrated operation where national awareness, economic, scientific and technological development play a major role, just as cultural, social and creative merging play essential roles that are of the very essence of the peace process and fortify it.

I review all this as I recall the difficult peace journey we have traveled, we have only covered a short distance. We have to arm ourselves with courage and utmost temerity to cover the longer distance ahead, towards the home base of just and comprehensive peace, and to be able to assimilate that creative force of the deeper meanings of peace.

As long as we have decided to coexist in peace we must do so on a firm basis that will withstand time and for generations. A comprehensive withdrawal from the West Bank and the Gaza Strip requires an in-depth consideration of the settlements question, they cut across geographic and political union, impede free communication between the regions of the West Bank and the Gaza Strip and create foci of tension: this is contrary to the spirit of peace we seek and mars its serenity. The same applies to the question of Jerusalem, the spiritual haven for Moslems, Christians and Jews. It is the city of cities for Palestinians and where Jewish holy places are on an equal footing with Islamic and Christian holy places, so let us make it a world beacon for spiritual harmony, the radiance of civilization and religious heritage for all humanity. In this context, there is an urgent task that impels the peace process and will help it overcome deep-seated barriers, namely that of the detainees and prisoners. It is important that they be released, that their mothers, wives and children may smile again.

Let us protect this newborn infant from the winter winds, let us nurture it with milk and honey, from the land of milk and honey, and on the land of Salem, Abraham, Ismael and Isaac, the Holy Land, the Land of Peace.

Finally, I would like to congratulate my partners in peace Mr. Yitzhak Rabin, the Prime Minister of Israel, and Mr. Shimon Peres, the Israeli Foreign Minister on being awarded the Nobel Peace Prize.

My congratulations also go to the people of Norway, this friendly nation, for their sponsorship, for their warm hospitality, it betokens their history and nobility. I assure you, Ladies and Gentlemen, that we shall discover ourselves in peace more than we have with war and confrontation, as I am sure that the Israelis in turn shall find themselves in peace more than they have found it in war.

Glory to God almighty,

Peace on Earth,
and Goodwill to all People,

Thank you.

54 Nobel Lecture by Shimon Peres (December 10, 1994)

Your Majesties,
Members of the Nobel Committee,
Prime Minister Brundtland,
Prime Minister Yitzhak Rabin,
Chairman Arafat,
Members of the Norwegian Government,
Distinguished Guests,

I thank the Nobel Prize Committee for its decision to name me among the laureates of the Peace Prize this year.

I am pleased to be receiving this Prize together with Yitzhak Rabin, with whom I have labored for long years for the defence of our country and with whom I now labor together in the cause of peace in our region.

I believe it is fitting that the Prize has been awarded to Yasser Arafat. His abandonment of the path of confrontation in favor of the path of dialogue, has opened the way to peace between ourselves and the Palestinian people.

We are leaving behind us the era of belligerency and are striding together toward peace. It all began here in Oslo under the wise auspices and goodwill of the Norwegian people.

From my earliest youth, I have known that while one is obliged to plan with care the stages of one's journey, one is entitled to dream, and keep dreaming, of its destination. A man may feel as old as his years, yet as young as his dreams. The laws of biology do not apply to sanguine aspiration.

I was born in a small Jewish town in White Russia. Nothing Jewish now remains of it. From my youngest childhood I related to my place of birth as a mere way station. My family's dream, and my own, was to live in Israel, and our eventual voyage to the port of Jaffa was like making a dream come true. Had it not been for this dream and this voyage, I would probably have perished in the flames, as did so many of my people, among them most of my own family.

I went to school at an agricultural youth village in the heart of Israel. The village and its fields were enclosed by barbed wire which separated their greenness from the bleakness of the enmity all around. In the morning, we would go out to the fields with scythes on our backs to harvest the crop. In the evening, we went out with rifles on our shoulders to defend our village. On Sabbaths we would go out to visit our Arab neighbors. On Sabbaths, we would talk with them of peace, though the rest of the week we traded rifle fire across the darkness.

From the Ben Shemen youth village, my comrades and I went to Kibbutz Alumot in the Lower Galilee. We had no houses, no electricity, no running water. But we had magnificent views and a lofty dream: to build a new, egalitarian society that would ennoble each of its members.

Not all of it came true, but not all of it went to waste. The part that came true created a new landscape. The part that did not come true resides in our hearts.

For two decades, at the Ministry of Defence, I was privileged to work closely with a man who was and remains, to my mind, the greatest Jew of our time. From him I learned that the vision of the future should shape the agenda for the present; that one can overcome obstacles by dint of faith; that one may feel disappointment—but never despair. And above all, I learned that the wisest consideration is the moral one. David Ben-Gurion has passed away, yet his vision continues to flourish: to be a singular people, to live at peace with our neighbors.

The wars we fought were forced upon us. Thanks to the Israel Defence Forces, we won them all, but we did not win the greatest victory that we aspired to: release from the need to win victories.

We proved that the aggressors do not necessarily emerge as the victors, but we learned that the victors do not necessarily win peace.

It is no wonder that war, as a means of conducting human affairs, is in its death throes and that the time has come to bury it.

The sword, as the Bible teaches us, consumes flesh but it cannot provide sustenance. It is not rifles but people who triumph, and the conclusion from all the wars is that we need better people, not better rifles—to win wars, and mainly to avoid them.

There was a time when war was fought for lack of choice. Today it is peace that is the "no-choice" option. The reasons of this are profound and incontrovertible. The sources of material wealth and political power have changed. No longer are they determined by the size of territory obtained by war. Today they are a consequence of intellectual potential, obtained principally by education.

Israel, essentially a desert country, has achieved remarkable agricultural yields by applying science to its fields, without expanding its territory or its water resources.

Science must be learned; it cannot be conquered. An army that can occupy knowledge has yet to be built. And that is why armies of occupation are a thing of the past. Indeed, even for defensive purposes, a country cannot rely on its army alone. Territorial frontiers are no obstacle to ballistic missiles, and no weapon can shield from a nuclear device. Today, therefore the battle for survival must be based on political wisdom and moral vision no less than on military might.

Science, technology, and information are—for better or worse—universal. They are universally available. Their availability is not contingent on the color of skin or the place of birth. Past distinctions between West and East, North and South, have lost their importance in the face of a new distinction: between those who move ahead in pace with the new opportunities and those who lag behind.

Countries used to divide the world into their friends and foes. No longer. The foes now are universal—poverty, famine, religious radicalization, desertification, drugs, proliferation of nuclear weapons, ecological devastation. They threaten all nations, just as science and information are the potential friends of all nations.

Classical diplomacy and strategy were aimed at identifying enemies and confronting them. Now they have to identify dangers, global or local, and tackle them before they become disasters.

As we part a world of enemies, we enter a world of dangers. And if future wars break out, they will probably be wars of protest, of the weak against the strong, and not wars of occupation, of the strong against the weak.

The Middle East must never lose pride in having been the cradle of civilization. But though living in the cradle, we cannot remain infants forever.

Today as in my youth, I carry dreams. I would mention two: the future of the Jewish people and the future of the Middle East.

In history, Judaism has been far more successful than the Jews themselves. The Jewish people remained small but the spirit of Jerusalem went from strength to strength. The Bible is to be found in hundreds of millions of homes. The moral majesty of the Book of Books has been undefeated by the vicissitudes of history.

Moreover, time and again, history has succumbed to the Bible's immortal ideas. The message that the one, invisible God created Man in His image, and hence there are no higher and lower orders of man, has fused with the realization that morality is the highest form of wisdom and, perhaps, of beauty and courage too.

Slings, arrows and gas chambers can annihilate man, but cannot destroy human values, dignity, and freedom.

Jewish history presents an encouraging lesson for mankind. For nearly four thousand years, a small nation carried a great message. Initially, the nation dwelt in its own land; later, it wandered in exile. This small nation swam against the tide and was repeatedly persecuted, banished, and down-trodden. There is no other example in all of history, neither among the great empires nor among their colonies and dependencies—of a nation, after so long a saga of tragedy and misfortune, rising up again, shaking itself free, gathering together its dispersed remnants, and setting out anew on its national adventure. Defeating doubters within and enemies without. Reviving its land and its language. Rebuilding its identity, and reaching toward new heights of distinction and excellence.

The message of the Jewish people to mankind is that faith and moral vision can triumph over all adversity.

The conflicts shaping up as our century nears its close will be over the content of civilizations, not over territory. Jewish culture has lived over many centuries; now it has taken root again on its own soil. For the first time in our history, some five million people speak Hebrew as their native language. That is both a lot and a little: a lot, because there have never been so many Hebrew speakers; but a little, because a culture based on five million people can hardly withstand the pervasive, corrosive effect of the global television culture.

In the five decades of Israel's existence, our efforts have focused on reestablishing our territorial center. In the future, we shall have to devote our main effort to strengthen our spiritual center. Judaism—or Jewishness—is a fusion of belief, history, land, and language. Being Jewish means belonging to a people that is both unique and universal. My greatest hope is that our children, like our forefathers, will not make do with the transient and the sham, but will continue to plow the historical Jewish furrow in the field of the human spirit; that Israel will become the center of our heritage, not merely a homeland for our people; that the Jewish people will be inspired by others but at the same be to them a source of inspiration.

In the Middle East most adults are impoverished and wretched. A new scale of priorities is needed, with weapons on the bottom rung and a regional market economy at the top. Most inhabitants of the region—more than sixty percent— are under the age of eighteen. A new future can be offered to them. Israel has computerized its education and has achieved excellent results. Education can be computerized throughout the Middle East, allowing young people to progress not just from grade to grade, but from generation to generation.

Israel's role in the Middle East should be to contribute to a great, sustained regional revival. A Middle East without wars, without enemies, without ballistic missiles, without nuclear warheads.

A Middle East in which men, goods and services can move freely without the need for customs clearance and police licenses.

A Middle East in which every believer will be free to pray in his own language— Arabic, Hebrew, Latin, or whatever language he chooses—and in which the prayers will reach their destination without censorship, without interference, and without offending anyone.

A Middle East in which nations strive for economic equality and encourage cultural pluralism.

A Middle East where every young woman and man can attain university education.

A Middle East where living standards are in no way inferior to those in the world's most advanced countries.

A Middle East where waters flow to slake thirst, to make crops grow and deserts bloom, in which no hostile borders bring death, hunger, and despair.

A Middle East of competition, not of domination. A Middle East in which men are each other's hosts, not hostages.

A Middle East that is not a killing field but a field of creativity and growth.

A Middle East that honors its history so deeply that it strives to add to it new noble chapters.

A Middle East which will serve as a spiritual and cultural focal point for the entire world.

While thanking for the Prize, I remain committed to the process. We have reached the age where dialogue is the only option for our world.

55 Nobel Lecture by Yitzhak Rabin (December 10, 1994)

Your Majesty the King,
Your Royal Highness,
Esteemed Members of the Norwegian Nobel Committee,
Honorable Prime Minister, Madame Gro Harlem Brundtland,
Ministers,
Members of the Parliament and Ambassadors,
Fellow Laureates,
Distinguished Guests,
Friends,
Ladies and Gentlemen,

At an age when most youngsters are struggling to unravel the secrets of mathematics and the mysteries of the Bible; at an age when first love blooms; at the tender age of sixteen, I was handed a rifle so that I could defend myself—and also, unfortunately, so that I could kill in an hour of danger.

That was not my dream. I wanted to be a water engineer. I studied in an agricultural school and I thought that being a water engineer was an important profession in the parched Middle East. I still think so today. However, I was compelled to resort to the gun.

I served in the military for decades. Under my command, young men and women who wanted to live, wanted to love, went to their deaths instead. Under my command, they killed the enemy's men who had been sent out to kill us.

Ladies and Gentlemen,

In my current position, I have ample opportunity to fly over the State of Israel, and lately over other parts of the Middle East, as well. The view from the plane is breathtaking: deep-blue lakes, dark-green fields, dun-colored deserts, stone-gray mountains, and the entire countryside peppered with whitewashed, red-roofed houses.

And cemeteries. Graves as far as the eye can see.

[. . .]

Standing here today, I wish to salute loved ones—and foes. I wish to salute all the fallen of all the countries in all the wars; the members of their families who bear the enduring burden of bereavement; the disabled whose scars will never heal. Tonight I wish to pay tribute to each and every one of them, for this important prize is theirs, and theirs alone.

Ladies and Gentlemen,

[. . .]

As a former military man, I will also forever remember the silence of the moment before: the hush when the hands of the clock seem to be spinning forward, when time is running out and in another hour, another minute, the inferno will erupt.

In that moment of great tension just before the finger pulls the trigger, just before the fuse begins to burn; in the terrible quiet of that moment, there's still time to wonder, alone: Is it really imperative to act? Is there no other choice? No other way?

And then the order is given, and the inferno begins.

[. . .]

Just as no two fingerprints are identical, so no two people are alike, and every country has its own laws and culture, traditions and leaders. But there is one universal message which can embrace the entire world, one precept which can be common to different regimes, to races which bear no resemblance, to cultures alien to each other.

It is a message which the Jewish people has borne for thousands of years, a message found in the Book of Books, which my people has bequeathed to all civilized men: "V'nishmartem me'od lnafshoteichem", in the words in *Deuteronomy,* "Therefore take good heed to yourselves"—or, in contemporary terms, the message of the Sanctity of Life.

The leaders of nations must provide their peoples with the conditions—the "infrastructure", if you will—which enables them to enjoy life: freedom of speech and of movement; food and shelter; and most important of all: life itself. A man cannot enjoy his rights if he is not among the living. And so every country must protect and preserve the key element in its national ethos: the lives of its citizens.

To defend those lives, we call upon our citizens to enlist in the army. And to defend the lives of our citizens serving in the army, we invest huge sums in planes, and tanks, in armored plating and concrete fortifications. Yet despite it all, we fail to protect the lives of our citizens and soldiers. Military cemeteries in every corner of the world are silent testimony to the failure of national leaders to sanctify human life.

There is only one radical means of sanctifying human lives. Not armored plating, or tanks, or planes, or concrete fortifications.

The one radical solution is peace.

Ladies and Gentlemen,

The profession of soldiering embraces a certain paradox. We take the best and bravest of our young men into the army. We supply them with equipment which costs a virtual fortune. We rigorously train them for the day when they must do their duty—and we expect them to do it well. Yet we fervently pray that that day will never come—that the planes will never take flight, the tanks will never move forward, the soldiers will never mount the attacks for which they have been trained so well.

We pray it will never happen because of the Sanctity of Life.

[. . .]

Ladies and Gentlemen,

We are in the midst of building the peace. The architects and engineers of this enterprise are engaged in their work even as we gather here tonight, building the peace layer by layer, brick by brick, beam by beam. The job is difficult, complex, trying. Mistakes could topple the whole structure and bring disaster down upon us.

And so we are determined to do the job well—despite the toll of murderous terrorism, despite fanatic and scheming enemies.

We will pursue the course of peace with determination and fortitude.

We will not let up.

We will not give in.

Peace will triumph over all our enemies, because the alternative is grim for us all.

And we will prevail.

We will prevail because we regard the building of peace as a great blessing for us, and for our children after us. We regard it as a blessing for our neighbors on all sides, and for our partners in this enterprise—the United States, Russia, Norway, and all mankind.

We wake up every morning, now, as different people. Suddenly, peace. We see the hope in our children's eyes. We see the light in our soldier's faces, in the streets, in the buses, in the fields.

We must not let them down.

We will not let them down.

[. . .]

I am here as the emissary of Jerusalem, at whose gates I fought in days of siege; Jerusalem which has always been, and is today, the eternal capital of the State of Israel and the heart of the Jewish people, who pray toward it three times a day. . . .

With me here are five million citizens of Israel—Jews and Arabs, Druze and Circassians—five million hearts beating for peace—and five million pairs of eyes which look to us with such great expectations for peace.

Ladies and Gentlemen,

I wish to thank, first and foremost, those citizens of the State of Israel, of all generations and political persuasions, whose sacrifices and relentless struggle for peace bring us steadier closer to our goal.

I wish to thank our partners—the Egyptians, Jordanians, Palestinians, and the Chairman of the Palestinian Liberation Organization, Mr. Yasser Arafat, with whom we share this Nobel Prize—who have chosen the path of peace and are writing a new page in the annals of the Middle East.

I wish to thank the members of the Israeli government and above all my colleague Mr. Shimon Peres, whose energy and devotion to the cause of peace are an example to us all.

I wish to thank my family for their support.

And, of course, I wish to thank the members of the Nobel Committee and the courageous Norwegian people for bestowing this illustrious honor on my colleagues and myself.

Ladies and Gentlemen,

Allow me to close by sharing with you a traditional Jewish blessing which has been recited by my people, in good times and in bad, from time immemorial, as a token of their deepest longing:

"The Lord will give strength to his people; the Lord will bless his people—all of us—with peace."

Part V

From Interim Agreements (1995) to the Present Time

56 Israeli-Palestinian Interim Agreement on the West Bank and the Gaza Strip (September 28, 1995)

September 28, 1995

The Government of the State of Israel and the Palestine Liberation Organization (hereinafter "the PLO"), the representative of the Palestinian people;

PREAMBLE

WITHIN the framework of the Middle East peace process initiated at Madrid in October 1991;

REAFFIRMING their determination to put an end to decades of confrontation and to live in peaceful coexistence, mutual dignity and security, while recognizing their mutual legitimate and political rights;

REAFFIRMING their desire to achieve a just, lasting and comprehensive peace settlement and historic reconciliation through the agreed political process;

RECOGNIZING that the peace process and the new era that it has created, as well as the new relationship established between the two Parties as described above, are irreversible, and the determination of the two Parties to maintain, sustain and continue the peace process;

RECOGNIZING that the aim of the Israeli-Palestinian negotiations within the current Middle East peace process is, among other things, to establish a Palestinian Interim Self-Government Authority, i.e. the elected Council (hereinafter "the Council" or "the Palestinian Council"), and the elected Ra'ees of the Executive Authority, for the Palestinian people in the West Bank and the Gaza Strip, for a transitional period not exceeding five years from the date of signing the Agreement on the Gaza Strip and the Jericho Area (hereinafter "the Gaza-Jericho Agreement") on May 4, 1994, leading to a permanent settlement based on Security Council Resolutions 242 and 338;

REAFFIRMING their understanding that the interim self-government arrangements contained in this Agreement are an integral part of the whole peace process, that the negotiations on the permanent status, that will start as soon as possible but not later than May 4, 1996, will lead to the implementation of Security Council Resolutions 242 and 338, and that the Interim Agreement shall settle all the issues of the interim period and that no such issues will be deferred to the agenda of the permanent status negotiations;

REAFFIRMING their adherence to the mutual recognition and commitments expressed in the letters dated September 9, 1993, signed by and exchanged between the Prime Minister of Israel and the Chairman of the PLO;

DESIROUS of putting into effect the Declaration of Principles on Interim Self-Government Arrangements signed at Washington, D.C. on September 13, 1993, and the Agreed Minutes thereto (hereinafter "the DOP") and in particular Article III and Annex I concerning the holding of direct, free and general political elections for the Council and the Ra'ees of the Executive Authority in order that the Palestinian people in the West Bank, Jerusalem and the Gaza Strip may democratically elect accountable representatives;

RECOGNIZING that these elections will constitute a significant interim preparatory step toward the realization of the legitimate rights of the Palestinian people and their just requirements and will provide a democratic basis for the establishment of Palestinian institutions;

REAFFIRMING their mutual commitment to act, in accordance with this Agreement, immediately, efficiently and effectively against acts or threats of terrorism, violence or incitement, whether committed by Palestinians or Israelis;

FOLLOWING the Gaza-Jericho Agreement; the Agreement on Preparatory Transfer of Powers and Responsibilities signed at Erez on August 29, 1994 (hereinafter "the Preparatory Transfer Agreement"); and the Protocol on Further Transfer of Powers and Responsibilities signed at Cairo on August 27, 1995 (hereinafter "the Further Transfer Protocol"); which three agreements will be superseded by this Agreement;

HEREBY AGREE as follows:

CHAPTER I—THE COUNCIL

ARTICLE I: Transfer of Authority

1. Israel shall transfer powers and responsibilities as specified in this Agreement from the Israeli military government and its Civil Administration to the Council in accordance with this Agreement. Israel shall continue to exercise powers and responsibilities not so transferred.

2. Pending the inauguration of the Council, the powers and responsibilities transferred to the Council shall be exercised by the Palestinian Authority established

in accordance with the Gaza-Jericho Agreement, which shall also have all the rights, liabilities and obligations to be assumed by the Council in this regard. Accordingly, the term "Council" throughout this Agreement shall, pending the inauguration of the Council, be construed as meaning the Palestinian Authority.

3. [. . .]

4. [. . .]

5. After the inauguration of the Council, the Civil Administration in the West Bank will be dissolved, and the Israeli military government shall be withdrawn. The withdrawal of the military government shall not prevent it from exercising the powers and responsibilities not transferred to the Council.

6. [. . .]

7. The offices of the Council, and the offices of its Ra'ees and its Executive Authority and other committees, shall be located in areas under Palestinian territorial jurisdiction in the West Bank and the Gaza Strip.

ARTICLE II: Elections

1. In order that the Palestinian people of the West Bank and the Gaza Strip may govern themselves according to democratic principles, direct, free and general political elections will be held for the Council and the Ra'ees of the Executive Authority of the Council in accordance with the provisions set out in the Protocol concerning Elections attached as Annex II to this Agreement (hereinafter "Annex II").

2. These elections will constitute a significant interim preparatory step towards the realization of the legitimate rights of the Palestinian people and their just requirements and will provide a democratic basis for the establishment of Palestinian institutions.

3. [. . .]

4. [. . .]

ARTICLE III: Structure of the Palestinian Council

1. The Palestinian Council and the Ra'ees of the Executive Authority of the Council constitute the Palestinian Interim Self-Government Authority, which will be elected by the Palestinian people of the West Bank, Jerusalem and the Gaza Strip for the transitional period agreed in Article I of the DOP.

2. The Council shall possess both legislative power and executive power, in accordance with Articles VII and IX of the DOP. The Council shall carry out and be responsible

for all the legislative and executive powers and responsibilities transferred to it under this Agreement. The exercise of legislative powers shall be in accordance with Article XVIII of this Agreement (Legislative Powers of the Council).

3. The Council and the Ra'ees of the Executive Authority of the Council shall be directly and simultaneously elected by the Palestinian people of the West Bank, Jerusalem and the Gaza Strip, in accordance with the provisions of this Agreement and the Election Law and Regulations, which shall not be contrary to the provisions of this Agreement.

4. The Council and the Ra'ees of the Executive Authority of the Council shall be elected for a transitional period not exceeding five years from the signing of the Gaza-Jericho Agreement on May 4, 1994.

5. [. . .]

6. [. . .]

7. [. . .]

8. [. . .]

9. [. . .]

ARTICLE IV: Size of the Council

The Palestinian Council shall be composed of 82 representatives and the Ra'ees of the Executive Authority, who will be directly and simultaneously elected by the Palestinian people of the West Bank, Jerusalem and the Gaza Strip.

ARTICLE V: The Executive Authority of the Council

1. The Council will have a committee that will exercise the executive authority of the Council, formed in accordance with paragraph 4 below (hereinafter "the Executive Authority").

2. The Executive Authority shall be bestowed with the executive authority of the Council and will exercise it on behalf of the Council. It shall determine its own internal procedures and decision making processes.

3. [. . .]

4. [. . .]

ARTICLE VI: Other Committees of the Council [. . .]

ARTICLE VII: Open Government [. . .]

ARTICLE VIII: Judicial Review [. . .]

ARTICLE IX: Powers and Responsibilities of the Council [. . .]

CHAPTER 2—REDEPLOYMENT AND SECURITY ARRANGEMENTS

ARTICLE X: Redeployment of Israeli Military Forces [. . .]

ARTICLE XI: Land

1. The two sides view the West Bank and the Gaza Strip as a single territorial unit, the integrity and status of which will be preserved during the interim period.

2. The two sides agree that West Bank and Gaza Strip territory, except for issues that will be negotiated in the permanent status negotiations, will come under the jurisdiction of the Palestinian Council in a phased manner, to be completed within 18 months from the date of the inauguration of the Council . . .

ARTICLE XII: Arrangements for Security and Public Order

1. In order to guarantee public order and internal security for the Palestinians of the West Bank and the Gaza Strip, the Council shall establish a strong police force as set out in Article XIV below. Israel shall continue to carry the responsibility for defense against external threats, including the responsibility for protecting the Egyptian and Jordanian borders, and for defense against external threats from the sea and from the air, as well as the responsibility for overall security of Israelis and Settlements, for the purpose of safeguarding their internal security and public order, and will have all the powers to take the steps necessary to meet this responsibility.

2. [. . .]

ARTICLE XIII: Security

1. The Council will, upon completion of the redeployment of Israeli military forces in each district, as set out in Appendix 1 to Annex I, assume the powers and responsibilities for internal security and public order in Area A in that district.

2. a. There will be a complete redeployment of Israeli military forces from Area B. Israel will transfer to the Council and the Council will assume responsibility for public order for Palestinians. Israel shall have the overriding responsibility for security for the purpose of protecting Israelis and confronting the threat of terrorism.

b. In Area B the Palestinian Police shall assume the responsibility for public order for Palestinians and shall be deployed in order to accommodate the Palestinian needs and requirements in the following manner:

[. . .]

ARTICLE XIV: The Palestinian Police [. . .]

ARTICLE XV: Prevention of Hostile Acts [. . .]

ARTICLE XVI: Confidence Building Measures

With a view to fostering a positive and supportive public atmosphere to accompany the implementation of this Agreement, to establish a solid basis of mutual trust and good faith, and in order to facilitate the anticipated cooperation and new relations between the two peoples, both Parties agree to carry out confidence building measures as detailed herewith:

1. Israel will release or turn over to the Palestinian side, Palestinian detainees and prisoners, residents of the West Bank and the Gaza Strip. The first stage of release of these prisoners and detainees will take place on the signing of this Agreement and the second stage will take place prior to the date of the elections. There will be a third stage of release of detainees and prisoners. Detainees and prisoners will be released from among categories detailed in Annex VII (Release of Palestinian Prisoners and Detainees). Those released will be free to return to their homes in the West Bank and the Gaza Strip.

2. Palestinians who have maintained contact with the Israeli authorities will not be subjected to acts of harassment, violence, retribution or prosecution. Appropriate ongoing measures will be taken, in coordination with Israel, in order to ensure their protection.

[. . .]

CHAPTER 3—LEGAL AFFAIRS

ARTICLE XVII: Jurisdiction [. . .]

ARTICLE XVIII: Legislative Powers of the Council [. . .]

ARTICLE XIX: Human Rights and the Rule of Law

Israel and the Council shall exercise their powers and responsibilities pursuant to this Agreement with due regard to internationally-accepted norms and principles of human rights and the rule of law.

ARTICLE XX: Rights, Liabilities and Obligations [. . .]

ARTICLE XXI: Settlement of Differences and Disputes [. . .]

CHAPTER 4—COOPERATION

ARTICLE XXII: Relations between Israel and the Council [. . .]

ARTICLE XXIII: Cooperation with Regard to Transfer of Powers [. . .]

ARTICLE XXIV: Economic Relations [. . .]

ARTICLE XXV: Cooperation Programs [. . .]

ARTICLE XXVI: The Joint Israeli-Palestinian Liaison Committee [. . .]

ARTICLE XXVII: Liaison and Cooperation with Jordan and Egypt [. . .]

ARTICLE XXVIII: Missing Persons [. . .]

CHAPTER 5—MISCELLANEOUS PROVISIONS

ARTICLE XXIX: Safe Passage between the West Bank and the Gaza Strip [. . .]

ARTICLE XXX: Passages [. . .]

ARTICLE XXXI: Final Clauses [. . .]

Done at Washington DC, this 28th day of September, 1995.

[end]

Posted July 2003
Bureau of Near Eastern Affairs

57 Speech by Prime Minister Yitzhak Rabin to the Knesset Supporting the Israeli–Palestinian Interim Agreement (October 5, 1995)

We view the permanent solution in the framework of the State of Israel which will include most of the area of the Land of Israel as it was under the rule of the British Mandate, and alongside it a Palestinian entity which will be a home to most of the Palestinian residents living in the Gaza Strip and the West Bank. We would like this to be an entity which is less than a state, and which will independently run the lives of the Palestinians under its authority. The borders of the State of Israel, during the permanent solution, will be beyond the lines which existed before the Six-Day War. We will not return to the June 4, 1967, lines.

And these are the main changes, not all of them, which we envision and want in the permanent solution:

- First and foremost, united Jerusalem, which will include both Ma'ale Adumim and Givat Ze'ev—as the capital of Israel, under Israeli sovereignty, while preserving the rights of the members of the others faiths, Christianity and Islam, to freedom of access and freedom of worship in their holy places, according to the customs of their faiths.
- The security border of the State of Israel will be located in the Jordan Valley, in the broadest meaning of that term.
- Changes which will include the addition of Gush Etzion, Efrat, Betar and other communities, most of which are in the area east of what was the "Green Line," prior to the Six-Day War.
- The establishment of blocs of settlements in Judea and Samaria, like the one in Gush Katif. . . .

The first stage of this redeployment of IDF forces will be carried out in three areas, in order to enable the Palestinians to hold elections for the Palestinian Council, and for its chairman, without the IDF being permanently present in Palestinian communities:

[In] Area A, or the "brown" area, the redeployment of IDF forces will be carried out in three areas—will include the municipal areas of the six cities: Jenin, Nablus, Tulkarem, Kalkilyah, Ramallah, and Bethlehem. Responsibility for civilian security in this area will be transferred to the Palestinian Authority.

Area B, or the "yellow" area, includes almost all of the 450 towns and villages in which the Palestinians of the West Bank live. In this area, there will be a separation of responsibilities. The Palestinians will be responsible for managing their own lives, and Israel will have overall responsibility for the security of Israelis and the war against the terrorist threat. That is, IDF forces and the security services will be able to enter any place in Area B at any time.

The third area, Area C, or the "white" area, is everywhere that is not included in the areas that have been mentioned until now. In this area are the Jewish settlements, all IDF installations and the border areas with Jordan. This area will remain under IDF control.

Areas A and B constitute less than 30% of the area of the West Bank. Area C, which is under our control, constitutes more than 70% of the area of the West Bank. . . .

I want to remind you: we committed ourselves, that is, we came to an agreement, and committed ourselves before the Knesset, not to uproot a single settlement in the framework of the interim agreement, and not to hinder building for natural growth. . . . An examination of the maps and of the paragraphs of the agreement regarding the additional stages of the redeployment shows that Israel retains complete freedom of action, in order to implement its security and political objectives relating to the permanent solution, and that the division of the areas gives the IDF and the security branches complete security control in Areas B and C, except for the urban areas.

A difficult problem arose in Hebron, and with both sides in agreement it was determined that, prior to the completion of the Halhoul bypass road, there would not be a complete redeployment in the city of Hebron, and this will take another half a year from the signing of the agreement, that is, until March 28, 1996. In our assessment, six months are required in order to build this bypass road. When the Halhoul bypass road and the Hebron bypass road (in the Beit Hagai-Har Manoah-Kiryat Arba section) are built, this will enable the movement of Israelis without their passing through those sections of Hebron which do not have a Jewish presence. . . .

I should further emphasize that activity for providing security measures for the Israeli communities—fences, peripheral roads, lighting, gates—will continue on a wide scale. Bypass roads will be built, whose purpose will be to enable Israeli residents to move about without having to pass through Palestinian population centers in places which will be transferred to the responsibility of the Palestinian Authority. In any case, the IDF will not carry out a redeployment from the first seven cities, before the bypass roads are completed. In all, investment in the bypass roads will be about NIS 500 million [$166 million].

From the depths of our heart, we call upon all citizens of the State of Israel, certainly those who live in Judea, Samaria and the Gaza Strip, as well as the Palestinian residents to give the establishment of peace a chance, to give the end of acts of hostility a chance, to give another life a chance, a new life. We appeal to Jews and Palestinians alike to act with restraint, to preserve human dignity, to behave in a fitting manner—and, to live in peace and security.

58 Speech by Prime Minister Rabin at a Peace Rally (November 4, 1995)

"I was a soldier for 27 years. I fought as long as there was no prospect of peace. I believe that there is now a chance for peace, a great chance, which must be seized . . .

"I have always believed most of the nation wants peace and is prepared to take risks for peace. And you here, who have come to take a stand for peace, as well as many others who are not here, are proof that the nation truly wants peace and rejects violence. Violence is undermining the foundations of Israeli democracy. It must be rejected and condemned and it must be contained. It is not the way of the State of Israel. Democracy is our way . . . Peace is not just a prayer. It is at first a prayer, but it is also the realistic aspiration of the Jewish people. But peace has its enemies, who are trying to harm us, to torpedo the peace.

"We have found a partner in peace among the Palestinians as well—the PLO, which was an enemy and has now forsaken terrorism . . . There is no painless way forward for Israel. But the way of peace is preferable to war . . .

"This rally must send a message to the Israeli public, to the Jews of the world, to the multitudes in the Arab lands and in the world at large, that the nation of Israel wants peace, supports peace—and for this, I thank you."

59 Israel–Lebanon Ceasefire Understanding (April 26, 1996)

The United States understands that after discussions with the governments of Israel and Lebanon, and in consultation with Syria, Lebanon and Israel will ensure the following:

1. Armed groups in Lebanon will not carry out attacks by Katyusha rockets or by any kind of weapon into Israel.

2. Israel and those cooperating with it will not fire any kind of weapon at civilians or civilian targets in Lebanon.

3. Beyond this, the two parties commit to ensuring that under no circumstances will civilians be the target of attack and that civilian populated areas and industrial and electrical installations will not be used as launching grounds for attacks.

4. Without violating this understanding, nothing herein shall preclude any party from exercising the right of self-defense.

A Monitoring Group is established consisting of the United States, France, Syria, Lebanon and Israel . . .

In the event of a claimed violation of the understanding, the party submitting the complaint will do so within 24 hours. Procedures for dealing with the complaints will be set by the Monitoring Group.

The United States will also organize a Consultative Group, to consist of France, the European Union, Russia and other interested parties, for the purpose of assisting in the reconstruction needs of Lebanon.

It is recognized that the understanding to bring the current crisis between Lebanon and Israel to an end cannot substitute for a permanent solution. The United States understands the importance of achieving a comprehensive peace in the region.

Toward this end, the United States proposes the resumption of negotiations between Syria and Israel and between Lebanon and Israel at a time to be agreed upon, with the objective of reaching comprehensive peace.

The United States understands that it is desirable that these negotiations be conducted in a climate of stability and tranquility.

This understanding will be announced simultaneously at 1800 hours, April 26, 1996, in all countries concerned.

The time set for implementation is 0400 hours, April 27, 1996.

60 The Wye River Memorandum (October 23, 1998)

October 23, 1998

I. FURTHER REDEPLOYMENTS [. . .]

II. SECURITY

In the provisions on security arrangements of the Interim Agreement, the Palestinian side agreed to take all measures necessary in order to prevent acts of terrorism, crime and hostilities directed against the Israeli side, against individuals falling under the Israeli side's authority and against their property, just as the Israeli side agreed to take all measures necessary in order to prevent acts of terrorism, crime and hostilities directed against the Palestinian side, against individuals falling under the Palestinian side's authority and against their property. The two sides also agreed to take legal measures against offenders within their jurisdiction and to prevent incitement against each other by any organizations, groups or individuals within their jurisdiction.

Both sides recognize that it is in their vital interests to combat terrorism and fight violence . . . They also recognize that the struggle against terror and violence must be comprehensive in that it deals with terrorists, the terror support structure, and the environment conducive to the support of terror. It must be continuous and constant over a long-term, in that there can be no pauses in the work against terrorists and their structure. It must be cooperative in that no effort can be fully effective without Israeli-Palestinian cooperation and the continuous exchange of information, concepts, and actions. . . .

A. Security Actions

1. Outlawing and Combating Terrorist Organizations

The Palestinian side will make known its policy of zero tolerance for terror and violence against both sides.

[. . .]

The Palestinian side will apprehend the specific individuals suspected of perpetrating acts of violence and terror for the purpose of further investigation, and prosecution and punishment of all persons involved in acts of violence and terror.

2. Prohibiting Illegal Weapons

The Palestinian side will ensure an effective legal framework is in place to criminalize, in conformity with the prior agreements, any importation, manufacturing or unlicensed sale, acquisition or possession of firearms, ammunition or weapons in areas under Palestinian jurisdiction. . . .

3. Preventing Incitement

[. . .] the Palestinian side will issue a decree prohibiting all forms of incitement to violence or terror, and establishing mechanisms for acting systematically against all expressions or threats of violence or terror. This decree will be comparable to the existing Israeli legislation which deals with the same subject. . . .

B. Security Cooperation

The two sides agree that their security cooperation will be based on a spirit of partnership and will include, among other things, the following steps:

1. Bilateral Cooperation

There will be full bilateral security cooperation between the two sides which will be continuous, intensive and comprehensive.

2. Forensic Cooperation

There will be an exchange of forensic expertise, training, and other assistance.

3. Trilateral Committee

In addition to the bilateral Israeli-Palestinian security cooperation, a high-ranking U.S.-Palestinian-Israeli committee will meet as required and not less than biweekly to assess current threats, deal with any impediments to effective security cooperation and coordination and address the steps being taken to combat terror and terrorist organizations. The committee will also serve as a forum to address the issue of external support for terror. . . .

C. Other Issues

1. Palestinian Police Force

The Palestinian side will provide a list of its policemen to the Israeli side in conformity with the prior agreements. Should the Palestinian side request technical assistance, the U.S. has indicated its willingness to help meet these needs in cooperation with other donors. . . .

2. PLO Charter

The Executive Committee of the Palestine Liberation Organization and the Palestinian Central Council will reaffirm the letter of 22 January 1998 from PLO Chairman Yassir Arafat to President Clinton concerning the nullification of the Palestinian National Charter provisions that are inconsistent with the letters exchanged between the PLO and the Government of Israel on 9/10 September 1993. . . .

3. Legal Assistance in Criminal Matters . . .

4. Human Rights and the Rule of Law

[. . .] the Palestinian Police will exercise powers and responsibilities to implement this Memorandum with due regard to internationally accepted norms of human rights and the rule of law, and will be guided by the need to protect the public, respect human dignity, and avoid harassment.

III. INTERIM COMMITTEES AND ECONOMIC ISSUES

1. The Israeli and Palestinian sides reaffirm their commitment to enhancing their relationship and agree on the need actively to promote economic development in the West Bank and Gaza. . . .

2. The Israeli and Palestinian sides have agreed on arrangements which will permit the timely opening of the Gaza Industrial Estate. They also have concluded a "Protocol Regarding the Establishment and Operation of the International Airport in the Gaza Strip During the Interim Period."

3. Both sides will renew negotiations on Safe Passage immediately. As regards the southern route, the sides will make best efforts to conclude the agreement within a week of the entry into force of this Memorandum. Operation of the southern route will start as soon as possible thereafter. As regards the northern route, negotiations will continue with the goal of reaching agreement as soon as possible. Implementation will take place expeditiously thereafter.

4. The Israeli and Palestinian sides acknowledge the great importance of the Port of Gaza for the development of the Palestinian economy, and the expansion of Palestinian trade. They commit themselves to proceeding without delay to conclude an agreement to allow the construction and operation of the port in accordance with the prior agreements. . . .

5. The two sides recognize that unresolved legal issues adversely affect the relationship between the two peoples. They therefore will accelerate efforts through the Legal

Committee to address outstanding legal issues and to implement solutions to these issues in the shortest possible period. . . .

6. The Israeli and Palestinian sides also will launch a strategic economic dialogue to enhance their economic relationship. . . .

IV. PERMANENT STATUS NEGOTIATIONS

The two sides will immediately resume permanent status negotiations on an accelerated basis and will make a determined effort to achieve the mutual goal of reaching an agreement by May 4, 1999. The negotiations will be continuous and without interruption. The U.S. has expressed its willingness to facilitate these negotiations.

V. UNILATERAL ACTIONS

Recognizing the necessity to create a positive environment for the negotiations, neither side shall initiate or take any step that will change the status of the West Bank and the Gaza Strip in accordance with the Interim Agreement.

ATTACHMENT: Time Line

This Memorandum will enter into force ten days from the date of signature.

Done at Washington, D.C. this 23d day of October 1998.

For the Government of the State of Israel:
Benjamin Netanyahu

For the PLO:
Yassir Arafat

Witnessed by:
William J. Clinton
The United States of America

[. . .]

61 Address in the Knesset by Prime Minister-Elect Ehud Barak upon the Presentation of His Government (July 7, 1999)

Your Excellency President and Mrs. Weizman, Mr. Speaker, our friend Avraham Burg, please accept my heartfelt congratulations on your deserved election as Speaker of the Knesset.

[. . .]

Let me begin with a personal comment. I have been a soldier for practically all my adult life. I have known the pride of victory, but also the pain of failure. . . . I am not alone here today on this podium. Together with me are generations of IDF soldiers who withstood the most severe trials of fire in order to secure our liberty. Together with me are those who returned at dawn from the nighttime inferno, carrying on their shoulders the silent stretchers bearing their lifeless comrades.

[. . .]

I am proud to submit to the people and the House a new, broad-based, good, representative government, supported by the large majority of Knesset members and the citizens of the state. It was not in vain that I took advantage of the full time allotted by law to form the government. I did not take the easy way. The lessons of Jewish history and the depth of the social and political chasm in Israel today required me to choose the long and patient way in order to achieve the goal which I had set for myself: to form a government which will act during a time of difficult national decisions, through consent and balance between most sections of the people. I did not accept any disqualification of any side.

During the negotiations I seriously examined the possibility of expanding the basis of the coalition even further. This was not possible and in retrospect, this may have been best. In a democratic system, there is great importance to the role of a parliamentary opposition, and it is my intention to express my recognition of this by maintaining ongoing contacts with, providing information to and holding consultations with the heads of those factions which are not members of the coalition. I expect substantive and constructive criticism from the opposition which will also enable consideration of its opinion in managing affairs of state.

Mr. Speaker, Members of the Knesset,

The basic guidelines of the government and the coalition agreements are before you. Everything is open and fully disclosed. Nothing is concealed, there are no secret agreements, no "under-the-table" understandings, and as you have seen, there are neither financial commitments nor favors to specific sectors or groups.

[. . .]

The Zionist idea which was proclaimed in Basel over 100 years ago has brought about a revolution in the life of the Jewish people and restored it to the stage of history as a sovereign, independent, strong and prosperous people.

The ingathering of the exiles, the settlement of the land, the revival of the language, culture, and scientific and intellectual life, the creation of a splendid educational system and Torah institutions, the establishment of a strong national economy, an exemplary defense force and security services, sophisticated infrastructure systems and advanced health and welfare services, the creation of a democratic, free and diverse society based on the supremacy of the rule of law—all of these are achievements which are utterly unparalleled in the history of nations. They were achieved despite the Holocaust, which wiped out a third of our people, and during an unrelenting struggle and a bloody war in which the best of our children and comrades gave their lives. It is because of them that we are here—determined and confident and aspiring to historic acceptance and an end to wars and enmity.

We embrace the bereaved families and the families of the MIAs and POWs, the disabled and wounded of the security establishment. May peace ease their suffering. We know that the victory of Zionism will not be complete until the achievement of genuine peace, full security, and relations of friendship, trust and cooperation with all our neighbors. And therefore, the government's supreme goal will be to bring peace and security to Israel, while safeguarding the vital interests of the State of Israel. The great historic breakthrough to peace took place 20 years ago, through the vision and courage of two outstanding leaders: the late Menahem Begin and the late Anwar Sadat, may they rest in peace.

A further milestone was the Madrid Conference during the tenure of Prime Minister Yitzhak Shamir. Renewed and far-reaching impetus was imparted by Yitzhak Rabin, the courageous and unswerving leader, from whom I learned so much, and who was assassinated during the struggle for his path, the path of peace, and with him, by our friend Shimon Peres.

The government of Benjamin Netanyahu indeed opened with the Hebron agreement, but it was unable to implement the Wye accords which it had signed.

Now it is our duty to complete the mission, and establish a comprehensive peace in the Middle East which has known so much war. It is our duty to ourselves and our children to take decisive measures to strengthen Israel by ending the Arab-Israeli conflict. This government is determined to make every effort, pursue every path and do everything necessary for Israel's security, the achievement of peace and the prevention of war.

We have an historic obligation to take advantage of the "window of opportunity" which has opened before us in order to bring long-term security and peace to Israel. We know that comprehensive and stable peace can be established only if it rests, simultaneously, on four pillars: Egypt, Jordan, and Syria and Lebanon, in some sense as a single bloc, and of course the Palestinians. As long as peace is not grounded on all these four pillars, it will remain incomplete and unstable. The Arab countries must know that only a strong and self-confident Israel can bring peace.

Here, today, I call upon all the leaders of the region to extend their hands to meet our outstretched hand, and toward a "peace of the brave", in a region which has known so much war, blood and suffering. To our neighbors the Palestinians, I wish to say: The bitter conflict between us has brought great suffering to both our peoples. Now, there is no reason to settle accounts over historical mistakes. Perhaps things could have been otherwise, but we cannot change the past; we can only make the future better. I am not only cognizant of the sufferings of my people, but I also recognize the sufferings of the Palestinian people. My ambition and desire is to bring an end to violence and suffering, and to work with the elected Palestinian leadership, under Chairman Yasser Arafat, in partnership and respect, in order to jointly arrive at a fair and agreed settlement for co-existence in freedom, prosperity and good neighborliness in this beloved land where the two peoples will always live.

To Syrian President Hafez Assad, I say that the new Israeli government is determined, as soon as possible, to advance the negotiations for the achievement of a full, bilateral treaty of peace and security, on the basis of Security Council Resolutions 242 and 338.

We have been tough and bitter adversaries on the battlefield. The time has come to establish a secure and courageous peace which will ensure the futures of our peoples, our children and our grandchildren.

It is my intention to bring an end to the IDF presence in Lebanon within one year, to deploy the IDF, through agreement, along the border, and to bring our boys home while also taking the necessary measures to guarantee the welfare and security of residents along the northern border, as well as the future of the Lebanese security and civilian assistance personnel who have worked alongside us, over all these years, for the sake of the residents of the region.

[. . .]

Mr. Speaker, distinguished Knesset,

These two missions—arriving at a permanent settlement with the Palestinians, and achieving peace with Syria and Lebanon—are, in my eyes, equally vital and urgent. One neither outranks the other, nor has priority over it.

The government's objective will be to act, at the same time, to bring peace closer on all fronts, but without compromising on Israel's security needs and most vital interests—first and foremost among them, a united Jerusalem, the eternal capital of Israel, under our sovereignty. We will not be deterred by the difficulties.

I know very well that difficult negotiations, replete with crises and ups-and-downs, await us before we reach our desired goal. I can only promise that, if the other side displays the same degree of determination and good will to reach an agreement as on our side, no force in the world will prevent us from achieving peace here.

In this context, I attach the greatest importance to the support of our partners to peace treaties: Egypt and Jordan. I believe that President Hosni Mubarak and King Abdullah can play a vital role in creating the dynamics and an atmosphere of trust so needed for progress toward peace. They can also advance education for peace among the children of Egypt and Jordan, the Palestinians and, in the future, also of Syria and Lebanon—education for peace, which is a condition for any long-term, stable peace. I am convinced that King Hassan of Morocco can also contribute to this, as can other countries who already, in the past, opened channels of communication with Israel, cooperating with the peace process in various spheres. My aspiration will be to firmly resume these contacts in order to create a favorable regional atmosphere that can assist the negotiations.

It goes without saying that the assistance of the United States is a fundamental condition for any progress toward resolving the conflict in the region. The friendship of America, under the leadership of President Clinton, its generosity and the intensity of its support for the peace process in the Middle East constitute a vital component in the chance to achieve our goal. I will soon leave for the United States, at the invitation of President Clinton, a loyal friend of Israel, in order to discuss the gamut of issues facing us: first and foremost, the renewal of the peace process on all tracks, and the fortification of the strength and security of Israel.

[. . .]

In the coming days, I will bring before the Knesset a proposal to change the Basic Law: The Government, for an increase in the number of ministers, as required by the size of the coalition and the composition of the Knesset. In any form, this is the best government for the State of Israel at this time. We are the bearers of the torch which our predecessors have transferred to us, and we assume full responsibility for moving forward. Today, the government requests the confidence of the 15th Knesset in the knowledge that the eyes of all Israelis are focused thereon, in prayer and with great hope.

[. . .]

Accompanied by the blessings and concern of everyone, we embark today on the long and arduous path. I would be most appreciative if you would express your confidence in the government today and wish it well and God speed.

62 Sharm el-Sheikh Memorandum (September 4, 1999)

The Government of the State of Israel ("GOI") and the Palestine Liberation Organization ("PLO") commit themselves to full and mutual implementation of the Interim Agreement and all other agreements concluded between them since September 1993 (hereinafter "the prior agreements"), and all outstanding commitments emanating from the prior agreements. Without derogating from the other requirements of the prior agreements, the two Sides have agreed as follows:

1. Permanent Status negotiations:

1. In the context of the implementation of the prior agreements, the two Sides will resume the Permanent Status negotiations in an accelerated manner and will make a determined effort to achieve their mutual goal of reaching a Permanent Status Agreement based on the agreed agenda i.e. the specific issues reserved for Permanent Status negotiators and other issues of common interest.

2. The two Sides reaffirm their understanding that the negotiations on the Permanent Status will lead to the implementation of Security Council Resolutions 242 and 338;

3. The two Sides will make a determined effort to conclude a Framework Agreement on all Permanent Status issues in five months from the resumption of the Permanent Status negotiations;

4. The two Sides will conclude a comprehensive agreement on all Permanent Status issues within one year from the resumption of the Permanent Status negotiations;

5. . . . .

2. Phase One and Phase Two of the Further Redeployments

The Israeli Side undertakes the following with regard to Phase One and Phase Two of the Further Redeployments:

1. On September 5, 1999, to transfer 7% from Area C to Area B;

2. On November 15, 1999, to transfer 2% from Area B to Area A and 3% from Area C to Area B;

3. On January 20, 2000, to transfer 1% from Area C to Area A, and 5.1% from Area B to Area A.

3. Release of Prisoners

1. The two Sides shall establish a joint committee that shall follow-up on matters related to release of Palestinian prisoners.

2. The Government of Israel shall release Palestinian and other prisoners who committed their offences prior to September 13, 1993, and were arrested prior to May 4, 1994. . . .

3. The first stage of release of prisoners shall be carried out on September 5, 1999 and shall consist of 200 prisoners. The second stage of release of prisoners shall be carried out on October 8, 1999 and shall consist of 150 prisoners;

4. . . .

5. The Israeli side will aim to release Palestinian prisoners before next Ramadan.

4. Committees [. . .]

5. Safe Passage

1. The operation of the Southern Route of the Safe Passage for the movement of persons, vehicles, and goods will start on October 1, 1999. . . .

2. The two Sides will agree on the specific location of the crossing point of the Northern Route of the Safe Passage . . . not later than October 5, 1999;

3. [. . .]

4. [. . .]

5. In between the operation of the Southern crossing point of the Safe Passage and the Northern crossing point of the Safe Passage, Israel will facilitate arrangements for the movement between the West Bank and the Gaza Strip, using non-Safe Passage routes other than the Southern Route of the Safe Passage;

6. [. . .]

6. Gaza Sea Port

The two Sides have agreed on the following principles to facilitate and enable the construction works of the Gaza Sea Port. . . .:

1. The Israeli Side agrees that the Palestinian Side shall commence construction works in and related to the Gaza Sea Port on October 1, 1999;

2. The two Sides agree that the Gaza Sea Port will not be operated in any way before reaching a joint Sea Port protocol on all aspects of operating the Port, including security;

3. The Gaza Sea Port is a special case, like the Gaza Airport, being situated in an area under the responsibility of the Palestinian Side and serving as an international passage. Therefore, until the conclusion of a joint Sea Port Protocol, all activities and arrangements relating to the construction of the Port shall be in accordance with the provisions of the Interim Agreement, especially those relating to international passages, as adapted in the Gaza Airport Protocol;

4. [. . .]

5. In this context, the Israeli side will facilitate on an on-going basis the works related to the construction of the Gaza Sea Port, including the movement in and out of the Port of vessels, equipment, resources, and material required for the construction of the Port;

6. [. . .]

7. Hebron Issues

1. The Shuhada Road in Hebron shall be opened for the movement of Palestinian vehicles in two phases. . . . ;

2. The wholesale market-Hasbahe will be opened not later than November 1, 1999, in accordance with arrangements which will be agreed upon by the two Sides;

3. [. . .]

8. Security

1. The two Sides will, in accordance with the prior agreements, act to ensure the immediate, efficient and effective handling of any incident involving a threat or act of terrorism, violence or incitement, whether committed by Palestinians or Israelis. To this end, they will cooperate in the exchange of information and coordinate policies and activities. Each side shall immediately and effectively respond to the occurrence or anticipated occurrence of an act of terrorism, violence or incitement and shall take all necessary measures to prevent such an occurrence;

2. Pursuant to the prior agreements, the Palestinian side undertakes to implement its responsibilities for security, security cooperation, on-going obligations and other issues emanating from the prior agreements, including, in particular, the following obligations emanating from the Wye River Memorandum:

1. continuation of the program for the collection of the illegal weapons, including reports;

2. apprehension of suspects, including reports;

3. forwarding of the list of Palestinian policemen to the Israeli Side not later than September 13, 1999;

4. beginning of the review of the list by the Monitoring and Steering Committee not later than October 15, 1999.

9. The two Sides call upon the international donor community to enhance its commitment and financial support to the Palestinian economic development and the Israeli-Palestinian peace process.

10. [. . .]

11. Obligations pertaining to dates, which occur on holidays or Saturdays, shall be carried out on the first subsequent working day.

This memorandum will enter into force one week from the date of its signature.

Made and signed in Sharm el-Sheikh, this fourth day of September 1999.
For the Government of the State of Israel

For the PLO

Witnessed by
For the Arab Republic of Egypt
For the United States of America
For the Hashemite Kingdom of Jordan

63 Protocol Concerning Safe Passage Between the West Bank and the Gaza Strip (October 5, 1999)

1. Preamble

A. Pursuant to the Wye River Memorandum of October 23, 1998 and the Sharm el-Sheikh Memorandum on Implementation Timeline of Outstanding Commitments of Agreements Signed and the Resumption of Permanent Status Negotiations of September 4, 1999; and

In accordance with the Israeli-Palestinian Interim Agreement on the West Bank and the Gaza Strip, signed in Washington, D.C. on September 28, 1995 (hereinafter "the Agreement"); . . .

both sides hereby agree to the following "Protocol Concerning Safe Passage between the West Bank and the Gaza Strip" (hereinafter the "Protocol").

B. This Protocol establishes the modalities for the use of safe passage. . . .

C. This Protocol may be amended by a decision of both sides.

D. This Protocol will come into force upon the signing thereof by both parties.

E. This Preamble is an integral part of this Protocol.

2. General Provisions

A. [. . .]

B. 1. Israel will ensure safe passage for persons and transportation during daylight hours (from sunrise to sunset) or as otherwise agreed, but in any event not less than 10 hours a day.

2. Travelers will be required to commence their journey as follows,
1. one and a half hours for travelers using private vehicles and taxis;
2. two hours for commercial traffic and buses,
before sunset on the day of the journey.

C. 1. Safe passage will be effected by means of privately owned road vehicles and public transportation, as detailed in paragraph 5 below.

2. Safe passage shall be via the following designated crossing points:
1. the Erez crossing point (for persons and vehicles only);
2. the Karni crossing point (Commercial) (for goods only);
3. the Tarkumya crossing point (for persons, vehicles and goods); and
4. an additional crossing point around Mevo Horon.

D. 1. The safe passage arrangements will not be available on Yom Kippur, Israel's Memorial Day and Israel's Independence Day.

2. Both sides may make special arrangements for other designated days, as agreed between them.

E. Israel shall signpost the safe passage routes clearly and shall take all necessary measures to ensure smooth movement while preserving safety and security on the route or routes in use on any specific day.

F. Except as provided in paragraph 3.H.2 below, the use of safe passage by residents of the West Bank and the Gaza Strip does not afford them license to be present in Israel except along the safe passage routes designated for their use.

G. Israel may, for security or safety reasons, temporarily halt the operation of a safe passage route or modify the passage arrangements while ensuring that one of the routes is kept open for safe passage. Notice of such temporary closure or modification shall be given to the Palestinian side, through agreed channels, as far in advance as the circumstances will allow.

H. Israel may deny the use of its territory for safe passage by persons who have seriously or repeatedly violated the safe passage provisions detailed in this Protocol or in the Agreement. Israel will notify the Palestinian side, through agreed channels, of any decision to deny the use of its territory as a result of such violations. The notification shall include details of the violations giving rise to the denial. The individual in question shall have the right to request, through the Palestinian side, that Israel reconsider its decision.

I. Nothing in this Protocol will be construed as derogating from Israel's right to apply inspection measures necessary for ensuring security and safety at the crossing points of the safe passage. Maximum efforts will be made to maintain the dignity of persons using safe passage and to implement inspection measures relying heavily on brief and modern procedures.

J. Israel shall notify the Palestinian side of incidents involving persons using safe passage routes through the agreed channels.

K. It is understood that the safe passage shall be operated on a cost-reimbursement basis, in accordance with an agreement on the modalities to be reached in the Joint Economic Committee.

L. Israel shall be compensated for damages incurred by Israel, Israelis or their property as a result of the use of safe passage, in accordance with an agreement on the modalities to be reached in the Joint Economic Committee.

3. Use of Safe Passage

A. Residents of the West Bank and the Gaza Strip wishing to make use of safe passage shall arrive with a safe passage card at the safe passage terminal at one of the crossing points specified at paragraph 2.C.2 above, where they will identify themselves by means of identification documents . . .

B. After identification at the terminal, and after the validity check of the safe passage card, travelers will be issued with safe passage slips subject to the provisions of this Protocol and the Agreement, . . .

C. [. . .]

D. A safe passage card shall be valid for one year for multiple two-way journeys on the safe passage routes. . . .

E. Upon completion of the journey, the safe passage slips and safe passage stickers shall be returned to the Israeli authorities at the destination crossing point.

F. Residents of the West Bank and the Gaza Strip in possession of permits enabling them to enter Israel will be able to use these permits as safe passage cards, subject to the conditions of such permits and to the modalities set out in this Protocol.

G. 1. Individual safe passage slips will be issued and stamped by the Israeli authorities at the crossing points, with the time of departure from the crossing point and the estimated time of arrival (hereinafter "the designated time").

2. The designated time shall enable completion of the journey within a reasonable time.

H. 1. Persons and vehicles using safe passage under these arrangements shall neither break their journey nor depart from the designated routes, and shall complete the passage within the designated time, unless a delay is caused by a medical emergency or a technical breakdown.

2. Notwithstanding paragraph 3.H.1 above, in the case of a medical emergency travelers may drive directly to the nearest hospital or first aid station. Such travelers will be required to report the incident to the relevant authorities at the destination crossing point as soon as circumstances allow.

3. In the case of a technical breakdown, travelers must remain on the safe passage route with their vehicles until the arrival of the Israeli police and follow their instructions. In addition, travelers may stop another vehicle using safe passage and request the driver to inform the authorities at the destination crossing point of the case.

I. [. . .]

J. Persons and vehicles shall not carry explosives, firearms or other weapons or ammunition except for special cases that may be agreed by both sides. Transportation of dangerous substances shall be in accordance with the provisions of the Agreement.

4. Use of Safe Passage Routes by Visitors from Abroad

[. . .]

5. Use of Vehicles on Safe Passage Routes

A. 1. Residents of the West Bank and the Gaza Strip wishing to use their privately owned vehicles to travel along the safe passage shall apply for a vehicle safe passage permit through the Palestinian side. The Israeli side shall respond to such applications within five working days. . . .

2. In addition to the above, the two sides may agree on specific categories or persons who may use a vehicle not owned by them. . . .

B. 1. On the day of the journey, the drivers will arrive at the safe passage terminal at the departure crossing point with their vehicle safe passage permits; safe passage cards or permits enabling them entry into Israel; identity cards; valid drivers' licenses; valid vehicle licenses; valid insurance policies; and, if applicable, the permit referred to in paragraph 5.A.2 above. After identification, and after the validity check of the vehicle safe passage permit, drivers will be issued with an individual safe passage slip and a safe passage sticker, to be displayed on the right-hand side of the front windshield of the vehicle.

2. The names of all passengers traveling in the vehicle shall be listed on a separate document to be attached to the driver's safe passage slip.

3. [. . .]

C. Residents of the West Bank or the Gaza Strip in possession of valid permits enabling them to enter Israel with their vehicles, will be able to use these permits as vehicle safe passage permits, subject to the conditions of such permits and to the modalities set out in this Protocol.

D. 1. Vehicle safe passage permits shall be valid for not less than three months from the date of issuance, for multiple two-way journeys.

2. [. . .]

E. [. . .]

F. All vehicles used for the purpose of safe passage shall meet Israeli standards and applicable Israeli law.

G. [. . .]

H. In special emergency related cases, to be handled through agreed channels, safe passage may be used by privately owned vehicles without having submitted an application in advance.

6. Use of Safe Passage by Persons Denied Entry into Israel

A. Persons who are denied entry into Israel will use safe passage by means of shuttle buses which will he escorted by Israeli security forces vehicles, and which will operate from 7:00 AM to 2:00 PM on Mondays and Wednesdays of every week.

B. Applications by persons denied entry into Israel to use the safe passage must be submitted to, and agreed upon, at least five working days prior to the planned journey.

C. Cases of persons denied entry into Israel whose applications to use safe passage are not agreed upon shall be discussed in the agreed channels.

D. 1. Persons denied entry into Israel who have used the safe passage will be able to return that same day to their original point of departure . . .

2. [. . .]

E. [. . .]

7. Passage of Palestinian Police

A. . . . uniformed and plainclothes Palestinian policemen required to use the safe passage so as to perform their duty in the West Bank and the Gaza Strip, . . . will be able to use the safe passage after the Palestinian police has submitted an application and after that application was approved, . . .

B. [. . .]

C. When in safe passage, the weapons of the Palestinian policemen will be handed over to the Israeli police and placed in a closed trailer affixed to the Israel police vehicle. . . .

D. [. . .]

8. Use of Safe Passage for Commercial Traffic [. . .]

9. Future Meetings for Improving Operation of the Safe Passage [. . .]

10. Use of Safe Passage by the Ra'ees of the Executive Authority

Arrangements for the use of safe passage by the Ra'ees of the Executive Authority shall be discussed in a special sub-committee through the JSC.

11. Final Clauses

[. . .]

Done at Jerusalem, this 5th day of October, 1999.

64 Trilateral Statement on the Middle East Peace Summit at Camp David (July 25, 2000)

President William J. Clinton
Israeli Prime Minister Ehud Barak
Palestinian Authority Chairman Yasser Arafat

Between July 11 and 24, under the auspices of President Clinton, Prime Minister Barak and Chairman Arafat met at Camp David in an effort to reach an agreement on permanent status. While they were not able to bridge the gaps and reach an agreement, their negotiations were unprecedented in both scope and detail. Building on the progress achieved at Camp David, the two leaders agreed on the following principles to guide their negotiations:

1) The two sides agreed that the aim of their negotiations is to put an end to decades of conflict and achieve a just and lasting peace.

2) The two sides commit themselves to continue their efforts to conclude an agreement on all permanent status issues as soon as possible.

3) Both sides agree that negotiations based on UN Security Council Resolutions 242 and 338 are the only way to achieve such an agreement and they undertake to create an environment for negotiations free from pressure, intimidation and threats of violence.

4) The two sides understand the importance of avoiding unilateral actions that prejudge the outcome of negotiations and that their differences will be resolved only by good faith negotiations.

5) Both sides agree that the United States remains a vital partner in the search for peace and will continue to consult closely with President Clinton and Secretary Albright in the period ahead.

65 Sharm El-Sheikh Fact-Finding Committee Final Report (April 30, 2001)

April 30, 2001

SHARM EL-SHEIKH

FACT-FINDING COMMITTEE

FINAL REPORT

The Honorable George W. Bush
President of the United States
The White House
Washington, DC 20500

Dear Mr. President,

We enclose herewith the report of the Sharm el-Sheikh Fact-Finding Committee. We sought and received information and advice from a wide range of individuals, organizations, and governments. However, the conclusions and recommendations are ours alone.

We are grateful for the support that you and your administration have provided to the Committee.

Respectfully,

Suleyman Demirel
Thorbjoern Jagland
Warren B. Rudman
Javier Solana
George J. Mitchell, Chairman

SUMMARY OF RECOMMENDATIONS

The Government of Israel (GOI) and the Palestinian Authority (PA) must act swiftly and decisively to halt the violence. Their immediate objectives then should be to rebuild confidence and resume negotiations.

During this mission our aim has been to fulfill the mandate agreed at Sharm el-Sheikh. We value the support given our work by the participants at the summit, and we commend the parties for their cooperation. Our principal recommendation is that they recommit themselves to the Sharm el-Sheikh spirit and that they implement the decisions made there in 1999 and 2000. We believe that the summit participants will support bold action by the parties to achieve these objectives.

The restoration of trust is essential, and the parties should take affirmative steps to this end. Given the high level of hostility and mistrust, the timing and sequence of these steps are obviously crucial. This can be decided only by the parties. We urge them to begin the process of decision immediately.

Accordingly, we recommend that steps be taken to:

END THE VIOLENCE

- The GOI and the PA should reaffirm their commitment to existing agreements and undertakings and should immediately implement an unconditional cessation of violence.
- The GOI and PA should immediately resume security cooperation.

REBUILD CONFIDENCE

- The PA and GOI should work together to establish a meaningful "cooling off period" and implement additional confidence building measures, some of which were detailed in the October 2000 Sharm el-Sheikh Statement and some of which were offered by the U.S. on January 7, 2001 in Cairo (see Recommendations section for further description).
- The PA and GOI should resume their efforts to identify, condemn and discourage incitement in all its forms.
- The PA should make clear through concrete action to Palestinians and Israelis alike that terrorism is reprehensible and unacceptable, and that the PA will make a 100 percent effort to prevent terrorist operations and to punish perpetrators. This effort should include immediate steps to apprehend and incarcerate terrorists operating within the PA's jurisdiction.
- The GOI should freeze all settlement activity, including the "natural growth" of existing settlements.
- The GOI should ensure that the IDF adopt and enforce policies and procedures encouraging non-lethal responses to unarmed demonstrators, with a view to minimizing casualties and friction between the two communities.
- The PA should prevent gunmen from using Palestinian populated areas to fire upon Israeli populated areas and IDF positions. This tactic places civilians on both sides at unnecessary risk.

- The GOI should lift closures, transfer to the PA all tax revenues owed, and permit Palestinians who had been employed in Israel to return to their jobs; and should ensure that security forces and settlers refrain from the destruction of homes and roads, as well as trees and other agricultural property in Palestinian areas. We acknowledge the GOI's position that actions of this nature have been taken for security reasons. Nevertheless, the economic effects will persist for years.
- The PA should renew cooperation with Israeli security agencies to ensure, to the maximum extent possible, that Palestinian workers employed within Israel are fully vetted and free of connections to organizations and individuals engaged in terrorism.
- The PA and GOI should consider a joint undertaking to preserve and protect holy places sacred to the traditions of Jews, Muslims, and Christians.
- The GOI and PA should jointly endorse and support the work of Palestinian and Israeli non-governmental organizations involved in cross-community initiatives linking the two peoples

RESUME NEGOTIATIONS

In the spirit of the Sharm el-Sheikh agreements and understandings of 1999 and 2000, we recommend that the parties meet to reaffirm their commitment to signed agreements and mutual understandings, and take corresponding action. This should be the basis for resuming full and meaningful negotiations.

[. . .]

The parties are at a crossroads. If they do not return to the negotiating table, they face the prospect of fighting it out for years on end, with many of their citizens leaving for distant shores to live their lives and raise their children. We pray they make the right choice. That means stopping the violence now. Israelis and Palestinians have to live, work, and prosper together. History and geography have destined them to be neighbors. That cannot be changed. Only when their actions are guided by this awareness will they be able to develop the vision and reality of peace and shared prosperity.

Suleyman Demirel
9th President of the Republic of Turkey

Thorbjoern Jagland
Minister of Foreign Affairs of Norway

George J. Mitchell, Chairman
Former Member and Majority Leader of the United States Senate

Warren B. Rudman
Former Member of the United States Senate

Javier Solana
High Representative for the Common Foreign and Security Policy, European Union

66 Roadmap to a Solution of the Israeli–Palestinian Conflict (April 30, 2003)

U.S. DEPARTMENT OF STATE
Office of the Spokesman
April 30, 2003

A PERFORMANCE-BASED ROADMAP TO A PERMANENT TWO-STATE SOLUTION TO THE ISRAELI–PALESTINIAN CONFLICT

The following is a performance-based and goal-driven roadmap, with clear phases, timelines, target dates, and benchmarks aiming at progress through reciprocal steps by the two parties in the political, security, economic, humanitarian, and institution-building fields, under the auspices of the Quartet [the United States, European Union, United Nations, and Russia]. The destination is a final and comprehensive settlement of the Israeli–Palestinian conflict by 2005, as presented in President Bush's speech of 24 June, and welcomed by the EU, Russia and the UN in the 16 July and 17 September Quartet Ministerial statements.

A two state solution to the Israeli–Palestinian conflict will only be achieved through an end to violence and terrorism, when the Palestinian people have a leadership acting decisively against terror and willing and able to build a practicing democracy based on tolerance and liberty, and through Israel's readiness to do what is necessary for a democratic Palestinian state to be established, and a clear, unambiguous acceptance by both parties of the goal of a negotiated settlement as described below. The Quartet will assist and facilitate implementation of the plan, starting in Phase I, including direct discussions between the parties as required. The plan establishes a realistic timeline for implementation. However, as a performance-based plan, progress will require and depend upon the good faith efforts of the parties, and their compliance with each of the obligations outlined below. Should the parties perform their obligations rapidly, progress within and through the phases may come sooner than indicated in the plan. Non-compliance with obligations will impede progress.

A settlement, negotiated between the parties, will result in the emergence of an independent, democratic, and viable Palestinian state living side by side in peace and security with Israel and its other neighbors. The settlement will resolve the Israel-Palestinian conflict, and end the occupation that began in 1967, based on the foundations of the Madrid Conference, the principle of land for peace, UNSCRs 242, 338 and 1397, agreements previously reached by the parties, and the initiative of

Saudi Crown Prince Abdullah—endorsed by the Beirut Arab League Summit—calling for acceptance of Israel as a neighbor living in peace and security, in the context of a comprehensive settlement. This initiative is a vital element of international efforts to promote a comprehensive peace on all tracks, including the Syrian-Israeli and Lebanese-Israeli tracks.

The Quartet will meet regularly at senior levels to evaluate the parties' performance on implementation of the plan. In each phase, the parties are expected to perform their obligations in parallel, unless otherwise indicated.

PHASE I: ENDING TERROR AND VIOLENCE, NORMALIZING PALESTINIAN LIFE, AND BUILDING PALESTINIAN INSTITUTIONS— PRESENT TO MAY 2003

In Phase I, the Palestinians immediately undertake an unconditional cessation of violence according to the steps outlined below; such action should be accompanied by supportive measures undertaken by Israel. Palestinians and Israelis resume security cooperation based on the Tenet work plan to end violence, terrorism, and incitement through restructured and effective Palestinian security services. Palestinians undertake comprehensive political reform in preparation for statehood, including drafting a Palestinian constitution, and free, fair and open elections upon the basis of those measures. Israel takes all necessary steps to help normalize Palestinian life. Israel withdraws from Palestinian areas occupied from September 28, 2000 and the two sides restore the status quo that existed at that time, as security performance and cooperation progress. Israel also freezes all settlement activity, consistent with the Mitchell report.

At the outset of Phase I:

— Palestinian leadership issues unequivocal statement reiterating Israel's right to exist in peace and security and calling for an immediate and unconditional ceasefire to end armed activity and all acts of violence against Israelis anywhere. All official Palestinian institutions end incitement against Israel.

— Israeli leadership issues unequivocal statement affirming its commitment to the two-state vision of an independent, viable, sovereign Palestinian state living in peace and security alongside Israel, as expressed by President Bush, and calling for an immediate end to violence against Palestinians everywhere. All official Israeli institutions end incitement against Palestinians.

SECURITY

— Palestinians declare an unequivocal end to violence and terrorism and undertake visible efforts on the ground to arrest, disrupt, and restrain individuals and groups conducting and planning violent attacks on Israelis anywhere.

— Rebuilt and refocused Palestinian Authority security apparatus begins sustained, targeted, and effective operations aimed at confronting all those engaged in terror and dismantlement of terrorist capabilities and infrastructure. This includes commencing confiscation of illegal weapons and consolidation of security authority, free of association with terror and corruption.

— GOI takes no actions undermining trust, including deportations, attacks on civilians; confiscation and/or demolition of Palestinian homes and property, as a

punitive measure or to facilitate Israeli construction; destruction of Palestinian institutions and infrastructure; and other measures specified in the Tenet work plan.
— Relying on existing mechanisms and on-the-ground resources, Quartet representatives begin informal monitoring and consult with the parties on establishment of a formal monitoring mechanism and its implementation.
— Implementation, as previously agreed, of U.S. rebuilding, training and resumed security cooperation plan in collaboration with outside oversight board (U.S.-Egypt-Jordan). Quartet support for efforts to achieve a lasting, comprehensive cease-fire.

* All Palestinian security organizations are consolidated into three services reporting to an empowered Interior Minister.
* Restructured/retrained Palestinian security forces and IDF counterparts progressively resume security cooperation and other undertakings in implementation of the Tenet work plan, including regular senior-level meetings, with the participation of U.S. security officials.
[. . .]

— As comprehensive security performance moves forward, IDF withdraws progressively from areas occupied since September 28, 2000 and the two sides restore the status quo that existed prior to September 28, 2000. Palestinian security forces redeploy to areas vacated by IDF.

PALESTINIAN INSTITUTION-BUILDING
— Immediate action on credible process to produce draft constitution for Palestinian statehood. . . .
— Appointment of interim prime minister or cabinet with empowered executive authority/decision-making body.

[. . .]

— As early as possible, and based upon the above measures and in the context of open debate and transparent candidate selection/electoral campaign based on a free, multi-party process, Palestinians hold free, open, and fair elections.

— GOI facilitates Task Force election assistance, registration of voters, movement of candidates and voting officials. Support for NGOs involved in the election process.

— GOI reopens Palestinian Chamber of Commerce and other closed Palestinian institutions in East Jerusalem based on a commitment that these institutions operate strictly in accordance with prior agreements between the parties.

HUMANITARIAN RESPONSE
— Israel takes measures to improve the humanitarian situation. Israel and Palestinians implement in full all recommendations of the Bertini report to improve humanitarian conditions, lifting curfews and easing restrictions on movement of persons and goods, and allowing full, safe, and unfettered access of international and humanitarian personnel.

[. . .]

CIVIL SOCIETY
— Continued donor support, including increased funding through PVOs/NGOs, for people to people programs, private sector development and civil society initiatives.

SETTLEMENTS
— GOI immediately dismantles settlement outposts erected since March 2001.

— Consistent with the Mitchell Report, GOI freezes all settlement activity (including natural growth of settlements).

PHASE II: TRANSITION—JUNE 2003–DECEMBER 2003
In the second phase, efforts are focused on the option of creating an independent Palestinian state with provisional borders and attributes of sovereignty, based on the new constitution, as a way station to a permanent status settlement. As has been noted, this goal can be achieved when the Palestinian people have a leadership acting decisively against terror, willing and able to build a practicing democracy based on tolerance and liberty. With such a leadership, reformed civil institutions and security structures, the Palestinians will have the active support of the Quartet and the broader international community in establishing an independent, viable, state.

Progress into Phase II will be based upon the consensus judgment of the Quartet of whether conditions are appropriate to proceed, taking into account performance of both parties. Furthering and sustaining efforts to normalize Palestinian lives and build Palestinian institutions, Phase II starts after Palestinian elections and ends with possible creation of an independent Palestinian state with provisional borders in 2003. Its primary goals are continued comprehensive security performance and effective security cooperation, continued normalization of Palestinian life and institution-building, further building on and sustaining of the goals outlined in Phase I, ratification of a democratic Palestinian constitution, formal establishment of office of prime minister, consolidation of political reform, and the creation of a Palestinian state with provisional borders.

— INTERNATIONAL CONFERENCE: Convened by the Quartet, in consultation with the parties, immediately after the successful conclusion of Palestinian elections, to support Palestinian economic recovery and launch a process, leading to establishment of an independent Palestinian state with provisional borders.

* Such a meeting would be inclusive, based on the goal of a comprehensive Middle East peace (including between Israel and Syria, and Israel and Lebanon), and based on the principles described in the preamble to this document.
* Arab states restore pre-intifada links to Israel (trade offices, etc.).
* Revival of multilateral engagement on issues including regional water resources, environment, economic development, refugees, and arms control issues.

— New constitution for democratic, independent Palestinian state is finalized and approved by appropriate Palestinian institutions. Further elections, if required, should follow approval of the new constitution.

[. . .]

— Creation of an independent Palestinian state with provisional borders through a process of Israeli-Palestinian engagement, launched by the international conference. As part of this process, implementation of prior agreements, to enhance maximum territorial contiguity, including further action on settlements in conjunction with establishment of a Palestinian state with provisional borders.
— Enhanced international role in monitoring transition, with the active, sustained, and operational support of the Quartet.
— Quartet members promote international recognition of Palestinian state, including possible UN membership.

PHASE III: PERMANENT STATUS AGREEMENT AND END OF THE ISRAELI-PALESTINIAN CONFLICT—2004–2005

Progress into Phase III, based on consensus judgment of Quartet, and taking into account actions of both parties and Quartet monitoring. Phase III objectives are consolidation of reform and stabilization of Palestinian institutions, sustained, effective Palestinian security performance, and Israeli-Palestinian negotiations aimed at a permanent status agreement in 2005.

— SECOND INTERNATIONAL CONFERENCE: Convened by Quartet, in consultation with the parties, at beginning of 2004 to endorse agreement reached on an independent Palestinian state with provisional borders and formally to launch a process with the active, sustained, and operational support of the Quartet, leading to a final, permanent status resolution in 2005, including on borders, Jerusalem, refugees, settlements; and, to support progress toward a comprehensive Middle East settlement between Israel and Lebanon and Israel and Syria, to be achieved as soon as possible.

[. . .]

— Parties reach final and comprehensive permanent status agreement that ends the Israel-Palestinian conflict in 2005, through a settlement negotiated between the parties based on UNSCR 242, 338, and 1397, that ends the occupation that began in 1967, and includes an agreed, just, fair, and realistic solution to the refugee issue, and a negotiated resolution on the status of Jerusalem that takes into account the political and religious concerns of both sides, and protects the religious interests of Jews, Christians, and Muslims worldwide, and fulfills the vision of two states, Israel and sovereign, independent, democratic and viable Palestine, living side-by-side in peace and security.

— Arab state acceptance of full normal relations with Israel and security for all the states of the region in the context of a comprehensive Arab-Israeli peace.

67 The Disengagement Plan from Gaza Strip and Northern Samaria (April 18, 2004)

1. General

Israel is committed to the peace process and aspires to reach an agreed resolution of the conflict on the basis of the principle of two states for two peoples, the State of Israel as the state of the Jewish people and a Palestinian state for the Palestinian people, as part of the implementation of President Bush's vision.

Israel is concerned to advance and improve the current situation. Israel has come to the conclusion that there is currently no reliable Palestinian partner with which it can make progress in a bilateral peace process. Accordingly, it has developed a plan of unilateral disengagement, based on the following considerations:

i. The stalemate dictated by the current situation is harmful. In order to break out of this stalemate, Israel is required to initiate moves not dependent on Palestinian cooperation.

ii. The plan will lead to a better security situation, at least in the long term.

iii. The assumption that, in any future permanent status arrangement, there will be no Israeli towns and villages in the Gaza Strip. On the other hand, it is clear that in the West Bank, there are areas which will be part of the State of Israel, including cities, towns and villages, security areas and installations, and other places of special interest to Israel.

iv. The relocation from the Gaza Strip and from Northern Samaria (as delineated on Map) will reduce friction with the Palestinian population, and carries with it the potential for improvement in the Palestinian economy and living conditions.

v. The hope is that the Palestinians will take advantage of the opportunity created by the disengagement in order to break out of the cycle of violence and to reengage in a process of dialogue.

vi. [. . .]

vii. . . . When there is evidence from the Palestinian side of its willingness, capability and implementation in practice of the fight against terrorism and the institution of reform as required by the Road Map, it will be possible to return to the track of negotiation and dialogue.

2. Main elements

i. Gaza Strip:

1. Israel will evacuate the Gaza Strip, including all existing Israeli towns and villages, and will redeploy outside the Strip. . . .

2. Upon completion of this process, there shall no longer be any permanent presence of Israeli security forces or Israeli civilians in the areas of Gaza Strip territory which have been evacuated.

3. As a result, there will be no basis for claiming that the Gaza Strip is occupied territory.

ii. West Bank:

1. Israel will evacuate an Area in the Northern Samaria Area (see Map), including four villages and all military installations, and will redeploy outside the vacated area.

2. Upon completion of this process, there shall no longer be any permanent presence of Israeli security forces or Israeli civilians in the Northern Samaria Area.

3. The move will enable territorial contiguity for Palestinians in the Northern Samaria Area.

4. [. . .]

5. [. . .]

6. The Security fence: Israel will continue to build the security fence, in accordance with the relevant decisions of the government. The route will take into account humanitarian considerations.

3. Security situation following the disengagement

i. The Gaza Strip:

1. Israel will guard and monitor the external land perimeter of the Gaza Strip, will continue to maintain exclusive authority in Gaza air space, and will continue to exercise security activity in the sea off the coast of the Gaza Strip.

2. The Gaza Strip shall be demilitarized and shall be devoid of weaponry, the presence of which does not accord with the Israeli-Palestinian agreements.

3. Israel reserves its inherent right of self defense, both preventive and reactive, including where necessary the use of force, in respect of threats emanating from the Gaza Strip.

ii. The West Bank:

1. Upon completion of the evacuation of the Northern Samaria Area, no permanent Israeli military presence will remain in this area.

2. Israel reserves its inherent right of self defense, both preventive and reactive, including where necessary the use of force, in respect of threats emanating from the Northern Samaria Area.

3. . . . However, as circumstances permit, Israel will consider reducing such activity in Palestinian cities.

4. Israel will work to reduce the number of internal checkpoints throughout the West Bank.

4. Military Installations and Infrastructure in the Gaza Strip and Northern Samaria

In general, these will be dismantled and removed, with the exception of those which Israel decides to leave and transfer to another party.

5. Security assistance to the Palestinians

Israel agrees that by coordination with it, advice, assistance and training will be provided to the Palestinian security forces for the implementation of their obligations to combat terrorism and maintain public order, by American, British, Egyptian, Jordanian or other experts, as agreed with Israel. No foreign security presence may enter the Gaza Strip or the West Bank without being coordinated with and approved by Israel.

6. The border area between the Gaza Strip and Egypt . . .

Initially, Israel will continue to maintain a military presence along the border between the Gaza Strip and Egypt . . .

Subsequently, the evacuation of this area will be considered. Evacuation of the area will be dependent, inter alia, on the security situation and the extent of cooperation with Egypt in establishing a reliable alternative arrangement.

If and when conditions permit the evacuation of this area, Israel will be willing to consider the possibility of the establishment of a seaport and airport in the Gaza Strip, in accordance with arrangements to be agreed with Israel.

7. Israeli towns and villages

Israel will strive to leave the immovable property relating to Israeli towns and villages intact. The transfer of Israeli economic activity to Palestinians carries with it the potential for a significant improvement in the Palestinian economy. . . .

Israel reserves the right to request that the economic value of the assets left in the evacuated areas be taken into consideration.

8. Civil Infrastructure and Arrangements

Infrastructure relating to water, electricity, sewage and telecommunications serving the Palestinians will remain in place. Israel will strive to leave in place the infrastructure relating to water, electricity and sewage currently serving the Israeli towns and villages. In general, Israel will enable the continued supply of electricity, water, gas and petrol to the Palestinians, in accordance with current arrangements. Other existing arrangements, such as those relating to water and the electro-magnetic sphere shall remain in force.

9. Activity of International Organizations

Israel recognizes the great importance of the continued activity of international humanitarian organizations assisting the Palestinian population. Israel will coordinate with these organizations arrangements to facilitate this activity.

10. Economic arrangements

In general, the economic arrangements currently in operation between Israel and the Palestinians shall, in the meantime, remain in force. These arrangements include, inter alia:

i. the entry of workers into Israel in accordance with the existing criteria.
ii. the entry and exit of goods between the Gaza Strip, the West Bank, Israel and abroad.
iii. the monetary regime.
iv. tax and customs envelope arrangements.
v. postal and telecommunications arrangements.

In the longer term, and in line with Israel's interest in encouraging greater Palestinian economic independence, Israel expects to reduce the number of Palestinian workers entering Israel. Israel supports the development of sources of employment in the Gaza Strip and in Palestinian areas of the West Bank.

11. Erez Industrial Zone

The Erez industrial zone, situated in the Gaza Strip, employs some 4000 Palestinian workers. The continued operation of the zone is primarily a clear Palestinian interest. Israel will consider the continued operation of the zone on the current basis, on two conditions:

i. The existence of appropriate security arrangements.
ii. The express recognition of the international community that the continued operation of the zone on the current basis shall not be considered continued Israeli control of the area.

Alternatively, the industrial zone shall be transferred to the responsibility of an agreed Palestinian or international entity.

Israel will seek to examine, together with Egypt, the possibility of establishing a joint industrial area in the area between the Gaza Strip, Egypt and Israel.

12. International passages

i. The international passage between the Gaza Strip and Egypt
    1. The existing arrangements shall continue.
    2. Israel is interested in moving the passage to the "three borders" area, approxi-

mately two kilometers south of its current location. This would need to be effected in coordination with Egypt. This move would enable the hours of operation of the passage to be extended.
ii. The international passages between the West Bank and Jordan:
The existing arrangements shall continue.

13. Erez Crossing Point

The Israeli part of Erez crossing point will be moved to a location within Israel in a time frame to be determined separately.

14. Timetable

The process of evacuation is planned to be completed by the end of 2005. The stages of evacuation and the detailed timetable will be notified to the United States.

15. Conclusion

Israel looks to the international community for widespread support for the disengagement plan. This support is essential in order to bring the Palestinians to implement in practice their obligations to combat terrorism and effect reforms, thus enabling the parties to return to the path of negotiation.
[. . .]

68 Prime Minister Ariel Sharon's Address to the Knesset – The Vote on the Disengagement Plan (October 25, 2004)

Mr. Speaker, Members of Knesset,

This is a fateful hour for Israel. We are on threshold of a difficult decision, the likes of which we have seldom faced, the significance of which for the future of our country in this region is consistent with the difficulty, pain, and dispute it arouses within us. You know that I do not say these things with a light heart to the representatives of the nation and to the entire nation watching and listening to every word uttered here in the Knesset today. This is a people that has courageously faced and still faces the burden and terror of the ongoing war, which has continued from generation to generation; in which, as in a relay race, fathers pass the guns to their sons; in which the boundary between the front line and the home front has long been erased; in which schools and hotels, restaurants and marketplaces, cafes and buses have also become targets for cruel terrorism and premeditated murder.

Today, this nation wants to know what decision this house will make at the end of this stormy discussion. What will we say to them, and what message will we convey to them? For me, this decision is unbearably difficult. During my years as a fighter and commander, as a politician, Member of Knesset, as a minister in Israel's governments and as prime minister, I have never faced so difficult a decision.

I know the implications and impact of the Knesset's decision on the lives of thousands of Israelis who have lived in the Gaza Strip for many years, who were sent there on behalf of the governments of Israel, and who built homes there, planted trees and grew flowers, and who gave birth to sons and daughters, who have not known any other home. I am well aware of the fact that I sent them and took part in this enterprise, and many of these people are my personal friends. I am well aware of their pain, rage, and despair. However, as much as I understand everything they are going through during these days and everything they will face as a result of the necessary decision to be made in the Knesset today, I also believe in the necessity of taking the step of disengagement in these areas, with all the pain it entails, and I am determined to complete this mission. I am firmly convinced and truly believe that this disengagement will strengthen Israel's hold over territory which is essential to our existence, and will be welcomed and appreciated by those near and far, reduce animosity, break through boycotts and sieges and advance us along the path of peace with the Palestinians and our other neighbors.

I am accused of deceiving the people and the voters, because I am taking steps which are in total opposition to past things I have said and deeds I have done. This is a false accusation. Both during the elections and as prime minister, I have repeatedly and publicly said that I support the establishment of a Palestinian state alongside the State of Israel. I have repeatedly and openly said that I am willing to make painful compromises in order to put an end to this ongoing and malignant conflict between those who struggle over this land, and that I would do my utmost in order to bring peace.

And I wish, Mr. Chairman, to say that many years before, in 1988, in a meeting with Prime Minister Yitzchak Shamir and with the ministers of the Likud, I said there that I believe that if we do not want to be pushed back to the 1967 lines, the territory should be divided.

As one who fought in all of Israel's wars, and learned from personal experience that, without proper force, we do not have a chance of surviving in this region, which does not show mercy towards the weak, I have also have learned from experience that the sword alone cannot decide this bitter dispute in this land.

I have been told that the disengagement will be interpreted as a shameful withdrawal under pressure, and will increase the terror campaign, present Israel as weak, and will show our people as a nation unwilling to fight and to stand up for itself. I reject that statement outright. We have the strength to defend this country, and to strike at the enemy which seeks to destroy us.

And there are those who tell me that, in exchange for a genuine signed peace agreement, they too would be willing to make these painful compromises. However, regrettably, we do not have a partner on the other side with whom to conduct genuine dialogue, in order to achieve a peace agreement. Even prime ministers of Israel who declared their willingness to relinquish the maximum territory of our homeland were answered with fire and hostility. Recently, the chairman of the Palestinian Authority declared that "a million shaheeds will break through to Jerusalem." In the choice between a responsible and wise action in history, which may lead to painful compromise and a "holy war" to destroy Israel, Yasser Arafat chose the latter—the path of blood, fire, and shaheeds. He seeks to turn a national conflict that can be terminated through mutual understanding into a religious war between Islam and Jews, and even to spill the blood of Jews who live far away.

Israel has many hopes and faces extreme dangers. The most prominent danger is Iran, which is making every effort to acquire nuclear weapons and ballistic missiles, and establishing an enormous terror network together with Syria in Lebanon.

And I ask you: What are we doing and what are we struggling over in the face of these terrible dangers? Are we not capable of uniting to meet this threat? This is the true question.

The Disengagement Plan does not replace negotiations and is not meant to permanently freeze the situation which will be created. It is an essential and necessary step in a situation which currently does not enable genuine negotiations for peace. However, everything remains open for a future agreement, which will hopefully be achieved when this murderous terror ends, and our neighbors will realize that they cannot triumph over us in this land.

Mr. Chairman, with your permission, I will read several lines from a famous essay which was published in the midst of the Arab Revolt of 1936—and we must bear in mind that the Jewish community in Israel numbered less than 400,000. This essay by Moshe Beilinson was published in "Davar", as I mentioned, during the murderous Arab Revolt of 1936 (and I quote): "How much longer? People ask. How much longer? Until the strength of Israel in its land will condemn and defeat in advance any enemy attack; until the most enthusiastic and bold in any enemy camp will know there are no means to break the strength of Israel in its land, because the necessity of life is with it, and the truth of life is with it, and there is no other way but to accept it. This is the essence of this campaign."

I am convinced that everything we have done since then confirms these emphatic words.

We have no desire to permanently rule over millions of Palestinians, who double their numbers every generation. Israel, which wishes to be an exemplary democracy, will not be able to bear such a reality over time. The Disengagement Plan presents the possibility of opening a gate to a different reality.

Today, I wish to address our Arab neighbors. Already in our Declaration of Independence, in the midst of a cruel war, Israel, which was born in blood, extended its hand in peace to those who fought against it and sought to destroy it by force (and I quote): "We appeal—in the very midst of the onslaught launched against us now for months—to the Arab inhabitants of the State of Israel to preserve peace and participate in the upbuilding of the state on the basis of full and equal citizenship and due representation in all its provisional and permanent institutions."

A long time has passed since then. This land and this region have known more wars, and have known all the wars between the wars, terrorism and the difficult counteractions undertaken by Israel, with the sole purpose of defending the lives of its citizens. In this ongoing war, many among the civilian population, among the innocent, were killed. And tears met tears. I would like you to know that we did not seek to build our lives in this homeland on your ruins. Many years ago, Ze'ev Jabotinsky wrote in a poem his vision for partnership and peace among the peoples of this land (and I quote): "There he will be saturated with plenty and joy, the son of the Arab, the son of Nazareth, and my son."

We were attacked and stood firm, with our backs to the sea. Many fell in the battle, and many lost their homes and fields and orchards, and became refugees. This is the way of war. However, war is not inevitable and predestined. Even today, we regret the loss of innocent lives in your midst. Our way is not one of intentional killing.

Forty-eight yeas ago, on the eve of our Independence Day in 1956, against the background of the return of the bodies of ten terrorists who committed crimes in Israel, murderous acts in Israel, and who were delivered in wooden coffins to the Egyptians at a border crossing in the Gaza Strip, on this, the Hebrew poet Natan Alterman wrote the following:

"Arabia, enemy unknown to you, you will awake when you rise against me, My life serves as witness with my back against the wall and to my history and my God, Enemy, the power of whose rage in the face of those who rise to destroy him until the day Will be similar only to the force of his brotherhood in a fraternal covenant between one nation and another."

This was during the time of the terrorist killings and our retaliatory raids.

Members of Knesset,

With your permission, I wish to end with a quotation from Prime Minister Menachem Begin, who at the end of December 1977 said on this podium (and I quote):

"Where does this irresponsible language come from, in addition to other things which were said? I once said, during an argument with people from Gush Emunim, that I love them today, and will continue to like them tomorrow. I told them: you are wonderful pioneers, builders of the land, settlers on barren soil, in rain and through winter, through all difficulties. However, you have one weakness—you have developed among yourselves a messianic complex.

"You must remember that there were days, before you were born or were only small children, when other people risked their lives day and night, worked and toiled, made sacrifices and performed their tasks without a hint of a messianic complex. And I call on you today, my good friends from Gush Emunim, to perform your tasks with no less modesty than your predecessors, on other days and nights.

"We do not require anyone to supervise the Kashrut of our commitment to the Land of Israel! We have dedicated our lives to the Land of Israel and to the struggle for its liberation, and will continue to do so."

I call on the people of Israel to unite at this decisive hour. We must find a common denominator for some form of "necessary unity" which will enable us to cope with these fateful days with understanding, and through our common destiny, and which will allow us to construct a dam against brotherly hatred which pushes many over the edge. We have already paid an unbearably high price for murderous fanaticism. We must find the root which brings us all together, and must carry out our actions with the wisdom and responsibility which allow us to lead our lives here as a mature and experienced nation. I call on you to support me at this decisive time.

Thank you.

69 U.N. Security Council: Resolution 1701 (August 11, 2006)

The Security Council,

Recalling all its previous resolutions on Lebanon, in particular resolutions 425 (1978), 426 (1978), 520 (1982), 1559 (2004), 1655 (2006) 1680 (2006) and 1697 (2006), as well as the statements of its President on the situation in Lebanon, in particular the statements of 18 June 2000 (S/PRST/2000/21), of 19 October 2004 (S/PRST/2004/36), of 4 May 2005 (S/PRST/2005/17), of 23 January 2006 (S/PRST/2006/3) and of 30 July 2006 (S/PRST/2006/35),

Expressing its utmost concern at the continuing escalation of hostilities in Lebanon and in Israel since Hizbollah's attack on Israel on 12 July 2006, which has already caused hundreds of deaths and injuries on both sides, extensive damage to civilian infrastructure and hundreds of thousands of internally displaced persons,

Emphasizing the need for an end of violence, but at the same time emphasizing the need to address urgently the causes that have given rise to the current crisis, including the unconditional release of the abducted Israeli soldiers,

Mindful of the sensitivity of the issue of prisoners and encouraging the efforts aimed at urgently settling the issue of the Lebanese prisoners detained in Israel,

Welcoming the efforts of the Lebanese Prime Minister and the commitment of the Government of Lebanon, in its seven-point plan, to extend its authority over its territory, through its own legitimate armed forces, such that there will be no weapons without the consent of the Government of Lebanon and no authority other than that of the Government of Lebanon, welcoming also its commitment to a United Nations force that is supplemented and enhanced in numbers, equipment, mandate and scope of operation, and bearing in mind its request in this plan for an immediate withdrawal of the Israeli forces from southern Lebanon,

Determined to act for this withdrawal to happen at the earliest,

Taking due note of the proposals made in the seven-point plan regarding the Shebaa farms area,

Welcoming the unanimous decision by the Government of Lebanon on 7 August 2006 to deploy a Lebanese armed force of 15,000 troops in South Lebanon as the Israeli army withdraws behind the Blue Line and to request the assistance of additional forces from the United Nations Interim Force in Lebanon (UNIFIL) as needed, to facilitate the entry of the Lebanese armed forces into the region and to restate its intention to strengthen the Lebanese armed forces with material as needed to enable it to perform its duties,

Aware of its responsibilities to help secure a permanent ceasefire and a longterm solution to the conflict,

Determining that the situation in Lebanon constitutes a threat to international peace and security,

1. Calls for a full cessation of hostilities based upon, in particular, the immediate cessation by Hizbollah of all attacks and the immediate cessation by Israel of all offensive military operations;

2. [. . .]

3. [. . .]

4. Reiterates its strong support for full respect for the Blue Line;

5. Also reiterates its strong support, as recalled in all its previous relevant resolutions, for the territorial integrity, sovereignty and political independence of Lebanon within its internationally recognized borders, as contemplated by the Israeli-Lebanese General Armistice Agreement of 23 March 1949;

6. Calls on the international community to take immediate steps to extend its financial and humanitarian assistance to the Lebanese people, . . .

7. Affirms that all parties are responsible for ensuring that no action is taken contrary to paragraph 1 that might adversely affect the search for a long-term solution, humanitarian access to civilian populations, including safe passage for humanitarian convoys, or the voluntary and safe return of displaced persons, and calls on all parties to comply with this responsibility and to cooperate with the Security Council;

8. Calls for Israel and Lebanon to support a permanent ceasefire and a longterm solution based on the following principles and elements:
– full respect for the Blue Line by both parties;
– security arrangements to prevent the resumption of hostilities, including the establishment between the Blue Line and the Litani river of an area free of any armed personnel, assets and weapons other than those of the Government of Lebanon and of UNIFIL as authorized in paragraph 11, deployed in this area;
– [. . .]

– provision to the United Nations of all remaining maps of landmines in Lebanon in Israel's possession;

9. [...]

10. [...]

11. [...]

12. [...]

13. [...]

14. Calls upon the Government of Lebanon to secure its borders and other entry points to prevent the entry in Lebanon without its consent of arms or related materiel and requests UNIFIL as authorized in paragraph 11 to assist the Government of Lebanon at its request;

15. Decides further that all States shall take the necessary measures to prevent, by their nationals or from their territories or using their flag vessels or aircraft:
(a) The sale or supply to any entity or individual in Lebanon of arms and related materiel of all types, including weapons and ammunition, military vehicles and equipment, paramilitary equipment, and spare parts for the aforementioned, whether or not originating in their territories; and
(b) The provision to any entity or individual in Lebanon of any technical training or assistance related to the provision, manufacture, maintenance or use of the items listed in subparagraph (a) above; except that these prohibitions shall not apply to arms, related material, training or assistance authorized by the Government of Lebanon or by UNIFIL as authorized in paragraph 11;

16. [...]

17. Requests the Secretary-General to report to the Council within one week on the implementation of this resolution and subsequently on a regular basis;

18. Stresses the importance of, and the need to achieve, a comprehensive, just and lasting peace in the Middle East, based on all its relevant resolutions including its resolutions 242 (1967) of 22 November 1967, 338 (1973) of 22 October 1973 and 1515 (2003) of 19 November 2003;

19. Decides to remain actively seized of the matter.

70 Announcement of Annapolis Conference (November 20, 2007)

20 Nov 2007
U.S. Department of State

On November 27, the United States will host Israeli Prime Minister Olmert, Palestinian Authority President Abbas, along with the Members of the Quartet, the Members of the Arab League Follow-on Committee, the G-8, the permanent members of the U.N. Security Council, and other key international actors for a conference at the U.S. Naval Academy in Annapolis, Maryland. Secretary Rice will host a dinner the preceding evening here in Washington, where President Bush will deliver remarks. President Bush and the Israeli and Palestinian leaders will deliver speeches to open the formal conference in Annapolis.

The Annapolis Conference will signal broad international support for the Israeli and Palestinian leaders' courageous efforts, and will be a launching point for negotiations leading to the establishment of a Palestinian state and the realization of Israeli-Palestinian peace.

Those invited to attend the conference are:

United States
Israel
Palestinian Authority
Algeria
Arab League Secretary General
Bahrain
Brazil
Canada
China
Egypt
EU Commission
EU High Rep
EU Pres Portugal
France
Germany
Greece
India

Indonesia
Iraq
Italy
Japan
Jordan
Lebanon
Malaysia
Mauritania
Morocco
Norway
Oman
Pakistan
Poland
Qatar
Russia
Saudi Arabia
Senegal
Slovenia
South Africa
Spain
Sudan
Sweden
Syria
Quartet Special Envoy Tony Blair
Tunisia
Turkey
United Arab Emirates
United Kingdom
UNSYG
Yemen

Observers:
IMF
World Bank

71 Joint Understanding on Negotiations (November 27, 2007)

The representatives of the Government of the State of Israel and the Palestine Liberation Organization (PLO), represented respectively by Prime Minister Ehud Olmert and President Mahmoud Abbas, in his capacity as Chairman of the PLO Executive Committee and President of the Palestinian Authority, have convened in Annapolis, Maryland, under the auspices of President George W. Bush of the United States of America, and with the support of the participants of this international conference, having concluded the following Joint Understanding:

We express our determination to bring an end to bloodshed, suffering and decades of conflict between our peoples, to usher in a new era of peace, based on freedom, security, justice, dignity, respect and mutual recognition, to propagate a culture of peace and non-violence, and to confront terrorism and incitement, whether committed by Palestinians or Israelis.

In furtherance of the goal of two states, Israel and Palestine, living side by side in peace and security:

- We agree to immediately launch good faith bilateral negotiations in order to conclude a peace treaty resolving all outstanding issues, including all core issues, without exception, as specified in previous agreements.
- We agree to engage in vigorous, ongoing and continuous negotiations, and shall make every effort to conclude an agreement before the end of 2008.
- For this purpose, a steering committee, led jointly by the head of the delegation of each party, will meet continuously, as agreed.
- The steering committee will develop a joint work plan and establish and oversee the work of negotiations teams to address all issues, to be headed by one lead representative from each party.
- The first session of the steering committee will be held on 12 December 2007.
- President Abbas and Prime Minister Olmert will continue to meet on a bi-weekly basis to follow up the negotiations in order to offer all necessary assistance for their advancement.

The parties also commit to immediately implement their respective obligations under the Performance-Based Road Map to a Permanent Two-State Solution to the Israel-Palestinian Conflict, issued by the Quartet on 30 April 2003 (hereinafter, "the Roadmap") and agree to form an American, Palestinian and Israeli mechanism, led by the United States, to follow up on the implementation of the Roadmap. The parties further commit to continue the implementation of the ongoing obligations of the Roadmap until they reach a peace treaty. The United States will monitor and judge the fulfillment of the commitments of both sides of the Roadmap.

Unless otherwise agreed by the parties, implementation of the future peace treaty will be subject to the implementation of the Roadmap, as judged by the United States.

In conclusion, we express our profound appreciation to the President of the United States and his Administration, and to the participants of this international conference, for their support for our bilateral peace process.

SOURCES

The documents included in this volume are all in the public domain. Most are available on the U.S. Government Department of State web site and are presented as full documents at http://www.state.gov/www/regions/nea/peace_process.html or another collection of Department of State documents at http://2001-2009.state.gov/p/nea/rt/c9679.htm. Alternatively, the Israeli Ministry of Foreign Affairs website has a very comprehensive collection of historical documents, too, found at http://www.mfa.gov.il/mfa/foreign%20relations/israels%20foreign%20relations%20since%201947/1947-1974/.

Listed below are locations where copies of the documents may be found from a variety of different sites, most of which present the full documents.

Web addresses of organizations and documents change over time. The addresses included here were correct at the time these documents were edited.

Reading 1:
http://www.geocities.com/Vienna/6640/zion/judenstaadt.html
http://www.jewishvirtuallibrary.org/jsource/Zionism/herzl2.html

Reading 2:
http://www.mideastweb.org/basleprogram.htm

Reading 3:
http://www.thejerusalemfund.org/carryover/documents/mcmahon.html

Reading 4:
http://www.mideastweb.org/mesykespicot.htm

Reading 5:
http://www.mfa.gov.il/MFA/Peace+Process/Guide+to+the+Peace+Process/The+Balfour+Declaration.htm

Reading 6:
http://www.mfa.gov.il/MFA/Peace+Process/Reference+Documents/The+Weizmann-Feisal+Agreement+3-Jan-1919.htm

Reading 7:
http://www.mideastweb.org/1922wp.htm

Reading 8:
http://www.mfa.gov.il/MFA/Peace+Process/Guide+to+the+Peace+Process/
The+Mandate+for+Palestine.htm

Reading 9:
Parliamentary Debates [Hansard] February 13, 1931; Vol. 248; Columns
751–757.

Reading 10:
http://unispal.un.org/unispal.nsf/0/08e38a718201458b052565700072b358?
OpenDocument

Reading 11:
http://unispal.un.org/unispal.nsf/0/4941922311b4e3c585256d17004bd2e2?
OpenDocument

Reading 12:
http://unispal.un.org/unispal.nsf/0/eb5b88c94aba2ae585256d0b00555536?Open
Document

Reading 13:
http://www.jewishvirtuallibrary.org/jsource/History/whitepapReaction.html

Reading 14:
http://www.mideastweb.org/biltmore_program.htm

Reading 15:
http://www.mideastweb.org/araboffice.htm

Reading 16:
http://www.mfa.gov.il/MFA/Peace+Process/Guide+to+the+Peace+Process/UN+
General+Assembly+Resolution+181.htm

Reading 17:
http://www.mfa.gov.il/MFA/Peace+Process/Guide+to+the+Peace+Process/
Declaration+of+Establishment+of+State+of+Israel.htm

Reading 18:
http://www.mfa.gov.il/MFA/Foreign+Relations/Israels+Foreign+Relations+
since+1947/1947-1974/Creation+of+a+Conciliation+Commission-+General+
Ass.htm

Reading 19:
http://www.mfa.gov.il/MFA/Foreign+Relations/Israels+Foreign+Relations+
since+1947/1947-1974/Admission+of+Israel+to+the+United+Nations-+
General.htm

Reading 20:
http://www.mideastweb.org/ga303.htm

Reading 21:
http://www.mfa.gov.il/MFA/MFAArchive/1950_1959/Law%20of%20Return%
205710-1950

Reading 22:
http://www.mideastweb.org/sc95.htm

Reading 23:
http://www.thejerusalemfund.org/carryover/documents/draft.html

Reading 24:
http://www.mfa.gov.il/MFA/Foreign%20Relations/Israels%20Foreign%20R
    Elations%20since%201947/1947-1974/19%20Statement%20to%20the%20
    Security%20Council%20by%20Foreign%20Mi

Reading 25:
http://www.mfa.gov.il/MFA/Peace+Process/Guide+to+the+Peace+Process/
    Protection+of+Holy+Places+Law.htm

Reading 26:
http://www.mfa.gov.il/MFA/Peace+Process/Guide+to+the+Peace+Process/The+
    Khartoum+Resolutions.htm

Reading 27:
http://usinfo.state.gov/regional/nea/summit/unres242.htm

Reading 28:
http://www.mfa.gov.il/MFA/Peace+Process/Guide+to+the+Peace+Process/The+
    Palestinian+National+Charter.htm

Reading 29:
http://www.jewishvirtuallibrary.org/jsource/Terrorism/fatah7.html

Reading 30:
http://usinfo.state.gov/regional/nea/summit/unres338.htm

Reading 31:
http://www.mideastweb.org/plo1974.htm

Reading 32:
http://www.knesset.gov.il/process/docs/egypt_interim_eng.htm

Reading 33:
http://www.knesset.gov.il/process/docs/beginspeech_eng.htm

Reading 34:
http://www.knesset.gov.il/process/docs/sadatspeech_eng.htm

Reading 35:
http://www.jewishvirtuallibrary.org/jsource/Terrorism/6point.html

Reading 36:
http://usinfo.state.gov/mena/Archive_Index/The_Camp_David_Accords.html

Reading 37:
http://www.mfa.gov.il/MFA/Peace+Process/Guide+to+the+Peace+Process/
    Israel-Egypt+Peace+Treaty.htm

Reading 38:
http://www.mfa.gov.il/MFA/MFAArchive/1980_1989/Basic+Law-+Jerusalem-
+Capital+of+Israel.htm

Reading 39:
http://www.knesset.gov.il/process/docs/fahd_eng.htm

Reading 40:
http://www.mfa.gov.il/MFA/Peace+Process/Guide+to+the+Peace+Process/
Golan+Heights+Law.htm

Reading 41:
http://www.mfa.gov.il/MFA/Foreign%20Relations/Israels%20Foreign%20R
Elations%20since%201947/1982-1984/55%20Address%20by%20Prime%20
Minister%20Begin%20at%20the%20National

Reading 42:
http://www.mfa.gov.il/MFA/Foreign%20Relations/Israels%20Foreign%20
Relations%20since%201947/1982-1984/114%20Agreement%20between%20
Israel%20and%20Lebanon-%2017%20May%201

Reading 43:
http://www.thejerusalemfund.org/carryover/documents/dec_independence.html

Reading 44:
http://www.mfa.gov.il/MFA/Peace+Process/Guide+to+the+Peace+Process/
Israel-s+Peace+Initiative+-+May+14-+1989.htm

Reading 45:
http://www.knesset.gov.il/process/docs/baker_eng.htm

Reading 46:
http://www.mfa.gov.il/MFA/Peace+Process/Guide+to+the+Peace+Process/
Madrid+Letter+of+Invitation.htm

Reading 47:
http://www.state.gov/p/nea/rls/22579.htm

Reading 48:
http://www.state.gov/p/nea/rls/22602.htm

Reading 49:
http://www.mfa.gov.il/MFA/Peace+Process/Guide+to+the+Peace+Process/
Israel-Jordan+Common+Agenda.htm

Reading 50:
http://www.state.gov/p/nea/rls/22676.htm

Reading 51:
http://www.mfa.gov.il/MFA/Peace+Process/Guide+to+the+Peace+Process/
The+Washington+Declaration.htm

Reading 52:
http://www.mfa.gov.il/MFA/Peace+Process/Guide+to+the+Peace+Process/
Israel-Jordan+Peace+Treaty.htm

Reading 53:
http://nobelprize.org/nobel_prizes/peace/laureates/1994/arafat-lecture.html

Reading 54:
http://nobelprize.org/nobel_prizes/peace/laureates/1994/peres-lecture.html

Reading 55:
http://nobelprize.org/nobel_prizes/peace/laureates/1994/rabin-lecture.html

Reading 56:
http://www.state.gov/p/nea/rls/22678.htm

Reading 57:
http://www.fmep.org/reports/vol05/no6/05-rabins_final_defense_of_oslo_ii.html

Reading 58:
http://www.mfa.gov.il/MFA/Foreign%20Relations/Israels%20Foreign%20
Relations%20since%201947/1995-1996/Excerpts%20from%20a%20
speech%20by%20Prime%20Minister%20Rabin%20at

Reading 59:
http://www.knesset.gov.il/process/docs/grapes_eng.htm

Reading 60:
http://www.state.gov/p/nea/rls/22694.htm

Reading 61:
http://www.mfa.gov.il/MFA/Foreign%20Relations/Israels%20Foreign%20Relatio
ns%20since%201947/1999-2001/1%20Address%20in%20the%20Knesset
%20by%20Prime%20Minister%20Elect%20E

Reading 62:
http://www.mfa.gov.il/MFA/MFAArchive/1990_1999/1999/9/Sharm+
el-Sheikh+Memorandum+on+Implementation+Timel.htm

Reading 63:
http://www.mfa.gov.il/MFA/Peace+Process/Guide+to+the+Peace+Process/
Protocol+ Concerning+Safe+Passage+between+the+West.htm

Reading 64:
http://www.mfa.gov.il/MFA/MFAArchive/2000_2009/2000/7/Trilateral+
Statement+ on+the+Middle+East+Peace+Summ.htm

Reading 65:
http://usinfo.state.gov/mena/Archive_Index/Sharm_ElSheikh_FactFinding_
Committee_Final_Report.html

Reading 66:
http://usinfo.state.gov/mena/Archive/2004/Feb/04-725518.html

Reading 67:
http://www.mfa.gov.il/MFA/Peace+Process/Reference+Documents/Disengagement+Plan+-+General+Outline.htm

Reading 68:
http://www.mfa.gov.il/MFA/Government/Speeches+by+Israeli+leaders/2004/PM+Sharon+Knesset+speech+-+Vote+on+Disengagement+Plan+25-Oct-2004.htm

Reading 69:
http://www.mfa.gov.il/MFA/Peace+Process/Reference+Documents/United+Nations+Security+Council+Resolution+1701+11-Aug-2006.htm

Reading 70:
http://www.mfa.gov.il/MFA/Peace+Process/Reference+Documents/Announcement+of+Annapolis+Conference+20-Nov-2007.htm

Reading 71:
http://www.mfa.gov.il/MFA/Peace+Process/Reference+Documents/Joint+Understanding+on+Negotiations+27-Nov-2007.htm

FURTHER READING

BIOGRAPHIES, MEMOIRS

Ashrawi, Hanan. *This Side of Peace: A Personal Account.* New York: Simon & Schuster, 1995.

Beilin, Yossi. *Touching Peace: From the Oslo Accord to a Final Agreement.* London: Weidenfeld & Nicolson, 1999.

Dayan, Moshe. *Breakthrough: A Personal Account of the Egypt-Israel Peace Negotiations.* New York: Knopf, 1981.

Eban, Abba. *Personal Witness: Israel Through My Eyes.* New York: G.P. Putnam's Sons, 1992.

Herzog, Chaim, *Living History: A Memoir.* New York: Pantheon Books, 1996.

Peres, Shimon, and David Landau. *Battling for Peace: A Memoir.* New York: Random House, 1995.

Rafael, Gideon. *Destination Peace: Three Decades of Israeli Foreign Policy: A Personal Memoir.* New York: Stein and Day, 1981.

Sadat, Anwar. *In Search of Identity: An Autobiography.* New York: Harper and Row, 1978.

Shlaim, Avi. *Lion of Jordan: The Life of King Hussein in War and Peace.* New York: Alfred A. Knopf, 2008.

Teveth, Shabtai. *Ben-Gurion and the Palestinian Arabs: From Peace to War.* New York: Oxford University Press, 1985.

Weizman, Ezer. *The Battle for Peace.* New York: Bantam Books, 1981.

GENERAL HISTORIES

Bar-On, Mordechai. *A Never-Ending Conflict: a Guide to Israeli Military History.* Westport, CT: Praeger, 2004.

Bar-On, Mordechai. *In Pursuit of Peace: A History of the Israeli Peace Movement.* Washington, DC: United States Institute of Peace Press, 1996.

Bickerton, Ian, and Carla Klausner. *A Concise History of the Arab-Israeli Conflict.* Upper Saddle River, NJ: Prentice Hall, 1998.

Cleveland, William. A *History of the Modern Middle East.* Boulder, CO: Westview Press, 2004.

Dowty, Alan. *Israel/Palestine.* Malden, MA: Polity, 2005.

Gilbert, Martin. *Israel: A History.* New York: Morrow, 1998.

Karsh, Efraim. *Fabricating Israeli History: The "New Historians."* Portland, OR: Frank Cass, 2000.

Kimmerling, Baruch, and Joel Migdal. *The Palestinian People: A History.* Cambridge, MA: Harvard University Press, 2003.

Morris, Benny. *Righteous Victims: A History of the Zionist-Arab Conflict, 1881–2001.* New York: Vintage Books, 2001.

Morris, Benny. *1948: A History of the First Arab–Israeli War.* New Haven, CT: Yale University Press, 2008.

Pappé, Ilan. *A History of Modern Palestine: One Land, Two Peoples.* New York: Cambridge University Press, 2004.

Reich, Bernard. *A Brief History of Israel.* New York: Facts On File, 2005.

Sachar, Howard. *The Course of Modern Jewish History.* New York: Vintage Books, 1990.

Sachar, Howard. *A History of Israel: From the Rise of Zionism to Our Time.* New York: Knopf, 2007.

Scheindlin, Raymond. *A Short History of the Jewish People: From Legendary Times to Modern Statehood.* New York: Oxford University Press, 2000.

Segev, Tom. *One Palestine, Complete: Jews and Arabs under the Mandate.* New York: Metropolitan Books, 2000.

Sternhell, Zeev. *The Founding Myths of Israel: Nationalism, Socialism, and the Making of the Jewish State.* Princeton, NJ: Princeton University Press, 1998.

Tessler, Mark. *A History of the Israeli-Palestinian Conflict.* Bloomington: Indiana University Press, 1994.

THE PALESTINIANS

Aruri, Naseer. *Palestinian Refugees: The Right of Return.* Sterling, VA: Pluto Press, 2001.

Farsoun, Samih, and Naseer Aruri. *Palestine and the Palestinians: A Social and Political History.* Boulder, CO: Westview Press, 2006.

Hadawi, Sami. *Bitter Harvest: A Modern History of Palestine.* New York: Olive Branch Press, 1991.

Jamal, Amal. *The Palestinian National Movement: Politics of Contention, 1967–2003.* Bloomington: Indiana University Press, 2005.

McDowall, David. *The Palestinians: The Road to Nationhood.* London: Minority Rights Publications, 1994.

Nakhleh, Issa. *Encyclopedia of the Palestine Problem.* New York: Continental Books, 1991.

Sa'di, Ahmad, and Lila Abu-Lughod. *Nakba: Palestine, 1948, and the Claims of Memory.* New York: Columbia University Press, 2007.

Said, Edward. *The Politics of Dispossession: The Struggle for Palestinian Self-Determination, 1969–1994.* New York: Pantheon Books, 1994.

Schanzer, Jonathan. *Hamas vs. Fatah: The Struggle for Palestine.* New York: Palgrave Macmillan, 2008.

THE ARAB-ISRAEL DISPUTE

Baylis, Thomas. *How Israel was Won: A Concise History of the Arab-Israeli Conflict*. Lanham, MD: Lexington Books, 1999.

Benvenisti, Meron. *Intimate Enemies: Jews and Arabs in a Shared Land*. Berkeley: University of California Press, 1995.

Ben-Yehuda, Hemda, and Shmuel Sandler. *The Arab-Israeli Conflict Transformed: Fifty Years of Interstate and Ethnic Crises*. Albany: State University of New York Press, 2002.

Bregman, Ahron. *Israel's Wars, 1947–93*. New York: Routledge, 2000.

Harms, Gregory, and Todd Ferry. *The Palestine–Israel Conflict: A Basic Introduction*. Ann Arbor, MI: Pluto, 2005.

Herzog, Chaim and Shlomo Gazit. *The Arab-Israeli Wars: War and Peace in the Middle East from the 1948 War of Independence to the Present*. New York: Vintage Books, 2005.

Pappé, Ilan. *The Israel/Palestine Question*. New York: Routledge, 1999.

Peretz, Don. *The Arab-Israel Dispute*. New York: Facts On File, 1996.

Shipler, David. *Arab and Jew: Wounded Spirits in a Promised Land*. New York: Penguin Books, 2002.

Shlaim, Avi. *The Iron Wall: Israel and the Arab World*. New York: W.W. Norton, 2000.

Smith, Charles. *Palestine and the Arab-Israeli Conflict*. New York: St. Martin's Press, 1996.

JERUSALEM

Armstrong, Karen. *Jerusalem: One City, Three Faiths*. New York: A.A. Knopf, 1996.

Benvenisti, Meron. *City of Stone: The Hidden History of Jerusalem*. Los Angeles: University of California Press, 1996.

Breger, Marshall, and Ora Ahimeir. *Jerusalem: A City and its Future*. Syracuse, NY: Syracuse University Press, 2002.

Dumper, Michael. *The Politics of Jerusalem Since 1967*. New York: Columbia University Press, 1997.

Friedland, Riger, and Richard Hecht. *To Rule Jerusalem*. New York: Cambridge University Press, 1996.

Gilbert, Martin. *Jerusalem in the Twentieth Century*. New York: J. Wiley & Sons, 1996.

Kark, Ruth, and Michal Oren-Nordheim, *Jerusalem and Its Environs*. Detroit: Wayne State University Press, 2001.

Palestinian Academic Society for the Study of International Affairs. *Documents on Jerusalem*. Jerusalem: PASSIA, 1996.

Sharkansky, Ira. *Governing Jerusalem: Again on the World's Agenda*. Detroit: Wayne State University Press, 1996.

Wasserstein, Bernard. *Divided Jerusalem*. New Haven: Yale University Press, 2001.

THE PEACE PROCESS

Abraham, S. Daniel. *Peace is Possible: Conversations with Arab and Israeli Leaders from 1988 to the Present*. New York: Newmarket Press, 2006.

Bailey, Sydney. *Four Arab-Israeli Wars and the Peace Process*. New York: St. Martin's Press, 1990.

Bar-On, Mordechai. *In Pursuit of Peace: A History of the Israeli Peace Movement*. Washington, DC: United States Institute of Peace Press, 1996.

Ben-Dor, Gabriel, and David Dewitt. *Confidence Building Measures in the Middle East*. Boulder, CO: Westview Press, 1994.

Cobban, Helena. *The Israeli-Syrian Peace Talks: 1991–96 and Beyond*. Washington, DC: United States Institute of Peace Press, 1999.

Cordesman, Anthony. *Perilous Prospects: The Peace Process and the Arab-Israeli Military Balance*. Boulder, CO: Westview Press, 1996.

Eisenberg, Laura Zittrain, and Neil Caplan. *Negotiating Arab-Israeli Peace*. Bloomington: Indiana University Press, 1998.

Kaufman, Edy, and Walid Salem. *Bridging the Divide: Peacebuilding in the Israeli-Palestinian Conflict*. Boulder, CO: Lynne Rienner Publishers, 2006.

Lukacs, Yehuda. *Israel, Jordan, and the Peace Process*. Syracuse, NY: Syracuse University Press, 1997.

Peleg, Ilan, ed. *The Middle East Peace Process: Interdisciplinary Perspectives*. Albany: State University of New York Press, 1998.

Quandt, William. *The Middle East: Ten Years after Camp David*. Washington, DC: Brookings Institution, 1988.

Quray, Ahmad. *From Oslo to Jerusalem: The Palestinian Story of the Secret Negotiations*. New York: I.B. Taurus, 2006

Rabinovich, Itamar. *The Brink of Peace: The Israeli–Syrian Negotiations*. Princeton, NJ: Princeton University Press, 1998.

Rabinovich, Itamar. *Waging Peace: Israel and the Arabs, 1948–2003*. Princeton, NJ: Princeton University Press, 2004.

Said, Edward. *The End of the Peace Process: Oslo and After*. New York: Pantheon Books, 2000.

Said, Edward. *Peace and its Discontents: Essays on Palestine in the Middle East Peace Process*. New York: Vintage Books, 1995.

Savir, Uri. *The Process: 1,100 Days that Changed the Middle East*. New York: Random House, 1998.

Sela, Avraham, and Moshe Ma'oz. *The PLO and Israel: From Armed Conflict to Political Solution, 1964–1994*. New York: St. Martin's Press, 1997.

Sher, Gildead. *The Israeli–Palestinian Peace Negotiations, 1999–2001: Within Reach*. New York: Routledge, 2006.

Stein, Kenneth. *Heroic Diplomacy: Sadat, Kissinger, Carter, Begin and the Quest for Arab-Israeli Peace*. New York: Routledge, 1999.

Telhami, Shibley. *Power and Leadership in International Bargaining: The Path to the Camp David Accords*. New York: Columbia University Press, 1990.

Watson, Geoffrey. *The Oslo Accords: International Law and the Israeli-Palestinian Peace Agreements*. New York: Oxford University Press, 2000.

Wittes, Tamara Cofman. *How Israelis and Palestinians Negotiate: A Cross-Cultural Analysis of the Oslo Peace Process.* Washington, DC: United States Institute of Peace Press, 2005.

THE U.S. AND THE PEACE PROCESS

Aruri, Naseer. *Dishonest Broker: The U.S. Role in Israel and Palestine.* Cambridge, MA: South End Press, 2003.

Aruri, Naseer. *The Obstruction of Peace: The United States, Israel, and the Palestinians.* Monroe, ME: Common Courage Press, 1995.

Druks, Herbert. *The Uncertain Alliance: The U.S. and Israel from Kennedy to the Peace Process.* Westport, CT: Greenwood Press, 2001.

Lesch, David. *The Middle East and the United States: A Historical and Political Reassessment.* Boulder, CO: Westview Press, 1996.

Miller, Aaron David. *The Much Too Promised Land: America's Elusive Search for Arab–Israeli Peace.* New York: Bantam Books, 2008.

INTERNET-BASED RESOURCES ON THE MIDDLE EAST PEACE PROCESS

http://www.mfa.gov.il/mfa/ Israeli Ministry of Foreign Affairs Web page (*Facts About Israel* in box on left)

http://www.haaretz.com/ One of Israel's most prominent daily newspapers. The site is all in English. A liberal newspaper.

http://www.jpost.com/ One of Israel's most prominent daily newspapers. The site is all in English. A more conservative newspaper.

http://iba.org.il/ Israeli news (English button at top right corner). The IBA is the Independent Broadcasting Authority, which runs some radio and television channels.

http://www.israelemb.org/ The site of Israel's Embassy in Washington, D.C.

http://www.knesset.gov.il/ The site of the Knesset, Israel's Parliament. Lots of information on political institutions and elections

http://www.iris.org.il/ Information Regarding Israel's Security

http://www.peacenow.org.il/site/en/homepage.asp?pi=25 Shalov Achshav, Israel's *Peace Now* organization.

http://www.state.gov/p/nea/ U.S. Department of State, Middle East and North Africa Desk

http://www.jewishagency.org/JewishAgency/English/Home/ The Jewish Agency for Israel.

http://www.fmep.org/maps/ A site with many maps of the Middle East

http://www.palestine-un.org/ Palestine's Office at the United Nations

http://www.passia.org/links.htm The site of the Palestinian Academic Society for the Study of International Affairs. They sponsor workshops and conferences, and have put together this list of links to other sources of information.

http://www.embassyworld.com/embassy/palestine.htm Information about the Embassies of Palestine around the world

http://www.arabicnews.com/ansub/index.html A translation into English of newspapers from around the Arab world. You can find "Palestine" listed in the box on the left.

http://www.hejleh.com/countries/palestine.html This is a very good site because if you scroll down halfway through the document you'll come to lists of *links* that will take you to other sites—media, history, institutions, etc. You can find everything you could possibly want to know about Palestine here

http://www.thisweekinpalestine.com/ An on-line resource on Palestinian news, culture, and society

Index